RONA MUNRO

Rona Munro has written extensively for stage, radio, film and television including the award-winning plays *Iron* (Traverse Theatre and Royal Court, London), *Bold Girls* (7:84 and Hampstead Theatre) and *The Maiden Stone* (Hampstead Theatre).

Other credits include *Scuttlers* for the Royal Exchange Theatre, Manchester, *The Last Witch* for the Traverse Theatre and the Edinburgh International Festival, *Long Time Dead* for Paines Plough and the Drum Theatre Plymouth, *The Indian Boy* and *Little Eagles* for the Royal Shakespeare Company and *Pandas* for the Traverse in Edinburgh. She is the co-founder, with actress Fiona Knowles, of Scotland's oldest continuously performing, small-scale touring theatre company, The Msfits. Their one-woman shows have toured every year since 1986.

Film and television work includes the Ken Loach film *Ladybird Ladybird*, *Aimee and Jaguar* and television dramas *Rehab* (directed by Antonia Bird) and BAFTA-nominated *Bumping the Odds* for the BBC. She has also written many other single plays for television and contributed to series including *Casualty* and *Dr Who*. Most recently, she wrote the screenplay for *Oranges and Sunshine*, directed by Jim Loach and starring Emily Watson and Hugo Weaving.

She has contributed several radio plays to the Stanley Baxter Playhouse series on BBC Radio 4.

Other Titles in this Series

Rona Munro

THE JAMES PLAYS

NICK HERN BOOKS
London
www.nickhernbooks.co.uk

A Nick Hern Book

The James Plays first published in Great Britain as a paperback original in 2014 by Nick Hern Books Limited, The Glasshouse, 49a Goldhawk Road, London W12 8QP, in association with the National Theatre of Scotland, the Edinburgh International Festival and the National Theatre of Great Britain

This revised edition published in 2016

The James Plays copyright © 2014, 2016 Rona Munro

Rona Munro has asserted her right to be identified as the author of this work

Cover photograph by David Eustace

Designed and typeset by Nick Hern Books, London
Printed and bound in Great Britain by CPI Group (UK) Ltd

A CIP catalogue record for this book is available from the British Library

ISBN   978 1 84842 560 6

Contents

Introduction
Rona Munro

The process of writing these plays has been long (though not as long as you might suppose) and, at the time of writing this introduction, it's ongoing. I am currently in rehearsal with the most extraordinary company of actors in the longest, most challenging, most terrifying and most exhilarating rehearsal process I have ever experienced.

I've long had the ambition to write on this scale. However, having the ambition is one thing. You also need the ability and the opportunity. It's an unfortunate fact that very few contemporary playwrights get the writing commissions that allow them to develop the ability to write on a large scale, still fewer get the opportunities thereafter.

If you enjoy these plays at all you should understand that I owe a debt to a series of theatre companies and other organisations who support and develop new writing for the stage and who have allowed me to grow to the point where I felt able to go for the big dream.

These plays are set within a period of Scottish history which is virtually unknown. I feel a certain responsibility, therefore, to alert you to the fact that some small liberties have been taken with known events in order to serve our stories.

Certain characters represent amalgamations of many characters or stand for political forces within Scotland. Certain events have had their timelines altered to maximise the drama.

However, as far as narrative imperatives allow, I've followed history and used primary sources.

We cannot know the character and thoughts of these dead kings and queens and long-gone Scots. We can speculate a whole series of possibilities from the few hard facts we can rely on, the slim historical evidence of their actions. However, I feel robustly certain that whatever their thoughts and feelings might have been, human nature is exactly the same now as it was then. Only culture and circumstances have changed.

I've translated and used words from the fifteenth century within the plays, so you'll read songs with lyrics taken from *The Kingis Quair*, the love poem written by James I himself. There are versions of work by the wonderful poet Robert Henryson and of anonymous authors whose words have still come down to us.

If any ghosts are offended by my appropriation and free interpretation of their work, I hope they'll still appreciate the wider publicity.

In the delightful possibility that you are reading these plays with the view to giving them further production, here are some guidelines and warnings. All stage directions are suggestions only, you can take enormous liberties with those and emerge unscathed.

Lines are very definitely not, tweak at your peril, you'll find you're pulling on a thread that could unravel all your plans.

Various solutions were found to represent some large moments and staging problems which are quite baldly stated in the text.

The rhythm and language of the dialogue is contemporary Scots. Apart from Joan and Henry V in *The Key Will Keep the Lock* and Margaret in *The True Mirror*, all characters are speaking Scots.

Acknowledgements

A work on this scale requires a list of itemised gratitude that would run to another three volumes. However, there are some thank-yous which simply have to be immortalised in print.

For not only encouraging the original idea but taking the reckless step of commissioning all three plays at once, a huge thank-you to Vicky Featherstone.

For endless patience, quiet wisdom and encouragement and nurturing of all kinds, George Aza-Selinger.

For many things but chiefly for the solid help that actually kept me afloat at the moment of greatest need, Caroline Newall.

For providing the best writing environment I have ever had, huge thanks to Julian Forrester and all the staff at Cove Park, these plays could not have been completed in this timescale without that refuge.

To Linda McLean and John Ferris for providing me with another calm refuge at times of personal and professional need, as well as the best support friends could ever offer an overwrought writer.

To Dr Michael Brown and Dr Christine McGladdery for their tolerance of every liberty I've taken with 'their' kings and all their help and support.

To the most amazing company of actors I could ever have imagined, they shaped this text, you did the impossible, guys, and you did it with style – Cameron Barnes, Daniel Cahill, Ali Craig, Blythe Duff, Nick Elliott, Peter Forbes, Andrew Fraser Sofie Gråbøl, Sarah Higgins, Stephanie Hyam, Gordon Kennedy, Alasdair Macrae, David Mara, Beth Marshall, James McArdle, Rona Morison, Andrew Rothney, Mark Rowley, Jamie Sives and Fiona Wood.

A massive thank-you also goes to the actors who contributed to three development workshops, one for each play. Emun Elliott, Lex Shrapnel, Billy Riddoch, Phil Cairns, Lorraine McIntosh, Karen Fishwick, Jessica Clark, Rodney Matthew, Keith McPherson, Liam Brennan, Deirdre Davis, Ruth Milne, James Rottger, Joanne McGuinness, Joe McFadden, Sam Heughan, Stuart Martin and Emma Hamilton.

Everyone in the huge list of creatives, stage management, administrators, publicity, casting and support of all kinds who brought their talent and more to the monumental task of these plays' first production.

And a thank-you too large to ever be adequately expressed anywhere, in any way, to Laurie Sansom. This was insane and it was impossible. Thank you for embracing the insanity. Thank you for making it work.

R.M.

The James Plays comprising *James I: The Key Will Keep the Lock*, *James II: Day of the Innocents*, and *James III: The True Mirror* were revived at the Festival Theatre Edinburgh on 6 February 2016, prior to a UK and international tour.

The James Plays is a co-production between the National Theatre of Scotland, Edinburgh International Festival and the National Theatre of Great Britain.

Director	Laurie Sansom
Set and Costume Designer	Jon Bausor
Lighting Designer	Philip Gladwell
Movement Director	Neil Bettles
Original Sound Designer (James I & II)	Christopher Shutt
Sound Designers for 2016 revival of James II	Christopher Shutt & Nick Sagar
Sound Designer (James III)	Nick Sagar
Composer (James I & II)	Paul Leonard-Morgan
*Composer (*James III)	Will Gregory
Fight Directors	Ruth Cooper-Brown Rachel Bown-Williams of RC Annie Ltd
Associate Director	Luke Kernaghan
Associate Set and Costume Designer	Jean Chan
Associate Lighting Designer	Rob Casey
Sound Associate (James I & James II)	Nick Sagar
Sound Associate	Kevin Murray
Musical Director	Alasdair Macrae
Assistant Director	Caitlin Skinner
Casting Director	Laura Donnelly

'Robin' composed by Will Gregory and Alasdair Macrae

Pre-show arrangements, additional arranging and hammered dulcimer by Alasdair Macrae

Additional piping arrangements by Cameron Barnes

Additional voice work by Ros Steen

	JAMES I	**JAMES II**	**JAMES III**
Rosemary Boyle	Joan, *an English noblewoman, later wife to James I*	Joan, *mother to James II* Mary, *wife to James II*	Ensemble
Daniel Cahill	Alisdair Stewart	Earl of Douglas	Jamie, *eldest son of James and Margaret*
Ali Craig	Big James Stewart	Ensemble/Hume	John, *Head of the Privy Council*
Malin Crépin			Margaret, *Queen of Scots*
Blythe Duff	Isabella Stewart, *Regent Consort*	Isabella Stewart	Annabella, *the King's aunt*
Nicholas Elliott	Ensemble	John Stewart, *a Scottish lord*	Ensemble
Peter Forbes	Balvenie, *of the Douglas family*	Balvenie, *of the Douglas family*	
Andrew Fraser	Ensemble	Davey Douglas, *the Earl's younger brother*	Ramsay, *the King's personal servant*
Dani Heron	Ensemble	Annabella, *the King's sister*	Phemy, *a lady of the court*
Brian James O'Sullivan	Ensemble	Ensemble	Tam, *a member of the household/* Musician
Sian Mannifield	Ensemble	Ensemble	Ensemble
David Mara	Ensemble	Crichton, *Earl and Keeper of Edinburgh Castle*	Ensemble/ Musician
Steven Miller	James I	Ensemble	Sandy, *the King's younger brother*

	JAMES I	JAMES II	JAMES III
Calum Morrison	Ensemble/ Musician	Ensemble/ Musician	Ensemble/ Musician
Matthew Pidgeon	Henry V, *King of England*		James III
Sally Reid	Meg, *a lady of the Scottish court*	Meg, *a lady of the Scottish court*	Ensemble
Andrew Rothney	Walter Stewart	James II	Cochrane, *a lord of the court*
John Stahl	Murdac Stewart, *Regent of Scotland*	Livingston, *Earl and Keeper of Stirling Castle*	
Andrew Still	Ensemble	William Douglas, *Balvenie's son*	Ross, *middle son of James III and Margaret*
Fiona Wood	Ensemble	Ensemble	Daisy, *a laundress*

The James Plays were premiered on 10 August 2014 as part of the Edinburgh International Festival, at the Festival Theatre Edinburgh, in a co-production between the National Theatre of Scotland, the Edinburgh International Festival and the National Theatre of Great Britain. The production opened in the Olivier auditorium of the National Theatre, London, on 25 September 2014. The original ensemble was as follows:

Cameron Barnes, Daniel Cahill, Ali Craig, Blythe Duff, Nicholas Elliott, Peter Forbes, Andrew Fraser, Sofie Gråbøl, Sarah Higgins, Stephanie Hyam, Gordon Kennedy, Alasdair Macrae, David Mara, Beth Marshall, James McArdle, Rona Morison, Andrew Rothney, Mark Rowley, Jamie Sives, Fiona Wood

JAMES I

THE KEY WILL KEEP THE LOCK

Characters

JAMES I, *King of Scots*
JOAN, *an English noblewoman, seventeen to twenty years old*
MEG, *a lady of the Scottish court, nineteen to twenty-two
    years old*
MURDAC STEWART, *Regent of Scotland*
WALTER STEWART, *a soldier and mercenary, twenty-three to
    twenty-six years old*
ALISDAIR STEWART, *a soldier and mercenary, twenty-two to
    twenty-five years old*
BIG JAMES STEWART, *a soldier and mercenary, twenty-one
    to twenty-four years old*
ISABELLA STEWART, *Regent Consort*
BALVENIE, *a member of the Douglas family*
HENRY V, *King of England, thirty-six years old*

And SERVANTS, *a* SCRIBE, *a* BISHOP, LORDS *and* LADIES
of the Scottish court, MUSICIANS, GUARDS, *etc*.

ACT ONE

Song.

> *L'homme armé doibt on douter.*
> *On a fait partout crier*
> *Que chascun se viengne armer*
> *D'un haubregon de fer*
> *L'homme armé doibt on douter.*

> [Fear the armed men,
> They're shouting everywhere,
> Get your armour on,
> Fear the armed men.]

The Edge of a Battlefield Beside a Castle

WALTER, ALISDAIR, BALVENIE *and* BIG JAMES *are Scottish prisoners of war. They are being herded into the courtyard where an execution is being prepared. Their English captors are taunting them.*

GUARD ONE. Bloody Scots!

GUARD TWO. Fucking French!

GUARD ONE. See what you're going to get!

GUARD TWO. See what's coming to you!

GUARD ONE *grabs* BALVENIE, *shaking him, showing him the execution platform.*

GUARD ONE. Think you'll hear your neck snap? Do you?

BALVENIE. Oh, Mary Mother of God...

GUARD TWO. I'll cut your throat if you like, make it quicker for you.

GUARD ONE. Fuck that, let the French-loving bastard choke.

WALTER. Christ this one's in a right mood, Alisdair.

ALISDAIR. They're all a wee bit tetchy, Walter.

WALTER. What's that about do you think, Big James?

BIG JAMES. They lost.

GUARD ONE. Oh, you think? You think we lost, do you? You murdering bastard! You're losing more than me today, you wait.

WALTER. How many English dead?

ALISDAIR (*pointing out over the battlefield*). They've barely got half the bodies buried. Smell them? Ripe English dead. Three quarters of their fucking army.

WALTER. And the rest of them ran away.

BIG JAMES. We could beat you even when we're tied up… wanna try?

GUARD ONE. You want a fight? Is that what you want?

The GUARDS *lay into* ALISDAIR, WALTER, BIG JAMES *and* BALVENIE, *who defend themselves as well as they can with bound hands.* ALISDAIR, WALTER *and* BIG JAMES *are trying to hit back,* BALVENIE *is shielding himself, trying to get away. All of them are shouting at once.*

BALVENIE. I'm no with them! No! No! Listen! Leave me! I'm no with these bastards!

GUARD ONE. Our King Henry is going to cut your tiny cocks off and make you *eat* them!

BIG JAMES. You lost! You lost! You're fucking losers 'cause we *gubbed* you!

GUARD TWO. Hold still, stay still, you fucking murdering prick!

WALTER. Aye, tie us up and have the fight then, eh? Only way you'll ever fucking win!

ALISDAIR. *Allez! Allez! Allez les Écossaises!*

HENRY V, JAMES *and other* GUARDS *enter over this.*

GUARD THREE. Order! Quiet! Order for His Majesty Henry the Fifth, King of England! Lord of Ireland! Regent and heir of France!

WALTER. In your fucking dreams, Henry boy!

GUARD ONE *knocks* WALTER *down and starts beating him again.* BIG JAMES *and* ALISDAIR *struggle to get to him as* GUARD TWO *holds them back, all of them yelling again.*

HENRY *pitches over this.*

HENRY. Oy! *Oy!!!* Stop that! Leave him! No killing! *No fucking killing!*

GUARD ONE *stops.*

No killing yet. Not yet.

Well. Here you all are, the gallant foe, eh? My defeated enemies.

WALTER. Aye, you're the one defeated the day!

BIG JAMES. Three hundred to you. Three thousand to us.

They shout together.

WALTER/BIG JAMES. Loser! Loser! Loser!

HENRY. Alright. Kill someone now.

The GUARDS *descend on* BALVENIE *who starts to scream.*

BALVENIE. No! No! Your Majesty! I never said a word! Please!

BIG JAMES. Oh! No fair!

WALTER. Let him go!

HENRY. You really want him to live!?

ALISDAIR. Come on, King Henry, play fair...

HENRY. Then *fucking shut up when I'm talking to you*!!

Silence. The GUARDS *back off* BALVENIE.

So. I suppose you think you're getting ransomed, do you? All this…

He indicates the scaffold.

That's just for show, is it? 'After all,' you'll be thinking, 'wasn't a great day for King Henry, was it? Lot of English prisoners over with the French and Scottish Army. He'll be wanting to do a prisoner exchange, won't he? Common sense.' Yeah. Common sense.

Not really in the mood for common sense. Sorry, boys. Not really in a good mood at all. Funny, that.

Do you know who this is?

He indicates JAMES.

All the Scotsmen down there. You recognise him surely?

The Scots shout suggestions.

(*To* JAMES.) Tell them who you are, James.

JAMES *looks at him but says nothing.*

Well, go on.

JAMES *still says nothing.*

He's usually so chatty, I don't know what's got into him.

This is your King, boys. This is King James of Scotland.

ALISDAIR (*to* WALTER *and* BIG JAMES). Is it?

WALTER. I don't know.

BALVENIE. Yes, it's him. It's James.

HENRY. You were all out there, fighting against me fighting for the French. Your King, *your very own King,* is standing here, with me, with the English. What does that make you? That makes you traitors. You're not prisoners of war, you're traitors against your King. Your lives are forfeit.

BALVENIE. Oh, Mary Mother of God.

BALVENIE *drops to his knees*.

WALTER. Get up, old man. Come on.

BALVENIE. You do what you like. I'm praying for my life.

HENRY. And who'd pay your ransom anyway?

ALISDAIR *calls to him*.

ALISDAIR. Our father's good for it!

WALTER. Murdac Stewart.

ALISDAIR. Regent of Scotland.

BIG JAMES. Ruler of Scotland.

HENRY. Murdac Stewart? He doesn't pay ransoms. Since when did he start paying ransoms?

(*Indicating* JAMES.) We've had this man, his nephew, his *King* a prisoner for eighteen years. I grew up watching this boy moulder in the dungeons of my castles. Murdac Stewart never paid the King of Scotland's ransom. Why's that?

BIG JAMES. Maybe we're not needing him back.

ALISDAIR. Will you stop cheeking the man! We're in negotiations here. Thing is, King Henry, you've priced him too expensive.

HENRY. Look, James, these are your cousins, isn't that nice? A family reunion. I'm filling up here. Though I have to tell you, I don't see a lot of family loyalty down there. I do not, I think they're traitors. What do you think?

WALTER. He's your *prisoner* King, he's no *my* King.

BALVENIE. Boys, do you want to just *think* before you speak just… listen to what you're saying.

HENRY (*to* JAMES). Are you listening to what they're saying? Did you hear them? Treason. They're traitors. What do you do with traitors? Show them you're a king. Go on.

BALVENIE. Oh Christ.

ALISDAIR. Your Majesty… I can see we need to put some figures on the table here. Will you let us name a price…

BALVENIE. Mary Mother of God.

WALTER (*to* BALVENIE). Will you stop that!

BIG JAMES. He's no my fucking King!

HENRY turns to the GUARDS.

HENRY. Make him kneel!

The GUARDS *wrestle* BIG JAMES *to the ground. All their weapons are out, ready to kill. Again everyone's talking at once, cutting over each other.*

ALISDAIR. Come on, King Henry, we were talking. Can't we talk here?

WALTER. No, no, no, no, you bastard. Leave him, you leave him, you leave my brother alone.

ALISDAIR. It's alright, big man, it's alright. He won't do it. Steady.

HENRY pitches over them all.

HENRY. On King James's command, boys, wait for the King of Scotland to speak.

Quiet as HENRY *talks just to* JAMES. BIG JAMES *is held, ready for execution.*

(*To* JAMES.) Show them what the King of Scotland does to traitors.

Those are your cousins down there, right? Your own flesh and blood. They took your throne, they took your youth and left you rotting in my father's prison for *eighteen years* while they stole your kingdom…

Show them you're a king.

BIG JAMES. Fucking do it!

JAMES. No.

He faces HENRY.

(*Quiet.*) Not playing this game, Henry. Stop it. Stop it now.

HENRY *is abruptly enraged*.

HENRY. It's not a fucking game, you stupid…!

I'm trying to teach you how to be a king, you ignorant little prick! We're running out of time here! When are you going to learn!? Jesus!

HENRY *doubles over, coughing. Looks at what he's coughed up*.

Jesus Christ…

JAMES *sees it, startled*.

JAMES. Is that blood?… Henry, are you sick?

HENRY. Yes. Yes, I'm sick of you, James. Sick and tired.

Right. Let's try that again.

These are your subjects. These are the most *unruly* of your subjects.

Why don't you show me how you plan to rule them. Demonstrate your kingship.

Just do it your way, James.

The Stewart boys are still held as if an execution might happen any moment.

JAMES *hesitates. Then he faces the prisoners*.

JAMES. You are prisoners of war. The laws of engagement and the rules of chivalry protect you. You will be ransomed or you will give service to His Majesty King Henry.

HENRY. That's it?

JAMES. Yes.

HENRY. They don't want you. They don't want you on the throne of Scotland. You're the king nobody wants. Tell them what they're missing, James, tell them what a brilliant king you'd be. Dazzle them. Let them see your regal power, your strength, they need to see your *strength*, James.

Talk to them again.

JAMES. This isn't the time or the place for that.

HENRY. No. *No*. This was the time to fucking *show them*.

(*To the prisoners*.) You don't want your King back, boys? No, no I don't blame you. What kind of king can't order an execution?

What kind of king is brought up in a prison reading books and writing poetry? What good will that do Scotland when I come to burn you down? What would you do, James? Stand at the border and shout a few verses at me to send me home? It might just work too, this stuff's diabolical. Want to hear some of this, boys?

HENRY *has taken some paper out and is waving it*. JAMES *recognises his poem*.

JAMES. What are you…?

Where did you get that!?

Give me that!?

JAMES *launches himself at* HENRY, *trying to get the poem back*. HENRY *throws it down and suddenly they are wrestling. The prisoners are cheering and egging them on. Their lines overlap, ragged and spontaneous*.

BIG JAMES. Go on, wee James!

WALTER. *Pas de chance!* I'm putting five hundred on King Henry.

ALISDAIR. No takers. *C'est le roi anglais!*… It's King Henry!

BIG JAMES. Aw come on, wee man! Make a fight of it! He's beating you!

JAMES *has an initial advantage but* HENRY *quickly overpowers and pins him*.

WALTER. You canny win a battle but you got him beat, Henry!

ALISDAIR (*shushing him*). Shush shush, dinny start him off again.

JAMES *is still down*, HENRY *gets up, breathless coughing*.

HENRY. Laws of engagement? Rules of chivalry? Bollocks to it. If you can promise me a ransom of five hundred I'll let you live. Anything less than that you can hang here while your King reads you verses.

(*To* GUARDS.) Get them out of here.

BALVENIE. My family is probably only going to offer about four hundred, Your Majesty, but it's a guaranteed four hundred. We're talking secure delivery of funds. I promise you! I promise you'd get the money in your hand, King Henry!!

HENRY. Five hundred or they hang!

The GUARDS *are pulling the prisoners away.*

BALVENIE. Boys! Come on! Help me here! The Earl of Douglas will thank you!

ALISDAIR. If he wants you, why won't he pay for you? Not even your own uncle cares if you hang.

BALVENIE. I'll pay you back.

WALTER. When?

HENRY. Get on with it, will you!

BALVENIE. It's… it's a cash-flow issue… I have the money in Scotland.

HENRY. Is he paying me or not!?

BALVENIE. Christ, are you helping them hang Scotsmen today? Is that what you're doing?!

The GUARDS *are pulling him off.*

BIG JAMES. Alright. Alright. (*To* HENRY.) He's with us. I'll pay his extra.

The GUARDS *let* BALVENIE *go.*

BALVENIE. Thank you. Thank you.

You'll have my service.

I'll give you service, my lords. I promise. I promise you.

WALTER. And what will we ever want from you, wee Douglas?

BIG JAMES. He's my wee Douglas now.

HENRY. Get them out of here!

WALTER. We'll see you soon though, eh? King Henry? See you soon?

The three brothers start to sing.

Song.

> *L'homme armé doibt on douter.*
> *On a fait partout crier*
> *Que chascun se viengne armer*
> *D'un haubregon de fer*
> *L'homme armé doibt on douter.*
> *L'homme armé doibt on douter.*

WALTER, ALISDAIR, BIG JAMES *and* BALVENIE *are led off. The Stewart boys still singing.*

JAMES *is recovering.*

HENRY *has another coughing fit. Again he looks at what he's coughed up.*

HENRY. Bloody Scots. Every time you turn around there's another one in your beard.

I'm not in the best of health today, James.

I would have thought… I would have imagined, you might have beaten me *today.*

But you've never beaten me. And you never will.

JAMES. Do you know why you lost the battle today?

HENRY. Do you?

JAMES. Yes. The enemy already knew all your battle positions, where you'd put the archers… where the horses were…

HENRY. What do you mean they already knew? Who told them?

JAMES. The ditch diggers. The farmers.

HENRY. Why?

JAMES. Because you rode down their ditches.

Do you know how long it takes to build a field-drainage system?

HENRY. No. Is it relevant?

JAMES. Days. Days and days. You have to excavate the ground. You have to line the base of your ditch with loose stone, not too big, not too small, you have to angle the sides so the wet earth can't collapse...

HENRY (*cutting him off*). Why the fuck did the farmers talk to the enemy?

JAMES. Their enemy is the man who rides down their ditches. Your knights did that.

HENRY. You *saw* this!?

JAMES. *You* saw it.

HENRY. When!?

JAMES. Yesterday. When we rode out to study the ground? There was that man, the farmer who shouted up at you... showing you what your men had done... your knights had made a playground of the farmland, practising war... the ditches are ruined... all the fields are flooded... the whole crop spoiled... everyone here will starve this winter, King Henry... and then...

HENRY. Which farmer?

JAMES. The one you stabbed in the throat for shouting at you.

HENRY. I've no memory of that.

JAMES. Well, you did it.

HENRY. Go on.

JAMES. Your men struck down his wife...

HENRY. This is starting to ring a bell.

JAMES. ...his sons were running away screaming curses at you... you had the archers fire...

HENRY. God yeah, I remember, useless fuckers missed, didn't they?

JAMES. And I said… 'Well, if I was them I'd go straight to the enemy now.'

HENRY. I didn't hear that.

JAMES. No. I don't think you were paying proper attention, Henry.

HENRY. You're probably right. That's probably what happened. Shouldn't have let them run. Wasn't fast enough cutting them down. Useless fucking archers.

JAMES. There's a *law* against trampling a man's crops, Henry. A law with your name on it. If you were the kind of king who cared about the law and the ditch diggers maybe…

HENRY *has a knife at* JAMES*'s throat.*

HENRY. I hold two kingdoms! Two! And you're my fucking prisoner, King James of Scotland! Aren't you?

(*Shaking him.*) Can't hear you?

JAMES (*quiet*). Yes.

HENRY *lets him go.*

HENRY. Yes you are. And always will be. My vassal King.

(*Studies* JAMES.) What's going on in there now? Are you dreaming of stabbing me or have you stopped thinking at all? No telling is there. Never is.

(*To* GUARDS.) After we're done here send out a battalion to round up the farmers. All of them. Cut their throats. Burn their crops.

JAMES. Then what will you eat, Henry?

HENRY. Shut up.

You don't need to worry about that, little King James. You won't be here.

(*Re: the poem.*) James is ready for love. He's pouring out romantic verses to unknown beauties.

Gives poem back to JAMES.

Actually some of it's quite touching. I was genuinely moved.
Time to get serious now though. You're going back to
England for your wedding.

JAMES. My wedding?

HENRY. Yes. Congratulations. You're marrying my cousin
Joan. Have you met her?

(*As* JAMES *says nothing.*) No. Well, don't worry. I think
you'll get on.

Jesus, I wish I could be there to see your face.

You'll need an English bride when we send you back to
Scotland.

(*Public announcement.*) King James of Scotland, I charge
you this day to return to your kingdom and command every
man there to cease their warring in France. I further charge
you to gather up the full price of your ransom as a prisoner
of England and pay that gold to the English crown. In token
of your agreement, kneel to me now.

JAMES *is just taking this in.*

Kneel.

Still nothing.

Fucking kneel, James.

JAMES. Are you really doing this?

HENRY. Yes. I'm really doing this.

JAMES. No.

HENRY. What?

JAMES. This will not work. This can't work.

HENRY. No, it's a useless plan but it's the best we've got. We
have to get the Scots out of France and we have to get more
gold in the treasury somehow.

It could have worked, James, it could have worked if you
had anything in you but dry ink and vinegar.

JAMES. Fuck you. I'm not going back to Scotland till we've got a proper plan, a strategy… I *had* a plan, you arse! We've been in negotiations for years! You just fucked every hour of that, didn't you!? How do you think I can rule the Scots when the story of your little display here gets back to them? I'm not doing it. I won't go.

HENRY. There's no time for plans, I'm dying, James.

(*Shows him the blood on his hand.*) It's black. Look. I am coughing up black blood. We all know what that means. We've seen it. First you cough, then your bowels go, then your reason, then there's just pain.

Two days from now I won't be able to sit up. A week from now I'll be dead.

JAMES. *Good!*

HENRY. No, you don't mean that. You'll be sorry you said that when I'm gone.

(*Calling to* GUARDS.) Assemble King James's escort.

(*To* JAMES.) You will swear allegiance to my son.

My son. Little Prince Henry. Heir to the thrones of England and France. He's still chewing his own fingers and burping milk but he is most definitely your future King, James.

You'll send him the gold Scotland owes and you'll bring no war against him, ever. Now kneel.

JAMES. Are you dying?

HENRY. I just lost a battle, didn't I? Bit of a giveaway when you think about it.

And now we all know. You can't even win a fight with a dying man. So shut up and do exactly what I say or I'll fucking haunt you.

JAMES. Why didn't you tell me!?

HENRY. I tried. I don't think you were paying proper attention, James.

GUARD. Your escort stands ready, James Stewart.

HENRY. It's time. There's no more time. And everything has come to ruin. Just do what I told you. You're right. They've seen the truth now.

Their King hasn't got the strength of a blind kitten. Keep reminding them that you're ours, you are England. The fear of my ghost might keep them off you for a while.

JAMES. I know how to be a king.

HENRY. Yes, you've had eighteen years to study that, haven't you? You can fake it for a while if you put your mind to it. If you remember the education I gave you here today.

HENRY *staggers*.

Oh Christ, the fire's in my gut. It's burning me already.

JAMES *tries to support him*.

Get off me. I can stand. They can't see me fall. Not yet.

JAMES *starts to exit*.

Will you light a candle for me?

JAMES. Yes.

HENRY. Thank you. What are you waiting for?… Fuck off.

HENRY *collapses*.

GUARDS *run and carry him off*.

A Castle in England, the Hall

A SCRIBE *is tailing* JOAN, *writing furiously. A* SERVANT *hovers, poised to take her orders.*

JOAN *is seventeen years old.*

JOAN (*rapid, urgent*). Two pigs, two bullocks, a dozen hens.

One beast roasted, the others in parts…

Five pounds of salt for what we don't eat.

A hundred loaves. Oat flour and wheat. Harder to chew but the flour won't last till February if we use all the wheat now.

(*Instructing the* SERVANT.) So we use the honey and we use ALL the butter. ALL of it.

SERVANT ONE. Yes, my lady, but…

JOAN. Oh! And… *and*… I was down the home farm last night and if they don't shift those cattle onto the far field by the river there won't be any butter at all, so get down there, tell the cattleman to get them onto green grass and tell him I know why he's not taking orders on it and tell him I *do* know his job better than he does and if he doubts it I can come down there with a three-foot cudgel and make my argument with that!

SERVANT ONE. Yes, my lady, but…

JOAN. Why are you still standing here! Go!

The SERVANT *runs off as* JOAN *turns straight onto the* SCRIBE, *looking at what he's written.*

How're we doing?

SCRIBE. I'm just… recording my lady's last…

JOAN (*cutting him off. Peering at the page*). You haven't written it all down. Don't pretend you've written it all down, I can see, I can read, the last thing you wrote down was 'salt', we're way past salt. Don't make me say it again, don't make me repeat myself.

The SCRIBE *is nodding, trying to placate her, scribbling frantically.*

Tell me you can write faster than that.

SCRIBE. It's just a question of clarity… forming the letters so that…

JOAN. What do you want to do, illuminate the margins?! *I don't have time for this!*

(*Reading as he scribbles.*) 'Bread', wonderful, you've caught up… Are we done on food? Can we leave the food? What comes after food?

Wine. Wine. I know baby King Henry won't want any but his retinue will definitely pack it away. Have to buy it. No way round it.

Another SERVANT *enters.*

SERVANT TWO. My lady, someone is here from…

JOAN *cuts him off with new instructions.*

JOAN. Right, take the second-best plate, cut it into coins, get yourself down to the port and get anything you can find. How close are they? That's what we need to know because if we've to send all the way to Dover for wine…

The SERVANTS *cross running in and out,* JOAN *is straight on the one returning.*

Have we seen any outriders yet?

SERVANT ONE. Yes, my lady, they're just…

JOAN. Oh God save me, they're nearly here!

It's alright, it's alright, we'll get the present first. They're bound to be sending someone ahead with a present. Please God let it be a minstrel. We've no one with a voice since Blind Eric choked on an apple. *I* might have to sing if they don't send a minstrel…

SERVANT ONE. It's…

JOAN (*cutting over her, pushing her off*). Get someone out on the roads and get them to grab anyone with a lute sticking out their pack. I'm not fussy at this point, as long as he can croak a madrigal.

The SERVANT *runs off as* MEG *enters and stands, waiting quietly.*

(*To* SCRIBE.) Where are we? Food, wine, music…

JOAN *sees* MEG *and stops.*

MEG. Everyone was busy so I just came in.

JOAN. Who are you?

MEG. I'm your present.

JOAN. What?

MEG. I'm your present. From the King.

JOAN. I see.

Are you a musician?

MEG (*laughing*). Oh, save us no! I can't keep tune better than a puddock.

JOAN. I see.

So… what can you do?

MEG. Anything you want me to, Lady Joan.

JOAN. What are my options?

MEG. I can milk a cow.

I can make a room smell sweet.

I can sew. Obviously.

JOAN. Anything more… interesting? I mean no offence but if you're a *present*…

MEG. Oh, I'm here to teach you Scots. Everything about the Scots. About Scotland. What we eat, how we talk, how we dance…

JOAN. And I need to know this because…?

MEG. Because you're marrying the King of Scots, of course!

JOAN. Oh!

Oh, I see.

They want me to marry the King of Scotland?

MEG. They're bringing King James here. To betroth you.

JOAN looks at the SCRIBE.

JOAN. Did you know about this?

SCRIBE. No, my lady. No.

JOAN. Well... it's time I was married, of course.

The SCRIBE *is bowing.*

SCRIBE. God's blessing on you, my lady, you will be...

JOAN (*cutting over him as she realises*). Oh, for... that means two Kings are coming... *two Kings*!

(*Pushing the* SCRIBE *out.*) Get down home farm and count the chickens, we're going to need more chickens, and a *load* more onions for the sauce because that's the only way we'll stretch any sauce far enough...

(*As the* SCRIBE *hurries off.*) Broilers, mind! Just count broilers! I'm not roasting them any layers no matter how royal they are. Make a list...

Put it on the list!

She's alone with MEG. *She considers her for a moment.*

I'm getting married.

I'm getting married?

Scotland's a long way to go to get married though. A long way.

What's he like? Is he kind? Is he fat? How's his breath?

MEG. He loves you already.

JOAN. Oh, he has to say that.

MEG. Does he?

JOAN. Oh yes. That's the polite way to court royalty. He'll have been writing love poems.

MEG. He has!

JOAN. Well, he'll have had them written. What they do is they put your name in when they know who they're marrying? They just write the name in.

MEG. No, he actually writes himself.

JOAN. Really?

Odd.

I hope he'll like the look of me.

MEG. Why wouldn't he?

JOAN. Yes, why wouldn't he? I'm pretty enough.

Oh, Mother of God! Mother of God, I'll be a queen!

MEG. Queen Joan of Scotland.

JOAN. Oh, you'll make me laugh! Really?

MEG. You're going to be Scottish. You're going to be more Scottish than me.

JOAN. No.

Queen Joan of Scotland.

MEG. Could you love him though?

Love makes you like bread soaking up their gravy. It makes you everything they are.

She looks round, admiring.

This is a lovely place. I'd never been away from home till they sent for me to be a present. I like moving around. You can feel your mind rolling out like spreading ribbons as your road unravels behind you.

I'm to take you home but I've barely got here, have I?

I like it here.

I'm to stay in your service until the end of my days or until you get weary of me. But you won't. We'll have a great time together. I've been in a great mood ever since I saw the sea and ate a fig. Have you ever eaten a fig? Of course you have. I thought they were just something out of the Bible but you can bite them and suck through all those little sweet seeds. So soft. Like biting into a wee bird that wants you to eat it.

So I'm thinking you'll maybe not like it in Scotland. Maybe you'll be wanting to visit France. I wouldn't mind that. I'll follow you to France no bother. I'm told the French have meat in sauces and soft wines that taste like the food and drink in paradise.

We eat stones in Scotland.

JOAN. You do not!

MEG. It's the truth. Our earth is so poor we have to suck the stones out of the fields instead of growing corn. We make a sauce of mud.

We've nothing sweet to eat at all. Do you like apples?

JOAN. Yes of course.

MEG. Well, there's no orchards in Scotland.

JOAN. No orchards?

MEG. We only dream of apples. You might get a lick of one at Christmas but it'll have a worm in it.

They won't have a crown for you, I'm telling you, we're poorer than beetles in a rotten log. They'll just have to give you a rather nice hat.

It'll be second-hand.

The Queen of France will let you have it out of pity. We'd be better going to stay with her.

JOAN. Are you trying to talk me out of this marriage?

MEG (*sighs*). No. You're right. We can't go to France.

Truth is you can't get out of this marriage. You've been promised.

JOAN. I could refuse.

MEG (*reaching out to* JOAN*'s dress*). Is that real silk?

JOAN. Yes.

MEG. Oh. Beautiful.

Your lady-in-waiting has one just like it, eh?

JOAN. You're saying no one in Scotland has the *sense* to make jam? Nothing sweet?

MEG. Alright, so we've lovely rowan trees. I can make a nice jelly out of rowan berries. And there's no much honey but it is good honey.

JOAN. Is it?

MEG. The best.

JOAN. Better than honey here?

MEG. Och, you're eating honey here all the time. You don't know what sweet is, your mouths are so full of sweetness you just think it's the taste of the air itself.

JOAN. What's the best thing?

MEG. The best thing about home?

Thinks about it.

You can understand folk better. What they say.

JOAN. But will I?

MEG. You make me out well enough, don't you? And the skies are bigger.

JOAN. How?

MEG. There's more light in them and you can see higher up into them. And the fish is fresher.

JOAN. I hate fish.

MEG. That's because you eat five-week-old herrings with salt. Our fish tastes like sweet white bread and clear water.

And the dancing's better.

JOAN. How?

MEG. More… (*Searches for the right words*.) Nobody sits down when the music gets going, you dance the soles off your shoes. Oh, I miss the dancing…

Maybe I do want to go home.

I do want to go home.

Will you go, lady? Will you say yes?

JOAN.…I'll understand the people…

MEG. You'll know what they mean.

JOAN.…There will be rowan trees and tall skies and fresh silver fish and dancing…

MEG. And King James will love you like you're the Queen of Heaven itself, all the days of your life.

JOAN. So we can sit in the two towers of our castle, the sun in the sky between us…

MEG. Ah now, I can't promise you sun. Not every day. There's usually some nice weather about September, when you've given up on there ever being any sun again ever… and that's nice for ripening the brambles and they're *delicious*.

JOAN. And he'll wave from his tower, and I'll wave from mine… and sometimes, in the evenings, we'll meet under the moon in the courtyard below…

MEG. If the wind's no in the east…

JOAN. And dance all night.

MEG. That's definitely possible.

JOAN. And eat rowan jelly.

MEG. And bramble jam.

I do love a bit of bramble jam.

JOAN *considers again*.

So will you do it? Will you marry him?

JOAN. I'm getting old. I'm seventeen already… but I might have a better marriage.

MEG. I don't know. I heard them talking about convents.

JOAN. And that would kill me.

MEG. It's not where I want to end my days. Not what I was hoping for when they put me in your service, my lady.

JOAN. Shall I marry him then?

MEG. I can live without figs. I can't get by without drinking and dancing, not when death comes so soon.

JOAN. Then I'll do it.

MEG. Aw, then you'll be my Queen, my lady, all the days I'm alive.

JOAN. Oh, this will be good! When will I meet him?

JAMES enters, he stops dead, staring at JOAN as she turns to face him, transfixed.

Southwark Cathedral

A CHOIR enters, singing. JAMES and JOAN are still facing each other as SERVANTS dress them in lavish wedding clothes. They process up to the altar. JAMES puts the ring on JOAN's finger and kisses her formally.

Singing over all of this.

Song.

> Busy ghost flit to and fro,
> Never quiet, you never rest,
> Till you go back to where you're from
> The dark was first, it's your last nest.
> Day after day life wraps you up in pain,
> If you wear flesh your waking hours are trouble
> That grows in sleep, so all your grief is double.
> And then you see –

A BISHOP *is blessing* JOAN *and* JAMES. *They kneel, facing the* CONGREGATION.

A white bird and a gilly flower
A white bird and a gilly flower
A white bird and a gilly flower
Wake up! Wake up! Lovers look what I've got
Good news, it's bliss, it's safe, it's sure
It's consolation. Laugh and play and sing
You're close to such a great adventure,
Look up, it's love, it's love, it's love…

The BISHOP *raises his hand in a final blessing.* JAMES *and* JOAN *bow their heads in prayer.*

The CONGREGATION *and the* CHOIR *file out leaving* JAMES *and* JOAN.

JOAN *keeps her head bowed. After a moment* JAMES *looks over at her.*

JAMES. Are you… sorry… are you still…?

JOAN (*looking round at him*). What?

JAMES. I don't want to disturb your prayers.

JOAN. Oh no, I'm finished. I was waiting on you.

JAMES. Good. No. I'm finished.

An awkward pause.

So now we're married.

JOAN. Yes.

JAMES. We'll have the wedding blessed again in Scotland.

Then we can have our wedding night.

JOAN. Yes.

JAMES. I think we can get up now.

JOAN. Sorry?

JAMES. I'm sure even the bishop will think we've prayed
    enough.

JOAN. Oh! Of course.

She's getting up, he does too.

JAMES. You look… Are you unhappy?

JOAN. No! No, of course not, I… It's exciting.

JAMES. What is?

JOAN. Being married.

I like your face.

JAMES. Do you?

JOAN. Yes. It's a nice face. Much nicer than your portrait.

JAMES. I couldn't believe it when I saw you. Couldn't believe it.

JOAN. No?

JAMES. It's you.

JOAN. It is me.

JAMES. No, I mean you're the woman I saw. In my dream. Out my window. In my poem.

JOAN. It's a lovely poem.

JAMES. You've read it?

JOAN. Oh! No I don't…

I mean I read, of course but…

Reading makes your eyes sore, doesn't it?

My ladies say it's a wonderful poem.

I will read it soon.

The box you sent it in is beautiful. Really beautiful.

JAMES. You should read the poem.

JOAN. Of course. I'm sorry.

JAMES. Some feelings… some things can't be conversational. Do you understand?

JOAN. I'm really sorry.

JAMES. No!

JOAN. I've disappointed you.

JAMES. No! You haven't! That's just it you see if you... just read the poem. You'll understand.

JOAN. I don't think I will disappoint you. I can keep a household, my lord. I am sure I can keep a court. I can plan. I can buy in. I can supervise the farms and the ponds, the linens and the cellars. You'll have a clean court with good food on the table every season of the year. I promise you. I can seat a bishop next to an ambassador and juggle the conversation between them. I'll remember the names of everyone you meet and how much charity they should receive. I can remember the total of your treasury without a scribe and add and subtract it so that your wealth will never escape you. Everything expected of a wife and the keeper of a castle I can do well. I will do well for you. I will give you children if I can. I'm sure I can.

We will do well together if it's in my power, we will do very well. I know how to be an excellent queen. You'll see.

Do you have a mistress at the moment?

JAMES. No!

JOAN. Because I'll make sure I never embarrass you.

JAMES. There's only you.

Jesus...

JOAN. You're very kind.

JAMES. There can't be anyone but you.

JOAN. That's so kind. What a lovely thing to say. I'm sure we will get on.

JAMES. Is there anything you want to know? Anything you wanted to ask me?

JOAN. Why were you England's prisoner? I've never really understood...

JAMES. Ah… it was… my brother… my elder brother was… he was… sick… he died… and I was only ten. They sent me away to France, to keep me safe… but I was captured by English pirates.

JOAN. But why weren't you safe in Scotland?

JAMES. Those were troubled times. It'll be different now.

JOAN. Meg… my woman says you don't even have apple trees in Scotland.

JAMES. No, we have apples… small ones maybe but… but… of course… of course we'll take a beautiful English apple tree.

JOAN. I can watch the birds in that.

JAMES. You see I love that too! I love watching the birds.

JOAN. Well… that'll be something we can do together.

(*Looking out of the church door.*) I think we're supposed to…

JAMES. Of course.

Our wedding procession.

She curtseys and waits. So does he. An impasse.

JOAN. You have to lead me to the coach.

JAMES. Aye! Of course… Just…

He gets tangled in her dress trying to get on the right side to lead her.

Sorry…

To Scotland, then.

JOAN. To Scotland.

The Scottish Throne Room / Great Hall, Stirling

A throne and some scattered precious objects. ISABELLA *is sorting through silver plate and cups.* BIG JAMES *comes quickly into the room with a bag.*

ISABELLA. Quick, quick, quick…!

He helps her bundle silver plates into the bag.

WALTER *and* ALISDAIR *enter, breathless.*

ALISDAIR. What next?

WALTER. Take the table.

ALISDAIR. Fuck that, take the throne.

They go and try and lift it.

ISABELLA. Will it even fit on the cart?

ALISDAIR. Cut the fucking legs off.

(*Strains.*) Big James, come and give us a hand.

BIG JAMES *goes to them.*

They all strain.

WALTER. *Allez mes braves! Encore une fois!*

ISABELLA. Watch yourselves! Watch!

They are all straining to lift the throne when MURDAC *enters.*

MURDAC. What are you doing!?

ALISDAIR. Hullo, Father.

BIG JAMES. Just helping the mother.

WALTER. Just giving the mother a wee hand with removals.

MURDAC. Put it back.

ALISDAIR. No, we can shift it see…

MURDAC. Put it back!

They put the throne down.

Now put the rest back.

ALISDAIR. There is a point where a man doesn't take orders...

WALTER. Except maybe from his mother.

MURDAC *moves in on* WALTER, *showdown*.

MURDAC. Well, maybe that man should leave his father's house and his father's horses and give back all the land his father gave him and wander about the hills in his semmet and a pair of leaking shoes having a wee think about all the many implications of defying the fifth commandment of God. Maybe that's what that man should be doing?

ALISDAIR. Well, maybe we honour our father *and* our mother.

BIG JAMES. Especially the mother.

They look at ISABELLA.

ISABELLA. We're leaving them the bloody crown, Murdac. What more do you want?

MURDAC. I thought we'd had this conversation. No. I know we did. Isabella, we've had this conversation and we agreed.

ISABELLA. I've changed my mind.

ALISDAIR, WALTER *and* BIG JAMES *exchange looks and then position themselves to watch the fight.* ISABELLA *is lifting a beautifully decorated stool*.

MURDAC. That's not yours.

ISABELLA *looks at it*.

ISABELLA. So whose is it then?

MURDAC. It stays here.

ISABELLA. Whose feet have been on it these last eighteen years?

MURDAC. It stays here.

ISABELLA (*showing him*). That's mud off my boots, look, here on the cloth.

MURDAC. It belongs here.

ISABELLA. You want me to leave them this?

MURDAC. Yes.

ISABELLA. My muddy footstool?

MURDAC. Yes.

ISABELLA. I suppose you want me to clean it for them too?

MURDAC. No, just put it back.

ISABELLA. Alright. If that's how we're doing things. If we're worried that they're going to count the furnishings.

She throws it down, a bit rough.

Ooops.

MURDAC. You're an oath-breaker.

ISABELLA. What did you call me?

WALTER *sucks in his breath. The brothers are enjoying this hugely.*

MURDAC. Were you with me when the families met?

Do you remember what was agreed?

ISABELLA. Are you going to keep asking me questions when we both know the answers?

MURDAC. Did you put your hand on mine and agree, before all the other families, that we'd step away from the throne, and all that belongs to the crown, when England sent the little King home?

ISABELLA. Yes. And now I've changed my mind about the silver.

MURDAC. Then you're an oath-breaker.

ALISDAIR. Fair point.

BIG JAMES. That's true enough, Mother, a promise is a promise.

MURDAC. Put the silver back, boys.

They start to do so.

We don't need the royal treasure. We've got our own. We're rich and we're none of us dead. God loves this family. Put the silver back.

ISABELLA *snatches silver away from* WALTER.

ISABELLA. That's my spoon.

MURDAC. It is not your spoon.

ISABELLA. It is my silver spoon and it's out of my mouth.

MURDAC. It's got the Scottish royal crest on it.

ISABELLA. It's got my teeth marks in it.

WALTER *shows* BIG JAMES. *They nod.*

BIG JAMES. She's right.

WALTER. I'd say anything we've had our teeth in we *couldny* let go.

ISABELLA. So we'll be having that and these plates *and* the bloody footstool. Get it, Walter.

BIG JAMES *is absorbed with the spoon.* WALTER *squares up to his father.* MURDAC *knocks him down and whacks* BIG JAMES*'s sword away before* BIG JAMES *realises what's going on.* ALISDAIR *is already holding up his hands in surrender, laughing.*

ALISDAIR. You're still the big man! We're doing it! Look! We're doing it!

He starts clearing up. BIG JAMES *and* WALTER *join in,* BIG JAMES *enthusiastic,* WALTER *sullen.*

BIG JAMES. Here's to you, Father! No way we could kill you yet, is there?

(*Looks to his brothers for agreement.*) No way!

ALISDAIR. None. He's still got it. For sure.

WALTER. He's near broken my bloody wrist.

ALISDAIR *cuffs him.*

ALISDAIR. Ach, stop your grietin, get faster, get stronger, go for his belly next time.

MURDAC. Back here as soon as you see the procession coming in the gate. And on your best behaviour, mind.

ALISDAIR. We're always on our best behaviour, Father. Don't you know that?

MURDAC is watching them exit with their loot and all their mess. He doesn't notice ISABELLA *creeping up to attack him until she's right on him. They're evenly matched. But* MURDAC *finds an advantage. He disarms her and pins her.*

MURDAC. Sweet Mary Mother of God, we don't have time for this, Isabella. I don't have the *energy* for this. Yield.

ISABELLA. No.

MURDAC. Come on. I beat you. Yield.

ISABELLA. No.

MURDAC. Will you at least admit I beat you?

ISABELLA. Yes.

She kisses him.

MURDAC. Thank God for that.

He lets her go. She trips him.

ISABELLA. But we wereny done.

MURDAC. We need to be out of this room. We can't be standing here as if we're welcoming the King into *our* hall.

ISABELLA. It *is* my hall!

MURDAC. No. We agreed. *All the families agreed.*

ISABELLA. I feel like we're robbing our own bairns.

MURDAC. If we are they'll rob us straight back, we both know that.

ISABELLA. They're good boys.

MURDAC. Isabella, do you never think it would be nice to have a bit of quiet conversation, a bit of reasoned argument without some muscly young fucker slamming an axe on the table before you get to the point!

ISABELLA. Murdac, often as I've wanted to kill you there has never been any other man in my heart... in my eyes... whose skin I've wanted to touch... even now... even now when we're down to the last warm coals in the fire. But I won't love you if you don't love our sons more than your breath.

A beat.

MURDAC. They're my sons. Blood is blood.

ISABELLA. There you go.

MURDAC. But… do you never worry that they've grown too… dangerous?

ISABELLA. For what?

MURDAC. For anything but war.

ISABELLA. Well, how else are they going to win wars?

He kisses her.

Alright. I'll make him welcome. You're right. I don't need the King's gold. I've got my own treasure.

MURDAC *kisses her.*

My boys are my treasure.

MURDAC. So what am I?

ISABELLA. Something to keep the bed warm if the fire dies down.

They kiss.

See? You're my warmth. You're my fire.

The sound of a LORD *and* LADY *of the Scottish court, both calling out, a formal cry and answer.*

LORD. The King's coming in.

LADY. So get his fire on.

LORD. The King's coming in.

LADY. Get him meat.

MURDAC *and* ISABELLA *talk over this.*

MURDAC. They're coming. Out of here. Don't be standing here like you own the place, Isabella!

ISABELLA *looks like she's following* MURDAC *but then stands waiting, a formal welcoming committee.*

The LORD *and* LADY *enter,* JAMES *is behind them. Behind him are* ALISDAIR, WALTER, BIG JAMES, BALVENIE *and all the rest of the* SCOTTISH LORDS *and* LADIES. *They all join in now, roaring the responses.*

LORD. The King's coming in.

LORDS *and* LADIES. Get his wine poured.

LORD. The King's coming in.

LORDS *and* LADIES. Gather round.

LORD. The King's coming in.

LORDS *and* LADIES. Gather Scotland.

LORD. The King's coming in.

LORDS *and* LADIES. See him crowned!

They're all cheering and clapping. JOAN *and* MEG *are the last to enter at the end of the procession.*

ISABELLA *is greeting* JAMES.

ISABELLA. King James, you're welcome home.

JAMES. Thank you, I...

BALVENIE *is trying to get* JAMES*'s attention.*

BALVENIE. King James, the Earl of Douglas sends his apologies, the war in France has delayed his...

The SCOTTISH LORD *shoulders past him, holding coronation robes.*

LORD. Your Majesty, it's my honour to dress you for your coronation.

ALISDAIR *and* BIG JAMES *are taking the robe off him.*

ALISDAIR. You're alright, we've got it. We'll do it.

BIG JAMES. Family business. This is our cousin you know.

They're helping JAMES *into the robes a bit rough. At the same time the* LADY *is carrying robes to* JOAN.

LADY. Your Highness, it's my honour to dress you for your coronation.

JOAN lets MEG and the LADY dress her. WALTER moves closer to watch her.

ALISDAIR. Good to see you again, Cousin James. Been a while, eh? When did we last see him, Big James?

BIG JAMES. Don't know, think it was at a hanging.

ALISDAIR. It *was* at a hanging, King Henry's wee execution party, that was it. Long time ago though, all forgotten now, eh?

They're getting a bit of the robing wrong, deliberately.

JAMES. That's not… You need to put it the other way.

BIG JAMES. You sure? I think it looks good like that.

MURDAC enters. He sees them. They see him. They back off JAMES.

ALISDAIR. Don't you worry, King James, just stick with us. We'll show you how it's all done.

Around them the room is being prepared, a throne, a crown, possibly a wedding bed. MEG is still fussing with JOAN's clothes.

JOAN. Leave that. That's not right.

MEG. You've got it all bumphled.

LADY. Are you ready, Your Highness?

JOAN (*to MEG*). I *want* it like that, that's how it's *supposed* to hang.

WALTER (*grinning at her*). I think you look great.

JOAN is startled.

LADY. Are you ready?

JOAN. Yes.

Thank you.

The LADY gives a signal. The BISHOP enters and calls out, formal.

BISHOP. In the name of God I call you all to witness! In the name of God!

Everyone falls silent and bows their heads as the BISHOP *processes up to the throne.*

MEG *tries to straighten* JOAN*'s dress again.* JOAN *hits at* MEG, MEG *hits back.*

JOAN (*whisper*). Stop hitting me! You can't *do* that! It's treason!

MEG (*whisper*). Well, stop slapping at me then! You're bumphled!

JOAN (*whisper*). I'm *not* bumphled. This is *my* coronation and this is how I *want* to look so…!

MEG. The *King*! *Go!*

JAMES *is waiting for* JOAN, *holding out his hand to her.*

JOAN *takes his hand and follows him up to the thrones.*

JAMES *sits on his throne.* JOAN *sits on hers. With slow ceremony the* BISHOP *lifts the crown. He raises it over* JAMES*'s head.*

BISHOP. King James, we crown you. We crown you King of Scots.

All the watching LORDS *shout together.*

LORDS. King James!

BISHOP. In God's name. In the sight of Scotland's lords, in the name of her people, we crown you King of Scots.

LORDS. King James!

The BISHOP *lowers the crown onto* JAMES*'s head. The watching* LORDS *cheer and then push close around the throne. They lift it, with* JAMES *seated in it. They carry it round the throne room, chanting, shouting.*

King James! King James!

They are shouting louder and louder, moving faster and faster. JAMES *clutches the arms of his throne as the roaring mob carries him off.* JOAN *is on her feet, terrified.*

ISABELLA (*calling after them*). Watch! Careful! Don't let the crown fall off his wee head!

JOAN. What are they doing!? Where are they taking him!?

BALVENIE. It's alright. It's perfectly normal, Queen Joan. It's part of the ceremony, they're showing him to the people.

He's King of Scots now. The Scots need to see him.

MEG. They'll be throwing flowers! And cakes even!

MEG *runs off after the throne. Only* BALVENIE, JOAN *and* ISABELLA *are left onstage.* BALVENIE *is close beside* JOAN.

BALVENIE (*soothing*). Please, Your Royal Highness, just sit back and wait. They'll bring him back to you soon, I promise you. There's nothing to worry about.

ISABELLA *is moving swiftly back to* JOAN *on her throne.*

ISABELLA. Aye, there is. She needs to worry about a wee creep like you putting his damp hands all over her coronation robes. Get away from her! Shoo now! Shoo!

BALVENIE *stands his ground.*

BALVENIE. I'm here for the Douglas family. I'm here for the Earl.

ISABELLA. You're no the Earl of Douglas.

BALVENIE. No, no, he's in France.

So I'm standing in.

ISABELLA. How can you stand in for the Earl of Douglas when you're no the Earl of Douglas?

BALVENIE. Because he's my un...

ISABELLA (*cutting him off*). You're just Balvenie, aren't you?

BALVENIE. And Dunkeld. I recently inherited...

I've got Dunkeld too.

ISABELLA. Really?

But when you've got Jedburgh, Galloway, Dumfries, Wigtown and all the other lands that make the Earl of

Douglas fit to sit by the Queen you can come back, till then go and stand over there and don't bother us. Go on!

She shoos him away.

There is the sound of roaring and shouting, off.

My lady, Your Majesty, I'm so pleased to meet you, I've only sons and I've aye wept for a daughter. Aw, Queen Joan, you'll be as dear as my ain bairns. I'll keep you close. See if I dinny.

JOAN (*uncertain*). Thank you...

ISABELLA. Oh, bless you, you can hardly mak me oot, eh?

JOAN. No, no, I...

ISABELLA (*cutting her off*). Never you mind, all you need to know is that you're welcome home and I'll be a mother to you if you let me.

JOAN. I don't even know who you are.

JAMES *is rushed back on, still clinging to his throne, the* LORDS *roaring round him. He's tipped out and half-jumps, half-falls. He keeps his feet. A cheer and applause.*

MURDAC. He's still standing. He's the King. Let's start the drinking, boys, we've got a king.

JAMES. No. No, not yet.

MURDAC. No, it's alright, King James, we're done. You can have a drink now.

JAMES. I'm not King yet, surely.

MURDAC. Aye, man, we had a bishop and everything.

JAMES. You have to kneel, I have to receive your homage. How can I be King without that? You have to kneel to me, and my Queen.

A nasty silence. JAMES *walks through it, going to* JOAN.

He takes her hand and they face the MEN *and* WOMEN *and* CLERGY *crowded in the throne room.*

You have to kneel.

When you kneel to me, then I'll say I'm your King.

No one moves.

WALTER. *Salup.*

MURDAC. Shoosht, Walter… Your Majesty… that's not how we do it.

JAMES. It's how they do it in every court in Europe.

BIG JAMES. *Va te faire foutre!* Get the wine. I'm no going on my knees till I fall over. No way.

MURDAC. *Quiet*, Big James! That might be the… English way, Your Majesty, but…

WALTER. You're in Scotland now, man, look about you!

JAMES. Oh. I see. I see. I understand.

WALTER. Good, now fetch the drink and let's get on.

JAMES. You think I'm an Englishman.

BIG JAMES. Yes!

JAMES. Do I sound like an Englishman?

MURDAC. You can sound like anything you like, Your Majesty! You're our King now! We *all* agreed on that!

JAMES. All of you?

MURDAC. Aye. Every man and woman here.

JAMES. Some of them don't look too happy about it.

WALTER. You want us to give you the throne and smile about it too?

JAMES. Yes. Yes that would be good. But you can't. You don't know who I am and it looks likely I'm an Englishman… or an English servant anyway. Of course you're not smiling.

I've not been here for eighteen years. You think I've forgotten who I am. Right enough, I was only a boy when I left.

Shall I tell you who I am now?

(*To* MURDAC.) We've got time for that, haven't we?

MURDAC. Aye but…

JAMES (*cutting him off*). Good.

People tell me they don't know what I'm thinking. That's because I don't often tell people what I'm thinking. But I tell you this, I think, I *know,* I can be a *really* good king. And I will be. I will be if you help me. — *He needs support (seen as weakness by the nobles)*

(*Searches their faces.*) No, no, you don't think I can do it. That's alright. I'll prove that I can.

I am so glad to be back here.

I annoyed you there, with the kneeling thing, eh? Of course I did. I should have known I would. After all, I never forgot the Scottish people, my people. *The people are independent, resilient & bow to no-one authority but their own* Not a courtier among you and everyone looking me in the eye. Every one of you kings and queens and every one of us poor as stones and not caring about it. Singing about it. Laughing about it because we can still stamp and shout and breathe in life.

Am I right? Is that who we are?

I don't want you to kneel to me, to King James. I want you to kneel to Scotland. That's who I am now, in my body, in my person, I'm the King of Scots. That's what I was born to. Wasn't it? Isn't that why you asked me back? Because of this… (*Holds up his wrist.*)

Blood. Royal blood. *Danger of power of blood (love of power with claims to the throne)*

Some quiet prison days all I did was sit and look at that, the little beat of it, under my skin. I'd just look at it and marvel. The same blood as my great great-grandfather, Robert the Bruce. The blood that made me a prisoner. The blood that made me a king.

But Murdac Stewart shares that blood, my cousins here share that blood, what else can I offer you?

I'm going to bring you peace.

I was sent home to bring peace between two kingdoms. We need peace. They want an end to our war against them in France. I want that too. They're losing their war but we're losing too many of our best warriors. I want those men home, in Scotland. So I'll give England its peace.

The Stewart brothers exchange a look. WALTER *makes a low noise of disgust.* MURDAC *shushes them again fiercely.*

But I'll give you this promise. That's all they're getting from me now.

You all know I've been sent home with a ransom on my head. They want me to gather up your money to pay for my eighteen years' board and lodging.

Well, I had an education in England. I learned history. England has pursued our wealth and bled our wealth for a hundred years or more and looks ready to do it for hundreds more until this is a nation of beggars. Then they'll flick us a coin of our own stolen gold and call it charity.

They think I'll help them in that work. They think that because in eighteen years *they* never knew what I was thinking. They never learned who I am.

I am the King of Scots. And they will get not *one* more penny that is yours!

The listening LORDS *and* LADIES *exchange glances. Some of them are starting to be won over, others less convinced.*

You'll lose no more of your wealth.

And look what I brought back to Scotland.

He raises JOAN's *hand, she's deeply embarrassed.*

The greatest jewel that England had is ours now. And that is how it will be from now on. What is Scotland's will stay with Scotland and the best that the world has will come to us as well.

I am the King of Scots. In eighteen years I never forgot that. You could keep a horse in a byre, doesny mak it a coo.

The last sight I had of Scotland was no sight at all, it was a wet wind, driving waves and rain in my face so I couldny see. I was ten years old. I was grietin more salt water than there was in the sea that was soaking me to the bone. I felt that the sky and the sea and the wind of Scotland were scolding me, shouting their anger at me. How could I leave my own country? How could I run away?

Eighteen years later I came up to the border and I saw the green hills, I saw the dark rocks and towering skies and the far-off mountains of home and I drew breath to shout a greeting into that dear country and – Bam! There it was again! A stour o' a wet wind, knocking me back south and roaring its disdain in my face.

And I tell you this, I *love* that gale. I've missed it! I am so ready for it!

And I tell you something else, if that wind had a human face, it would have been glowering at me just like you are! You're like a cold gale roaring in my eyes, shouting in my face, 'Who do you think you are, laddie?'

Well, I'll tell you! I'm your bloody King! I'm the King of Scots!

Kneel to me because I promise you, and I will prove to you by everything I do now… I *am* Scotland.

That Scotland will be small but it will be whole. It will be poor, but all its people will know their worth and know how to fight for it. It will be a tiny part of the world but it will know *all* the world knows. It will be assaulted but it will never be broken. It will make no quarrel where it isn't provoked… but it will bend to no other nation on this earth. That is Scotland. That is who I am.

So I'm asking you now… show me how much you love this country.

One by one they all drop to their knees. Last to go down is WALTER, *he holds* JAMES's *eye for a beat then he too kneels.*

And now I'm truly your King.

MEG *walks forward and curtseys deeply to* JOAN.

MEG. My lady, with your permission…

JOAN. Yes… what?

MEG (*calling to the room*). Time to make up the bed!

At once there's a great cheer, wine's brought out, the wedding bed is assembled. MEG is helping a bemused JOAN out of some of her coronation robes as the LORDS come close to JAMES, all carry cups, a party atmosphere.

MURDAC. King James, I want something from you.

JAMES. Yes?

MURDAC. Conversation. Man, I want a conversation with you. Just to talk some ideas, just to talk.

JAMES. We'll be talking in my council, won't we?

MURDAC. Aye but...

WALTER. Are we doing this or what's going on?

MURDAC. I speak first. *I* speak first and I'll do it when I'm ready.

He waits till WALTER steps back then turns to JAMES, formal.

King James, it is my honour to lie beside your bed to defend your royal person this night and all nights.

ALL MEN. King James!

JOAN (*to MEG*). That's just a theoretical honour though, isn't it?

BALVENIE. King James, it is my honour and my family's honour to lie at the head of your bed and defend your royal person this night and all nights.

ALL MEN. King James!

JOAN (*looking round*). No, because they have another room, don't they? At the English court there are several royal antechambers... where are the antechambers?

LORD. King James, it is my honour and my family's honour to lie at the foot of your bed and defend your royal person, this night and all nights.

ALL MEN. King James!

JOAN. Or at least there's a screen. Meg, tell me there's going to be a screen!

MEG. You're alright, Joan... Your Majesty, I mean... they'll be so drunk they won't be able to see anything anyway.

STEWART BROTHERS. King James, it is my honour to lie at the side of your bed to defend your royal person this night and all nights.

ALL MEN. King James!

BIG JAMES. Gentlemen, let's get Scotland drunk!

A cheer, they all pour more wine into JAMES *and each other.*

JOAN. What do I do? What am I supposed to do?

MEG *settles her on the bed, spreading her wedding dress out attractively.*

MEG. You just sit here, Your Highness... and wait.

BIG JAMES. Don't worry, Queen Joan, we'll send him to you soon enough.

JOAN. I thought this *was* an antechamber. It's tiny! How can the royal bedroom be so small? Why are all the rooms so small? This isn't a castle, it's a cottage perched on top of a rock!

WALTER. The lords of England have to witness each royal birth, in case a changeling's slipped in under the bedclothes.

BIG JAMES. Aye, that's the kind of trick they would pull.

ALISDAIR. But we're cannier than that, never mind who pulls the royal baby out, who put it in!? That's the trick you need to watch, eh? Eh?

BALVENIE. More wine, King James...

JAMES. Let me serve my Queen first...

He takes wine to JOAN *as they all erupt, 'Oh aye, you serve her, Jamie! We'll see you serve her!', etc.*

(*To* JOAN, *quiet.*) We'll wait for them to sleep. Don't worry, I'll be gentle, I'll be... eh... slow, it will be...

JOAN (*cuts him off*). No, honestly, just be quick. Please, please just be quick.

He goes back to the others, they are roaring and singing. She gulps her wine, it spills, red on her white dress.

Meg, I've spoiled my dress.

JAMES *comes to her on the bed. Everyone is round them, watching.*

I've spoiled my dress.

End of Act One.

ACT TWO

A Dining Tent in the Grounds of Falkland Palace

A long table laid out with food. JOAN *takes her place at the centre of the table.* MEG, BALVENIE, *the Stewart brothers,* MURDAC *and* ISABELLA *follow her in and take their own places.*

This is nine months after Act One. JOAN *is now very pregnant.*

The BISHOP *and* MUSICIANS *are waiting. Everyone waits in silence for a moment.*

JOAN. The King will be with us shortly.

They wait.

Any moment.

They wait.

He was called away. Someone needed to talk to him. Something important, he said. He did say it was important.

They wait.

I think we could have the grace and the music, don't you? I don't think he'd expect us to keep you waiting, bishop.

The BISHOP *rapidly delivers the grace in Latin and exits. The* MUSICIANS *start to play quietly. The Stewart boys start tearing into the food.*

Yes.

We should eat.

We should all eat. I don't think he would expect us to wait.

She turns to MURDAC.

We've had fine weather for the King's parliament anyway.

MURDAC. A soft summer.

JOAN. I thought he was joking, he told me he'd be holding his parliament in a garden and I laughed...

As the Stewart brothers finish meat, they throw the bones over their shoulders. MEG *has seen this. She is outraged.*

But he said there were no halls in Scotland large enough to hold the whole assembly, so...

ISABELLA (*cutting her off*). We don't need any.

JOAN. Sorry?

ISABELLA. There's no need to call the whole assembly. We don't need to ask every little lord how to go on. We don't need to be taking some abbot's advice. The families can run things. They've been doing that just fine.

MURDAC. Since when did you sit in the Three Estates, woman?

ISABELLA. I'm just saying.

(*Smiles at* JOAN.) Lovely chicken, pet.

MURDAC. This is new for all of us. These are the first parliaments that have been called for forty years.

JOAN. I do hope your accommodation is satisfactory. I didn't realise so many of the families would be housed in... tents.

ISABELLA. It's our own tent. It's what we use for war.

JOAN. Sorry?

ISABELLA. To sleep before a battle? It's a good big tent. Warm too. We're better in that than the spare rooms in Falkland Palace, there was only ever one room warm in that place and you're in that, eh?

JOAN. Yes, I...

ISABELLA. I had that fireplace made bigger. I hope you're getting the benefit?

JOAN. Yes, it's very... cosy.

ISABELLA. Good.

BALVENIE. We're waiting on the mutton ribs down this end if you're done with them, boys...

STEWART BROTHERS. We're not.

ISABELLA (*to* JOAN). Any more of this good French red?

She holds out her glass. JOAN *is really embarrassed.*

JOAN. No… no… We couldn't buy…

There's ale.

ISABELLA. My cleaning wifie drinks ale, I'm on the red.

JOAN. There's no more.

ISABELLA. You didn't buy any more of the French red?

Couldn't afford it, I suppose.

(*Laughs.*) Hear that, Murdac? The King's so broke he can't even buy us a glass of wine! Never mind, pet. Shall I treat you? We've got plenty in our tent…

MEG *has got up and is behind the Stewart brothers, she's been waiting for the next bone to come over. When it does she grabs it and hits* BIG JAMES *over the head with it.*

MEG. Where were you raised!? In a midden!?

(*To* ISABELLA.) Is this the way you raised them?

ISABELLA. What are they doing?

MEG. Chucking their bones on the floor!

ISABELLA. What!?

MEG. Aye! Did you not see them? Throwing their bones on the ground like a pack of great smelly bears that don't know how to use a plate!

ISABELLA (*shocked*). Boys!

WALTER *points at* JOAN.

WALTER. She's doing it!

JOAN. It's just a chicken bone…

MEG. Oh, that's just wonderful! That's a great example to be setting, isn't it? That's how they do it in England, is it?

Throw their chicken bones on the ground for the dogs to choke themselves on? Have you *any* sense? And you fretting yourself sick about money.

(*To the Stewart brothers.*) Well, she comes from a heathen country where they've got servants running round like ants clearing up after them, and all their big lords and ladies never think the servants have eyes and ears and they never know their names half the time. Here there's just me and *here* we need the bones for the soup tomorrow. So leave them on your bloody plates!

BIG JAMES. I bet you make great soup.

MEG. I'll make it out of your head if you don't behave.

BIG JAMES. I could marry you.

MEG. You could sit on the church roof and wait for a pigeon to lay a golden egg in your pocket but I wouldn't rate your chances of that either.

JAMES *comes in.*

JOAN. Oh, where have you *been*!?

(*Checks herself.*) I'm sorry, my lord. We waited for you but your guests were hungry.

JAMES. Of course.

There was a petition…

I was called to see this woman.

JOAN. Well, why did you go?

JAMES (*he's distracted*). Sorry?

JOAN. Don't we have servants? To meet your petitioners?

JAMES. I saw her…

I had to talk to her. It was important.

JOAN. What was?

JAMES. Not now. Not here.

He is watching the Stewart brothers.

JOAN. Of course. Excuse me, my lord.

　　Forgive me.

JAMES (*suddenly alert to her*). Are you upset?

JOAN. There's no more wine.

JAMES. You want wine? Why doesn't someone get you some wine?

ISABELLA. I've been trying.

JOAN. We've only beer left.

JAMES. I'll drink beer. I like beer.

　　MURDAC *serves him*.

MURDAC. Nothing wrong with beer, it's an honest drink.

JOAN. And we've hardly any flour, I've had them count the flour sacks. If you want to feed your whole parliament till the end of the week we need more bread. I've sent to the mill. Cheese we're alright, we're out the door with cheese but some of it's on the turn, we can cook it or we can feed it to the common folk.

JAMES. I'm sure it will all be…

ISABELLA. I can get you more meat if you're needing some…

JOAN (*cuts her off, icy and cutting*). I'm so sorry, Lady Isabella, is the food not to your liking?

ISABELLA. No, pet, what you've put out is fine I'm just…

JOAN (*driving over her again*). I'm just trying to organise my own household. I'm sure you understand. You'll have to excuse me. You'll have my attention again in a moment I promise you.

　　A pie is brought in and placed on the table. The Stewart boys roar in delight and all start trying to cut into it.

BALVENIE. Could you pass that down, boys, do you think?

　　They ignore him.

JAMES. What do you need, Joan?

JOAN. Oh, don't talk to me. Just don't talk to me!

Pass me the pickled onions.

JAMES. Don't you want some more meat? You've barely eaten…

JOAN. Just give them to me.

She takes some onions and starts to exit, JAMES *gets up from the table and stops her.*

JAMES. You're upset!

Christ, I'm sorry… stay… please stay. What's wrong? Let me…

JOAN. My lord! You're the *King*! Don't *chase me*!

You shouldn't…!

She breaks off in exasperation. She drops into a curtsey.

(*Toneless*.) I beg your pardon, Your Majesty. I'm feeling unwell, do I have your permission to leave your royal presence?

JAMES. No, no, stay please…

He takes the onions from her and puts them back on the table.

Well, if you're unwell…

I'm sorry. I'm sorry you're not well.

JOAN. This is a poor country. A poor, poor country.

JOAN *exits.*

JAMES *stands looking after her, completely bereft.*

ISABELLA. I don't know what her problem is. I offered her my wine.

JAMES. Fine. We'll do this here and now.

(*Turns to* MURDAC.) There's a woman over by the palace gate you should go and see. She lives on your land. On your son Walter's land. She came to petition me for justice.

ISABELLA. The cheeky bissum!

JAMES. Go and see her.

ISABELLA. We're not running off to talk to some woman with a grudge on my son...

JAMES. It's only a step outside. Go and hear her story.

(*To* MURDAC.) This is your business, your family's business.

MURDAC *hesitates*.

ISABELLA. Don't do it, Murdac, you're in the middle of your lunch.

JAMES. Go and look.

MURDAC *exits*.

ISABELLA. What woman's this?

MEG (*quiet to* JAMES). Should I go after the Queen?

ISABELLA. Walter? What woman is he talking about?

JAMES (*to* WALTER). You tortured her.

WALTER. I never did!

JAMES. You nailed horseshoes to her hands and feet.

ISABELLA. Oh, someone's making up stories!

WALTER (*realises*). Oh, *her*. Aye, but she was just an old biddy who keeps her cows on my land.

JAMES. On *her* land. Separated from yours and her grazing all her life.

WALTER. Like I said. She was just an old cow-wife.

JAMES. You broke her ditches down.

WALTER. You're not really going to make this fuss over a cow-wife, are you?

JAMES. While I am King, while *I* am King, the key will keep the lock and the broom bush will keep the cow and no man, *no man*, will stand above that law. You can read the law. You can read it in Latin and tell me it back in French. So keep it.

WALTER. Or?

MURDAC *is back on. He is shaken. He speaks to*
ISABELLA.

MURDAC. It's Ada Stewart, from Blairgowrie. He's crippled
her.

WALTER. Och, she wouldny shut up! Scolding me like I was a
bairn.

ISABELLA. She's *known* you since you were a bairn, Walter!

WALTER. She was *scolding me*!

JAMES. She came to him, her lord, the man who owed her
protection.

She asked for justice. He had her held down and shoed her
like a horse.

WALTER. It shut her up. I'll tell you that.

JAMES. You pay her restitution or I'll give her every field of
yours that touches hers.

WALTER. Oh, you've got your eyes on my *land*, you greedy
wee monarch.

ALISDAIR. Why not try and take it in fair fight.

BIG JAMES. 'Stead of weaseling it out of us with laws.

MURDAC. Big James, be quiet!

JAMES. You will pay her restitution.

WALTER. Make me.

JAMES. Fine. We'll do it that way.

JAMES *launches himself at* WALTER. *They wrestle.*

BIG JAMES. *Salup!*

ALISDAIR. Christ, Walter, get him, *get him*!

BIG JAMES. He's got nothing, Walter! Finish him!

JAMES *pins* WALTER.

(*Surprised.*) Oh, hullo!

JAMES *has beaten* WALTER.

JAMES (*to* WALTER). You are bound by the laws of this country!

You have to keep that law as much as the poorest beggar hiding in your barns. Do you hear me!?

WALTER. Oh, I hear you. I hear you.

JAMES. Will you pay the woman restitution?

MURDAC. He will.

ISABELLA. No, not our land…

MURDAC (*cutting her off*). He will! Walter!

WALTER. Aye. I'll pay her.

JAMES. Then here's my hand.

JAMES helps WALTER up, WALTER grips him and pulls him close.

WALTER. King Henry's prisoner. Not my King. Not my fucking King!

MURDAC. Get him away from here! Get away from here, all of you!

The Stewart brothers look at him a moment.

ALISDAIR. Papa's not happy, Big James.

BIG JAMES. *Tant pis.*

They exit.

ISABELLA. All I'm saying… she could be annoying, that Ada Stewart.

MURDAC. Isabella, just *don't*!

ISABELLA. Murdac! We are not giving up one spade of our earth! He's not having our land! Never!

MURDAC. Get out of here! Before I… *get out*!

ISABELLA exits. MURDAC looks at JAMES. A bell sounds off, distant.

JAMES. It's time for the afternoon session of parliament.

MURDAC *is still stuck.*

Tell them I'm on my way.

MURDAC *slowly exits.* JAMES *is getting himself together.* MEG *helps him.*

I could take him now.

MEG. Who?

JAMES. King Henry.

You see that? I win an argument and I win a fight and she doesn't even see it.

MEG. I'll tell her.

JAMES (*bitter*). Aye. You woo her for me, Meg. That'll work. Nothing else has.

JAMES *exits. After a moment* MEG *follows. As soon as she's gone* BALVENIE *starts helping himself to cakes.*

JOAN *enters,* BALVENIE *startles and drops all the cakes.*

BALVENIE. Oh Christ. They can make more though, eh?

JOAN. There's no time. They need a slow oven.

BALVENIE *groans in frustration. He starts beating his own head.*

BALVENIE. Aaaaaaach! You stupid greedy lump, Douglas.

God I'm sorry, I'm so sorry.

JOAN. You think I care? I just came for the onions.

She starts eating them.

BALVENIE. The thing is… I never get any. Those bastards above me on this table never pass them down.

It hurts me to watch them. They shovel in… (*Searches for word.*) ambrosia… like this and never even taste it. They don't care what they put in their mouths, all they care about's the booze. And they won't even pass me crumbs. You had nutmeg put in those, didn't you?

JOAN. And white cheese.

BALVENIE. Was *that* it? Man, that's genius! Makes them moist as Italian peaches. Now there's a taste of heaven, have you ever had one of those?

JOAN. No.

BALVENIE. We need to get you to Rome.

Looks down at the wreck on the ground.

See, I'd still eat that. But I don't suppose anyone else would, eh?

JOAN *says nothing.* BALVENIE *gets down and starts to scoop up the ruined cakes.*

JOAN. Who are you?

BALVENIE. Douglas of Balvenie, Queen Joan. I was at your wedding night.

JOAN. Everyone was at my wedding night.

BALVENIE. Aye, right enough.

You looked fantastic by the way.

JOAN. Don't.

BALVENIE. No... listen no... I would never... think about you like that.

(*Searching for the words.*) Looking at you... It's like looking at the Virgin on a church window. You see? You watch the light stream through her. You'd no more think of touching her than digging up the fields of heaven.

JOAN. You saw him touching me. You all saw him touching me.

BALVENIE. You were a little white flower bending in his wrestler's hands. That's what I saw.

JOAN. I don't like thinking about it.

BALVENIE. Well, when you do, know that I saw a white flower. Think about that.

I'd never harm you. I'll be your friend, Queen Joan. Always. I think you need one. Don't you?

You and the King.

Tell him to look to the wee men. Tell him to look to me. All I'm after is a wee bit more land, Queen Joan, enough to bring me up to the big boys' shoulders. I'm just a flea hopping about with no clue where to go, give me a warm place to land and I'll prove what my friendship could be worth.

JOAN. We have friends, I have my whole household…

BALVENIE. Ah… right enough.

JOAN. If you're my friend stop talking sideways! Tell me what you mean.

BALVENIE. Can't you feel it? There are too many royal Stewarts at the King's table. And they're hungry, every one of them could claim…

JOAN (*cutting him off*). James has the best… the *only* claim to be King…

BALVENIE. Well, his big brother's claim was better. And they killed him.

JOAN. His brother was sick…

BALVENIE. He didn't get sick till Murdac Stewart's father locked him in a cellar with no food or drink.

It was just over in Falkland Palace there. I can show you the room…

I'm nobody and he's a king… but I'd take better care of you if you were mine… that's all I'm saying.

He exits, after a moment she follows.

The Garden, Falkland Palace

Parliament is assembled on a green lawn.

A blast of music announces JAMES*'s arrival. The* LORDS,
CLERGY *and* COMMONERS *are assembled. We get a sense of
the crowd.* JAMES *strides into the middle of them and cuts off
the end of the fanfare. He's furious.*

JAMES. No, we'll not bother with the ceremony. We'll not
bother with the kneeling. Today I'm just going to tell you the
law of the land. Easy thing to forget when your lawful King
is locked up in England but I'm back to remind you.

Every man here is laird of his own land. And every man here
gathers the taxes from the folk on his land, doesn't he?
That's all great. That's the law doing what the law was
supposed to do, since the time of my great-grandfather, since
the time of the Bruce. But then we've got a problem, eh? A
wee memory lapse about what should happen to all that tax
money. Shall I remind you what the law says? The law says
it's due to me, *to the crown.*

And I will be having it, from now on, every farthing!

*The start of an uproar, the Stewart brothers are howling in
opposition. 'Thief!' 'We bled for that money!', etc.…* JAMES
pitches over this.

And any of you that haven't paid me that money, or won't
pay me that money or just plain forgot to pay me that money
I will be having your land off you because I am King of
Scots and I will make you keep the laws of Scotland!

*Uproar. The Stewart brothers are shouting at him, everyone
is rushing out of the parliament. Helpless,* JAMES *watches
them go as, unseen by him,* MURDAC *walks up to the
throne. When* JAMES *turns* MURDAC *is sitting on the
throne behind him.*

MURDAC. That's pretty much how it was when your father,
King Robert, held his parliaments. He didn't have lungs like
yours, though, he'd a wispy wee indecisive voice. And he
didn't have it in him to do what my father did, what I did.

JAMES. What you did?

MURDAC. Sit on the throne of Scotland and look like a real king.

JAMES. That's a good trick. Can you teach it to me?

MURDAC. When you think you can't do it a minute longer, stand up and let some other fool sit down.

MURDAC *stands up*.

JAMES. Oh nice, thanks for that.

MURDAC. So, King James, are you ready for that conversation now because I think…

JAMES (*cutting over him*). No, you do not… you do not talk to me here!

Talking about my father? Telling me what he was like? Aye, you knew him so well, didn't you? So well! I never knew my father, I barely remember my fucking father, do I?

I remember my brother, though. I remember David. What happened to him, Murdac Stewart? Where's my big brother David?

You murdered him. Your family murdered him, didn't they? Your fucking family…

What do you remember about him? About David?

JAMES. I have one clear memory of him. Just one. I'm sitting on his shoulders, we're walking down to the sea. He said 'When I'm King I'll take you all the way over the sea to France, Jamie… when I'm King.' Then he ran with me and I thought I was flying…

MURDAC. He was a useless prince and he'd have been a worse king.

Your brother David was a greedy wee bastard, he didn't care about the King's law, all he ever wanted was the King's gold, he'd have robbed us all and called it justice.

He needed to die.

But I think Scotland needs you to live, James Stewart.

JAMES. What do you want, Murdac?

MURDAC. I've listened to you. I've watched you. I think we want the same thing, King James. I do.

JAMES. Really.

MURDAC. A peaceful country, bound by law, ruled by a strong king.

JAMES. I can't begin to rule here! How can I rule without money? How can I pay crown officers without money? If we want law they have to pay! That's common sense!

MURDAC. Not to the men with the wealth and the lands.

JAMES. I had a plan. It was a good plan.

MURDAC. I heard you. It was a beautiful plan. Anyone could hear the sense in it. But this lot won't listen to any man until he proves he's as good as they think they are. You need to scare them.

JAMES. What do you suggest? I'll shout a bit louder, shall I?

MURDAC. Make some arrests.

JAMES. Who? Who can I arrest?

MURDAC. My sons. You have to arrest my sons. They shouted treason in your face. The whole world heard them.

JAMES. And how do you propose I arrest three warriors with their own private armies, their own defended castles...

MURDAC. There is only one place in this whole palace where there'll be good French red wine to drink tonight, that's our tent in the garden here. They'll be with me and Isabella tonight.

JAMES. What kind of father offers up his own children?

MURDAC. A father that loves the bravest sons that ever drew breath! Don't flatter yourself, wee King James. They could gobble you up and never even stop to pick their teeth, but after that... After that they'd be fighting for their chance to sit on your throne the rest of their days. No man can defeat every sword in Scotland.

No man can live in a war all his days and hope to live long.

> They'd probably kill each other in the end. But they'd kill me long before that. That's certain.

JAMES. So you give me your sons...

MURDAC. And you'll give me your word you'll keep them safe. Alive, unharmed. Your vow before God.

> And give me your word you'll not touch one blade of grass that belongs to me and mine. All that's ours will still be ours.

JAMES. Murdac Stewart... If I have your sons locked up... why would I ever let them loose again?

MURDAC. Because you'll need to keep my friendship, King James. You need the friendship of one great man at least. Otherwise you might as well have drowned eighteen years ago.

JAMES. You're trusting your children's lives to my word?

MURDAC. It's the only thing that makes sense, at this point. Isn't it?

JAMES. Yes.

MURDAC. Well, I trust you to know good sense when it offers itself up to you.

> I love them... but I could wish you'd been my son, James Stewart. I could.

JAMES. Thank you.

> JAMES *takes his hand*.

> You have my word. My solemn vow before God. Your lands will not be touched and your sons will not be harmed.

MURDAC. Then you can take them, you can take my boys.

JAMES. I thought I was alone here.

MURDAC. Well, you're not. I'm the only man alive who's sat where you're sitting. I know what it feels like.

> Let's hold onto that.

The Queen's Room

JOAN *and* MEG *are sorting dresses for remaking.* JOAN
busies herself unpicking stitches, MEG *is cutting embroidered
panels from another dress.*

MEG. You're very quiet.

JOAN *says nothing.*

Quiet as a mushroom.

JOAN. What does that even mean?

MEG. Eh?

JOAN. 'Quiet as a mushroom', what does that even *mean*?

MEG. It's just something I say.

JOAN. I don't understand a word you say!

MEG. Why are you picking a fight with me?!

JOAN. I can't imagine! I can't imagine, I mean if I was a proper
English princess I wouldn't even know your name, would I?
You'd just be a little ant scurrying about doing what I want
and never speaking.

MEG. Are you seriously still cross about that?

JOAN *says nothing, tearing cloth angrily.*

Well, Your Majesty, here's a limit to how nice I'm going to
be to you because you're stuffed full of crabbitnesses along
with your bairn so don't push my patience.

A beat.

You'll do fine. I've helped all my aunties and my big sister
and I'm telling you I know you'll do fine.

And you'll make the King so happy.

JOAN *sighs.*

Can I ask you something?

JOAN. Probably.

MEG. Have you never loved any man?

A beat.

JOAN (*quiet*). Love is a sweet, secret thing you do in cupboards.

JOAN has nicked her finger, she goes mad throwing the dress down, slapping at it.

Oh, the stupid thing, the *stupid* thing.

MEG is stopping her.

MEG. Stop it. Let me do it. You rest now.

JOAN. I hate small work, I *hate* it. My head starts buzzing as soon as I've got to look at anything as small as stitches! Oh, there's no air in this place. I've no more room to move than a nut tight in its shell! I'm trapped in another stupid little *hovel* of a castle!

MEG. What's wrong with it!?

JOAN. It has no empty cupboards.

ISABELLA enters right at the end of this. She's been listening outside.

ISABELLA. Anything you need you can fit in a kist.

She's carrying a covered bowl. She puts it down on a chest, beaming at them.

And it's proper furniture. A kist has a hundred uses, a table, a shelf, a chair. You could fit two bairns and a week's rations for a squadron of men in a kist like this. You can have all your wealth ready to carry the minute you smell smoke. And you could barricade a door with the thing. Drop it out the window and brain any bastard climbing up the castle. A cupboard is just a door in a wall. Get more kists. I'll have the man make you up a few.

JOAN. No, I can...

ISABELLA (*cuts her off*). Oh, it's no trouble!

JOAN. Thank you.

ISABELLA. What is it you're needing to put in store anyway?

JOAN. Just a few precious... personal...

ISABELLA. Oh ho! Secrets!

JOAN. My own things.

My own things. So I would like to order the work myself.

ISABELLA. Of course.

Of course… Your Highness.

Making boxes to keep your secrets in. Important. Important work indeed.

(*Abruptly to* MEG.) Are you going to get me a drink or do I need to sit here till I'm drooling dust?

MEG. Oh!… Sorry… I was just…

ISABELLA. Daydreaming. I'd beat you for it if you were mine.

JOAN (*smiling*). She'd likely beat you back.

ISABELLA. Well, then I'd have to get the sword out.

Can you use a blade?

JOAN. I can gut a fish. I can chop an onion. I could carve a spoon, if I had to.

ISABELLA. So could your cooks.

ISABELLA *gets a short sword out and swishes it through the air to demonstrate*.

My family's the oldest royal house in Scotland. Did you know that? My grandmother cut down all the robber lords invading her castle with her own blade. Royalty has the natural instinct for battle. That's what sets us apart.

JOAN. From what?

ISABELLA. From the likes of her.

MEG. Oh, I've killed plenty men, my lady.

ISABELLA. How do you figure that?

MEG. They all died of love.

ISABELLA (*stares at her, then decides to laugh*). More fool them.

So! Secrets! Secrets… what secrets does my bonny wee
Queen have to keep?

Of course you're worried about that bairn inside you.

JOAN. It's my first child. That's no secret.

ISABELLA. I didn't say it was, just making conversation. It'll
be a girl, of course.

No, it will. Get ready for the disappointment. Stewart seed
usually makes women first before it works up to breeding
boys. Strong women though. She'll likely fight her way out.
Get ready to bleed.

MEG. So you're here to frighten us, are you?

ISABELLA. A queen doesn't get frightened.

(*To* JOAN.) Do you?

Though I'd be frightened if my man had done what yours
has done. Beating my boy down. In front of us all. Taking
his land…

A beat.

JOAN. Your son broke the law, Lady Isabella. The King's law.

ISABELLA. And the King must have his way.

But maybe his way isn't the way things need to be done. The
way things have been done these last few years.

The lords are not happy. The great men are not happy. The
noble women are not laughing.

And you're scared.

JOAN. But a queen is never frightened.

ISABELLA. Away! I can smell that lie. It bursts out your oxters
with a reek like week-old cabbage.

MEG. What are you here to tell us, Lady Isabella?

ISABELLA. Well, madam, I'm not here to talk to you at all.

(*To* JOAN.) Send her out of here.

JOAN. No.

ISABELLA. Oh, wee girl.

Bless you, wee girl. Look at you, cooried in here, trembling, you sweet thing, like a cooshie doo on its nest with the fox climbing the tree.

You better learn how to make the right friends or you'll no get much older, will you?

My ancestors have been Kings of Scotland back to the start of recorded time. There's a lot of royalty in Scotland. Royalty should make friends with royalty, don't you think?

You can tell King James how he should go on. He should leave our land alone. Tell him. It's a wife's job to care for her husband. You'll know what's best, eh? He'll listen to you.

(*Offers the bowl.*) I brought you some soup. From one mother to another.

JOAN. Thank you. No.

ISABELLA. I'll put it here for you. (*Puts bowl down.*)

You should eat, my wee Queen. We don't want you wasting away, do we? And you should learn the sword, my lady. You never know when you'll need the knack, or at least you'll have a better way to slice an apple. Quick as you like.

ISABELLA *slices the sword through the air. It just misses* JOAN's *pregnant stomach.* JOAN *freezes.*

(*Laughs.*) Made you jump.

ISABELLA *exits.* JOAN *still seems frozen.* MEG *takes the cover off the bowl of soup. She's shocked.*

JOAN. What is it?

MEG. I'll take this out.

JOAN. Show me!

She goes to look. It shocks her.

What does she mean? One mother to another? What does she mean?

She has hold of the bowl, MEG *tries to take it from her.*

MEG. I'll take this out.

JOAN. You said I'd know what folk meant. You promised me I'd know what people meant...

She means to kill me.

JAMES *enters*.

MEG. I'll take this out.

MEG *exits with the bowl*.

JAMES. What was that?

JOAN. The Lady Isabella brought me some soup.

JAMES. Was it good?

JOAN. It was...

It was...

It was chickens...

JAMES. What's happened? Are you ill?

JOAN (*getting upset*). Baby chickens, unhatched. Dead baby chickens taken before they could hatch... She just broke the eggs in a bowl... and there were the tiny chicks, pink, with no feathers...

JAMES. What do you want me to do, Joan?

He tries to touch her.

JOAN. Oh, dear *God*!

(*Controls herself.*) Excuse me, Your Majesty, I...

JAMES (*cutting her off*). Look at the state of you! How am I supposed to understand you if you never explain anything to me? It's just this. It's always this. Tears and glum looks and no reason for it! No reason! Ever!

JOAN. I'm sorry, Your Majesty, if...

JAMES (*cutting her off*). Oh, you're not fucking sorry! You're sorry for yourself and that's an end to it!

Horrible silence.

If you told me what was wrong with you I could fix it. I would give my life and half my kingdom to fix it. If you show me the job you need me to do to make you happy I will get it done.

I can't bloody *guess*, Joan. I need information.

JOAN *goes and gets a box and takes papers out of it. The poem.*

What are you doing now!?

JOAN. You said I had to read it.

JAMES. You don't have to read it.

JOAN. No, I've been doing the best job I can, with *very* limited resources but it's not enough, is it? I'm still a disappointment, apparently. So I better read your poem too, hadn't I?

JAMES. You don't have to read it.

JOAN. No, you're not going to blame me for not reading your poem, I'm reading your poem.

JAMES. Then read it! Bloody read it to me!

He grabs it up, rifles pages, finds the place he wants.

Here! Here! Read that bit, read it to me! Go on!

JOAN *hesitates.*

JOAN. I don't always... I don't have the eyes for small work.

JAMES *says nothing.* JOAN *starts to read, haltingly.*

'And then... I cast down my eyes again
Where I saw walking under the tower,
Half hidden, a new thing, coming here to play,
The fairest and the freshest young flower
That I ever saw, I thought, before that hour...'

JAMES. I wrote that when I was prisoner in Windsor. Looking down into the garden from the tower.

JOAN. It... I used to run in that garden... in Windsor.

JAMES (*points*). Read.

JOAN (*reading again*)....

>   'I heard a little sound
>   And after it my eyes eagerly down
>   I cast, seeing there her little hound
>   That with his bells played on the ground,
>   Then I said, and sighed a little too
>   "Oh lucky dog that plays down there with you."'

(*Breaks off, agitated.*) I had a dog! I played in that garden with Bess and she had bells on her collar...

(*Gets it.*) This is about me.

JAMES. There were some years when they let me roam the court, more years when they kept me locked in my room. I never got out. I used to watch the birds in the tree outside my prison window. They were the only hopeful living thing I ever saw... until I saw you playing in that garden. I never thought I'd meet you. It was a dream. And then it was real.

JOAN. Why didn't you tell me?

JAMES. I did! I put it in a bloody poem and gave it to you!

JOAN. Well, how am I supposed to understand something if you put it in a poem! Why can't anyone here ever say anything in plain words!?

JAMES. I love you.

A beat.

Plain enough for you? How can you understand about eels and milk and sides of bacon and not see what's right in front of your eyes!

A beat.

JOAN. We'll have bacon now. We killed the pigs today. Did you hear them screaming?

The baby jumped to hear it.

There was a little boy watching, he was only about three, he was terrified. They make such a human sound, don't they, the pigs? And their feet were scrabbling on the bloody cobbles.

I saw the little boy's mother wrap her arms round him and
then his father picked him up and kissed his soft little cheek
and whispered in his ear... I knew what they were saying...
'This is alright. This is natural. This is just how it has to be.
We need salted meat for the winter. Who could get through a
winter without meat?'

And I thought, you can teach a child anything. Persuade it
into anything, can't you? Killing pigs or killing men. Just
kiss its soft little cheek and tell it why it has to be done.

'We need meat when we are hungry. We need salted meat to
last through the cold.'

It's always cold here. They won't suffer a winter without
meat. They're always hungry. And they all know what has to
be done.

I don't want my baby to be born here.

I don't want to be here.

Do you understand what's wrong now?

JAMES. You're frightened.

JOAN. Yes. Yes. Yes!

I have no friends here and I'm frightened all the time. All
the time!

JAMES. I've fixed it.

JOAN. What?

JAMES. Duke Murdac's sons will be in prison before the
    morning and any rebellion will be locked up with them
    for good.

JOAN. You can't...

JAMES. It's already as good as done.

JOAN (*wondering*). She won't dare hurt me if you have her sons.

JAMES. No one will.

JOAN. Is it true?

JAMES. Yes.

JOAN. Is it really true?

JAMES. Yes.

JOAN. I want to believe you…

JAMES. Believe me. It's true. In the morning you'll see it's true. You'll know you're safe.

JOAN. Oh, I'd love that… so much…

He kisses her. She kisses him back for a moment then pulls away.

I'm sorry… I think it's just the baby.

JAMES. It's fine. It's good. We're safe now. We have all the time you want.

JOAN. Can I tell you what I do want?

I'd like to lie beside you in the bed. I'd like to lie on your shoulder, on my side, so the baby can rest against you. I'd like you to put both your arms around me until I fall asleep. I'd like you to hold me like that all night, so I feel safe the whole night. That's what I want, that'll make me happy.

JAMES. Yes.

JOAN. The arm I lie on top of will go to sleep.

JAMES. I don't care.

JOAN. Good.

They get into bed. JOAN *positions herself against him, he wraps his arms round her.*

I'm going to sleep now.

JAMES. It will be alright.

JOAN. I'm asleep now.

You're certain? You're certain everything's going to be alright? You believe that?

JAMES. Yes.

JOAN *sighs in relaxation, they move closer into an embrace.*

Song.

> If my own love will love me best,
> And do the things I mean,
> I'll buy or make her such a dress,
> Her shape would match my dream.
> Her slip would lie against her skin,
> Soft, white and slipping free
> As white as shame, as white as dread,
> And perfect so to me.

A Tent in the Grounds of Falkland Palace

It's ISABELLA*'s and* MURDAC*'s tent.* ISABELLA *is drinking inside with the Stewart boys.* MURDAC *is outside or close to outside, watching the night. The song continues over this and under the following dialogue.*

Song.

> Her dress would so much match my dream
> With style to turn all heads,
> Beaded with pleasure in every seam,
> And furred to charm the dead.
> If she'd just wear this dress I mean,
> I swear upon my soul,
> That she could not wear grey or green,
> That showed her half as whole.

ISABELLA. You're welcome, you're welcome.

> ISABELLA *is greeting people as they enter the tent, getting them wine.*

You are all here because you're friends to this family, you'll eat with us, you'll drink with us…

ALISDAIR. You'll make war with us!

MURDAC *moves away.*

Dad?

ISABELLA. Never mind him.

ISABELLA and the Stewart boys are moving amongst their guests, giving them drink.

Take a drink. You're with us.

Take a drink to show you're with us.

GUARDS *have entered.* MURDAC *nods at them and steps clear to allow them to creep up on the tent.*

WALTER. If you're ready to stand with this family against the King, raise your glass. *Santé?*

Everyone cheers 'Santé!'

GUARD. In the name of King James – Walter, Alisdair and James Stewart, you are under arrest.

The GUARDS *charge into the tent and go for them.*

A fight.

ISABELLA. Get off them! Leave them! Leave my boys!

ISABELLA draws her weapon, screaming as she goes for the GUARDS. MURDAC *pulls her off and disarms her.*

What are you doing!?

Walter! Alisdair!

ALISDAIR. Run, Big James. Run!

ALISDAIR and WALTER *are captured.* BIG JAMES *gets away. The* GUARDS *are restraining* ALISDAIR *and* WALTER. *They are dragged off.*

A GUARD *hands* MURDAC *a ring.*

GUARD. The King sends you this ring as a token of his gratitude and of the oath between you.

The GUARD *exits.*

ISABELLA (*to* MURDAC). What have you done!?

What have you done to us!

MURDAC. What I thought best to do.

ISABELLA. I set you aside!

You're not my husband! Do you hear me?

He turns away from her.

I don't even want your name! When I see you next I will kill you, Murdac Stewart! Do you hear me? I will kill you and your pet King!

MURDAC *exits.* BALVENIE *and other* SCOTTISH LORDS *and* LADIES *are still just watching, shocked and uncertain.* ISABELLA *turns on them all, daring them to intervene.*

 What are you all looking at? Take your eyes to the ground.

You do not look at this, you do not.

ISABELLA *exits.*

LORD. Is it war now? Is that what's happening?

BALVENIE. I don't know.

LORD. I need to go home. I need to stand on my own land, with my own family.

The LORDS *and* LADIES *exit in all directions.* BALVENIE *goes to exit but* BIG JAMES *steps out of hiding and puts a knife to his throat.*

BIG JAMES. Quiet, old man, quiet... they'll be searching the bushes and the fields for me, the kitchens and the kirk. Look me in the eye...

He releases BALVENIE *so he can do so.*

I need to see the truth.

You know I could kill you.

BALVENIE. Yes.

BIG JAMES. You know I *would* kill you, if it suited me.

BALVENIE. Yes.

BIG JAMES. And do you know, do you believe that when I'm gone from here, I can still have you killed any time I like?

BALVENIE. It seems probable.

BIG JAMES. Not certain?

As BALVENIE *doesn't answer.*

No, not certain, but likely. Because who'd stand beside a creature like you?

A wee friendless, landless creature.

BALVENIE. I have lands.

BIG JAMES. King of a midden.

And you stand here and it's me that has to run for my life.

BALVENIE. There's no shame in it.

BIG JAMES. There's nothing *but* shame.

A LORD *runs through carrying belongings, a* LADY *chases him.* BIG JAMES *half-ducks back into hiding as they go.*

What's your life worth? Because I saved your life, as I remember it.

BALVENIE. And I paid. I did pay you.

BIG JAMES. You're my wee Douglas by rights. You owe me.

BIG JAMES *offers him the knife.*

You still sleep in the King's bedchamber. Don't you?

BALVENIE. If no higher member of the House of Douglas is ahead of me…

BIG JAMES. I want you to kill the King for me.

If you don't do us this one wee thing I will come back and strangle you with your own guts. Or someone who loves me will. You know that, don't you? That's what will *probably* happen, wee Douglas. I wouldn't gamble on another result. Would you?

BALVENIE. No.

BALVENIE *takes the knife*.

BIG JAMES. Have you ever been to The Lennox, old man?

BALVENIE. Yes.

BIG JAMES. There's a bonny bank, where the Kelvin bends round to Allander water, it's a bonny spot and the air is wet and clean, it clears your heart. Find me there when you're done, and show me his blood on this blade.

Don't keep me waiting there long, there's nothing to do but fish. Now get on with it.

They exit.

The Queen's Room

JOAN *and* JAMES *sleep*. BALVENIE *appears with a knife close to* JAMES*'s throat*. JAMES *wakes up*.

JAMES. Who's there?

BALVENIE. I sleep beside you this night and all nights.

JAMES (*peering*). Balvenie?

BALVENIE. Yes?

JAMES. What are you doing?

BALVENIE. I sleep beside you, King James... this night... all nights.

JAMES. Well, go to sleep then! You'll wake the Queen.

BALVENIE. Oh God... No. I can't. Sleep. Sorry. I'll just wait here... a bit... if that's alright.

JAMES. No. It's not. Lie down or fuck off, Balvenie. I need to sleep.

BALVENIE. I know. But I'm waiting. I'm always waiting you see, waiting to see which way it's safe to jump. Waiting till I know what's best. Waiting till I'm sure… Waiting to see what's going to happen next.

JAMES. What's going to happen next?

BALVENIE. Someone's going to try and kill you.

JAMES. Who? Who is going to try and kill me?

BALVENIE moves and JAMES sees the knife he holds for the first time.

BALVENIE. I'm not a gambling man. I'm not. I don't take chances. And if I did, would I gamble on your luck? Would I?

JOAN wakes and sees the knife. She screams.

JOAN. Murder! Help us! Help!

Neither JAMES nor BALVENIE move. MEG runs on. She sees the knife and stops dead.

JAMES. Balvenie… what do you want?

BALVENIE. Land. I just want more land. What else gives a man worth on this earth? A good life is invisible unless you own the land they bury you under.

JAMES. You're… you're petitioning me for land?

BALVENIE. That'd be nice.

But how can you give it to me when you're dead…?

He's still poised with the knife.

JOAN. You said you were my friend…

BALVENIE. Oh, what can I tell you. What do you want?

Maybe if you were mine I might fight every man alive for the chance to keep you safe. Looking at you might make me strong enough to do it.

But probably not. I'm not that kind of man. The question is, King James… what kind of man are you? I've no chance of a peaceful life now. He'll come for me, I know he will. I have to choose.

JAMES. Who'll come for you?

BALVENIE. Big James Stewart.

JAMES. Why will he come for you?

BALVENIE. Because he told me to kill you.

JAMES. Are you going to kill me?

BALVENIE. No... No, I... No.

He drops the knife. He crumples, terrified.

Oh Jesus, what have I done, what have I done, what have I done?

There was no safe choice, was there? This is the end of me. The end. I'm dead. You'll kill me now, won't you?

JAMES *secures the knife, moving slowly, careful.*

JAMES. No. No, not if you stand by me. Tell me what's happening.

JOAN. You told me we were safe, you promised me we were safe.

BALVENIE. He's gone to the south-west. He's raising an army against you. He'll bring war on us. Big James will raise their whole family and all the other families that run with them. And the rest of Scotland will sit and watch like it's a dog fight.

JOAN. We can run away. We can run south. We can go to my father's castle, we'll be safe there. We will. I know we will.

JAMES. I am the King of Scots and I won't be driven from Scotland again.

BALVENIE. Well, get ready to fight because Scotland's bringing war on you. Oh Jesus...

JAMES (*to* MEG). Bring my armour. Make me ready.

MEG *goes to get his war gear from a chest.* BALVENIE *helps. They dress* JAMES *for war.*

JOAN. I'm sorry.

JAMES. For what?

JOAN. Your armour. It hasn't been cleaned. I didn't think… I didn't want to think…

JAMES. It's fine.

JOAN. I don't want you to die. I don't want any harm to come to you. I feel that. You see? I do feel that. Look I'm shaking with it. That's how much I want you to be safe.

BALVENIE. What lands would you have given me?

JAMES. What?

BALVENIE. If either of us had lived, what lands would you have granted me?

JAMES. You'll have all of Big James Stewart's lands. I promise you.

BALVENIE takes a long sigh of happiness.

BALVENIE. So I hold those now? Already? Right this moment?

JAMES. Yes.

BALVENIE. Oh, maybe I can die happy then. Maybe I can.

I know where he is. I know where Big James Stewart will be waiting.

JAMES. Then take me to him.

He's armed and ready. He turns to JOAN.

JOAN. I could love you. I could. I'd love you if you could make me safe! I want to love you. I will love you. I promise.

JAMES. Good.   *love is conditional*

JOAN. Can you do this? Do you even know how to do this?

JAMES. I've watched… I've seen battle, I… Yes! Yes of course I know how to do this! I'm going to do this!

JOAN. Don't die. Don't. Please don't die.

He kisses her and exits. BALVENIE *follows.* JOAN *turns to* MEG, *holding her stomach.*

Tell them to arrest the Lady Isabella.

It's moving, it's frightened. It's so frightened.

A Battlefield, Morning

Drums. Two armies. JAMES *facing* BIG JAMES.

JAMES *is talking to himself, focusing himself.*

JAMES. I know how to do this. I know this work. I do. There is nothing but the sword in my hand. The sword and its weight and its use. I know this sword and I know its use.

(*Shouting to his men.*) Ready! Ready for my command!

Use breath, use weight, throat and arm and grip on horse and hilt and...

(*Roaring it as he urges the army forward.*) *Charge!*

Aw Christ, look at this morning... first smell of frost in the air. Last few yellow leaves hanging on the birches by the river, lit up like wee flames of morning light...

The GHOST OF HENRY *is there, taunting* JAMES.

HENRY'S GHOST. What kind of *king* is brought up in a prison reading books and writing poetry?

JAMES. Fuck the leaves!... light on the *blade,* on the sword.

The battle begins.

(*Shouting at* BIG JAMES.) That's right, you bastard! That's right! I'm coming for you!

HENRY. You? You can't even win a fight with a dying man.

JAMES. I'm ready. My sword's ready. Never mind that burn in your shoulder, keep it high, slash that burn down when it's time, when it's time, when it's time.

BIG JAMES *gives a yell of defiance at* JAMES.

That's right, you bastard! Your King's coming for you!
Death's coming for you!

HENRY. You've never beaten me. And you never will.

JAMES. I know this work! Nothing but the blade and... *NOW!*

JAMES *slashes his sword down, yelling. He's slashing to left
and right, in the thick of the battle.*

Drive them into the river!

*A chaotic press of men crammed together in bloody hacking
fury.*

BALVENIE. We're winning! We're winning!

(*Rallying the men around.*) King James! For King James!
Drive them into the river!

JAMES *is straight on* BIG JAMES. *He hacks down a man in
his way. The man becomes the* GHOST OF HENRY. *He
falls,* JAMES*'s sword is stuck in him. He roars in rage as he
tries to tug it loose. At the same moment* BIG JAMES *breaks
and runs.*

JAMES. Give me back my sword! You dare! You! I'll show you
how to be King! I'll show you!

BALVENIE. They're running! We've won! We've won!

The rest of BIG JAMES*'s forces run after him.* JAMES *is
still slashing at the fallen man again and again.*

JAMES. You dare stop me doing my work! You fucking dare
stop me!

The battle is over but JAMES *is still hacking.* BALVENIE
taps him.

BALVENIE. You're alright, I think that one's deid.

JAMES *whirls on him, the blade right at* BALVENIE*'s throat.*

JAMES. Did we win?

BALVENIE. Aye… Christ… aye… you annihilated them, King James…

JAMES *drops the sword and releases* BALVENIE, *giving in to tiredness.*

You could tell the ones that couldny swim, eh? The ones that died on the bank, more frightened of the dark, boiling flood than our blades.

Christ, look at me. I'm reborn. I could do that again.

JAMES. Big James Stewart?

BALVENIE. He ran.

JAMES. Not dead?

BALVENIE. No… he fled the field. But you're the victor. You're safe on your throne today, King James.

JAMES. No. No, that work's not finished. But it will be. Bury the dead and follow me to Stirling…

JAMES *moves through the applause of his army and the people to the throne room.* MURDAC *is there.*

MURDAC. Your Majesty, you've done what you had to. I know what has to happen now. I understand.

JAMES (*looking out the window*). This is a good view. You can see everything. The land our great-great-grandfather won.

MURDAC. He'll go to Ireland. He'll go to our family in Ireland. He won't be back unless there's another rising here and I won't let that happen. I promise you.

JAMES. Come and look. Look at it.

(*Looking round the whole view.*) The cold blue air. The great stone gateway to the high hills. The silver river. The sharp green marsh… Robert the Bruce might never have won if the ground hadn't been wet… he drove them onto the marsh and into the river, didn't he? If it had been a dry spring we might not be standing here, Murdac.

MURDAC. You have to take Big James's lands, I understand that, but he'll trouble you no more.

JAMES. How do you know that? I don't know that. I can't
know that. That doesn't seem likely. Does it?

A beat.

So now the next thing has to be done.

MURDAC. Yes… Yes… You'll need to hold my boys longer. I
understand. You've no choice.

JAMES. No, it's not enough. I have to execute them. I have to
execute every other man in your family.

A beat.

MURDAC. Oh Christ, no, listen to me.

James, now you've tamed them I can keep them in check. I
promise you.

JAMES. No, I have to execute you too. And the leader of every
family that rose with your son. You wouldn't give me peace
so I'll need to buy it. The crown will not be poor again. And
I can't look weak. Not even for one sunny afternoon. The
crown will have your lands. And theirs. And your cousins'
and your uncles'. All your lands and titles are forfeit to the
crown. We'll need the money for my ransom.

MURDAC. You're going to pay them? You're going to pay
England?

JAMES. I can't afford a war with England. Not until I'm safe
on my throne.

MURDAC. You're doing this for *money*!?

JAMES. I'm doing it because I have finally learned all the job
of a king.

MURDAC. Jesus, don't make me beg you, man… not all my
boys…

JAMES. Too many Stewarts. It has to be done.

MURDAC. No. It doesn't. It doesn't. You know. James, you
know better.

JAMES. I am the King of Scots, and I know my work, better than you, I will sit on this throne until I die, Murdac Stewart.

MURDAC. They will hate you till you die. Everyone would have understood if you'd cut me down in hot blood, slaughtered my sons in front of my eyes and screamed your rage at me. They'd've feared you for that. They might even have loved you in the end. But you're slaughtering me like a moneylender robbed of his interest. You're hacking my neck so it'll bleed gold for you. You're a cowardly little coin pusher, robbing his cousin's corpses. They'll despise you to death and beyond.

JAMES. Arrest Duke Murdac.

The GUARDS *move to take him*

MURDAC. You won't have a friend in the whole country when I'm gone.

JAMES. I never had a friend. I have the Queen.

(*To the* GUARDS.) Take him away.

MURDAC *pulls off the ring and gives it to* JAMES.

MURDAC. Your ring, Your Majesty. The token of your solemn vow.

The execution is prepared. JOAN *hurries out to watch.*
ISABELLA *is brought out under guard. She follows* JOAN.
She drops to her knees.

ISABELLA. Queen Joan. Your Highness… please… please…

JOAN *turns to her.*

Save my boys, Your Majesty. Save them or let me die with them.

JOAN. No. You did this! You did it to yourself! Your eggs are all broken, Isabella. You've smashed them all. And there are your little chicks. There they all are. Look. You look now.

The execution. JOAN, JAMES *and* ISABELLA *watch.*

Outside Stirling Castle

Song.

> Man is a withering weed,
> Woman is just smoke,
> His skin's a sack filled up with ash,
> She's a jar of dying coals.
> Like meat they'll dry,
> Like meat they'll hang,
> Like meat they'll stink,
> They'll be rubbed out...
> So... why are you wearing those jewels lady why the
>   gorgeous gown?
> Why are you wearing gold my lord?
> Why are you wearing that crown?

A deafening bang as the axe falls. ISABELLA *gives* JOAN
one deadly, desperate look.

The execution is over, JOAN *and* JAMES *still stand looking
down.*

JOAN. Did you watch? Did you keep your eyes open?

JAMES. Yes. Everyone was watching me.

JOAN. Me too. I forced them wide, wide open, I didn't even
dare blink.

I was shaking, but the wind was making all the folds of my
dress tremble anyway so I just kept my hands tight clasped
in my sleeves. No one saw me shiver, did they?

JAMES. No. No one saw.

He was a good axeman. He knew what he was doing.

JOAN. But it was so quick! And I didn't know, I'd never seen...

JAMES. Hadn't you?

JOAN. I'd seen hangings, of course, but not... the blood...

JAMES. Ah, that would be a shock.

JOAN. Did you see her? Did you see her look at me?

JAMES. It's over. The Lady Isabella will be imprisoned until she withers and dies. No one will look at you like that again. I won't allow it. I'm making a new world for you. Look.

He points.

They're planting roses. I'm planting a rose garden for you to walk in. You're safe now. And next year you'll have roses and gilly flowers in your garden.

MEG *enters with the baby.*

MEG. Here, you hold her. You hold her a while. She'll settle better with her mother.

JOAN. She's all sticky.

MEG. I tried her with honey.

JOAN. Did she take it?

MEG. Did she piddle! Mumbling and mewling like an old beggar lady chewing stones. Oh, the face on her! Nothing's as sweet as your mother at that age.

She hands the baby to JOAN.

JAMES. You are the dearest, sweetest thing I will ever know and I'll never stop loving you.

Looking at you is like looking at a green tree full of birds.

He kisses her.

JOAN (*looking at the baby*). Look at the blood moving under her skin, so thin... her skull is small as a robin's egg... Are we monsters now? We are. We are.

JAMES. No! Stop this, Joan. We are King and Queen and we'll be happy and I'll hold you safe in my arms every night. Every night.

JOAN. Yes, of course... She's cold... I'll take her in.

JAMES. It's not cold! This is our summer. A soft summer. I commanded it for you and here it is. Look at that view. Over the hills and all the way to the sea. How can you not love Scotland when she lays herself out for you to admire on a soft day like this?

JOAN. I'm sorry… I'm shivering still. I must be feeling cold, in the wind. I need to get her inside.

JOAN *exits*.

JAMES. It's a warm day.

MEG. Aye… she just… she's no long had the bairn… give her time…

JAMES. Yes… of course… There's three fulmars! See them? White. Riding the air high enough to look straight at us. You'd think they were gulls but they have blue eyes, really… dark, blue, human eyes, see them looking at us? They come inland to nest. They say they're the souls of dead men who couldn't find their way to heaven, lost for ever. But they look happy enough. They have the whole sky. She will love me now though… won't she, Meg? She will… surely?

MEG *just looks at him, a sad look. She exits.* JAMES *walks slowly to his throne.* ISABELLA *still sits looking out.*

ISABELLA. They've given me a view of the sea. They know its cruelty.

I curse them. I curse them with misery and demons till the end of their blood.

The waves in the sea beat on and on, carving up time into tiny grains of sand. And my blood beats in my ears. The only blood of mine still moving on this earth, every other darling young heart that carried this blood stilled and lying under the cold earth. I sit as still as my beloved dead and watch the seabirds slicing back and forth on the salty wind.

All I can do is wait and keep my hating sharp. The wheel will turn. The wheel always turns. The wheel will turn round again.

End.

JAMES II
DAY OF THE INNOCENTS

Characters

JAMES II, *King of Scots*
JOAN, *his mother*
ANNABELLA, *the King's sister*
MEG, *a lady of the Scottish court*
JOHN STEWART
LIVINGSTON, *Earl and Keeper of Stirling Castle*
CRICHTON, *Earl and Keeper of Edinburgh Castle*
BALVENIE, *senior statesman and lord, much older than
    appears*
ISABELLA, *noblewoman and long-term prisoner*
YOUNG DOUGLAS, *sixth Earl of Douglas, seventeen years old*
DAVID, *the Earl's younger brother, fifteen years old*
WILLIAM DOUGLAS, *Balvenie's son then eighth Earl of
    Douglas, eleven to twenty-two years old*
MARY, *the King's French wife, fifteen years old*
HUME, *a Scottish lord*
THE BULL-HEADED MAN, *a nightmare vision*

And LORDS, GUARDS, SERVANTS, SUPPORTERS, *etc.*

ACT ONE

Stirling Castle, Night / A Dream Memory

From now on everything we see is either nightmare or heightened memory. We hear, but don't see, MEG *calling off, desperate.*

MEG. Jamie! Jamie!

The closed chest sits in the centre of the room. Offstage, MEG *is still calling for* JAMES, *moving further away.*

WILLIAM *enters.*

He crosses to the chest and opens it, looking inside.

WILLIAM. I knew you'd be here. I won't tell them. They won't find you. I won't let them come in.

Slowly JAMES *climbs out of the box.*

Did they kill them both?

JAMES. Yes.

WILLIAM. It'll be fine. Just stay here with me a while. No one's after you. They never kill the wee bairns. Well, they might kill you because you're King but you'll be fine here with me. They won't find you. There's no one here but me. Look.

JAMES. There was all blood... on the floor.

WILLIAM. Did you see how they killed them? Did you not look? We need to look. A fighting man needs to be fit for that.

JAMES. I've dark blood, like snakes, under my skin.

WILLIAM. No you don't.

JAMES. It'll come out. I'll kill people.

WILLIAM. You might. But not with snakes.

When we're grown we can learn killing.

I'm nearly grown. Till then we need to learn how to bear looking at it. I'll teach you.

It's like when you take a beating. You think you can't stand it but if you just get used to what it feels like to get clouted round the heid, you can. Makes you stronger. I'll help you. I'm going to be the greatest warrior in Scotland. See when my father finds out what I can do? We'll be warriors, wee Jamie. We'll rule this country like roaring lions.

JAMES. I don't want to do that.

WILLIAM. Aye you do. I'll help you.

See if anything bad's happening all you need to do is call for me. Just…

WILLIAM *is suddenly wrenched away from* JAMES, *before he can finish the sentence, he's just gone, whipped away into the dark.*

JAMES *cries out, sitting up, looking round wildly for* WILLIAM.

WILLIAM *is gone.* JAMES *is sucked further into the nightmare.*

JAMES. Will?!

JOAN. Jamie?

JAMES. Mum? What is it?

JOAN. I need you to be a brave boy now, Jamie.

A brave, brave little boy.

Can you do that?

JAMES. I'm not a little boy. I'm six. I'm six whole years old.

JOAN. That's right. You're my brave little man. Come here, sweetheart.

JOAN*'s in a terrible state of fear and tension but covering. She has blood on her.*

JAMES. You're hurt.

JOAN. No, no, I'm fine.

JAMES. You're bleeding.

JOAN. It's not my blood, Jamie. It's from the men who killed your father.

JAMES. What are you doing?

JOAN *is finding and putting on jewellery.*

JOAN (*preoccupied with her task*). They'll have to tear them off me, they'll have to tear every jewel off me. They won't get them otherwise. This is my wealth, Jamie. This is half my power.

JAMES. I like that one.

JAMES *reaches out and touches a bracelet.*

JOAN *puts it on.*

JOAN. Your father gave me that, when Annabella was born. He should have known. Pearls are unlucky.

(*Shows* JAMES.) But I have the King's ring, look. I have your father's ring. And when you're big enough you'll wear it and be King yourself.

JAMES. I don't want to be King.

JOAN. Oh sweetheart, you're King already, but it's alright. I'll help you. I'll wear the ring and Mummy will be King for you till you're grown.

She hears shouts outside – looking round, sees the kist.

They won't stop me leaving if they think I'm alone…

JAMES. Who?

JOAN. …Bad men. Just bad men. They don't want Mummy to be Queen.

They've come to drive me away. Traitors!

MEG *enters with* ANNABELLA, *they're ready for a journey.*

MEG. What are you doing?

JOAN (*the kist*). This will work. Yes.

(*To* JAMES.) Come here, darling. I need you to hide in here.

MEG. Joan, no! I don't want to leave him either. But we can't take him with us!

JAMES. Why not? Where are you going? Meg?

JOAN. It's alright, darling. We're not leaving you behind.

JOHN STEWART *hurries on.*

JOHN STEWART. Queen Joan. Your guard is ready. They'll let you ride out.

JAMES. Who's that?

JOAN. Oh Christ save us, James, there's no time, please, please… you'll be safe in the box.

She helps him into the kist.

(*To* JOHN STEWART.) Save us, John Stewart. Save your King.

Save me and you'll win me. Look at me. It's true. You've seen how I've looked at you. I know you have. Help me now.

He hesitates.

JOHN STEWART. All the lords of Scotland would chase us if we took the little King.

JOAN. We can do this if we run now, *now*. John Stewart, I've watched you win every fight in the games. You can dare this too.

He's still unsure.

You'll be guardian of the King. We'll be rulers of Scotland. You will have Scotland's Queen.

MEG. Joan… no…

JOAN. Be quiet!

(*To* JOHN STEWART.) Well?

He decides.

JOHN STEWART. Aye, we can do it, we can do it. We can outrun them. I'll take you to my castle.

JOAN. Yes! You hear that, James? We'll be safe in John's castle.

You'll have a new pony and Meg will feed you as many honey cakes as you can eat.

JOHN STEWART. Quick then! Before they think to look for him. Hurry!

JOAN. Jamie, you just have to stay in the box a little while longer. Then we'll be safe and I'll never leave you again ever, not ever.

JAMES. Promise?

JOAN. I promise.

She closes the lid. A transition, a journey. JAMES *is being lifted, carried, buffeted. He's confined in a small, dark space.* JAMES *cries out.*

John Stewart's Castle

They've arrived. JOAN *opens the kist.*

JOAN. Jamie, look, look.

She's helping him out of the kist.

We're here. We're safe.

JAMES. Where are we?

JOAN. John Stewart's brought us safe to his castle.

JOHN. Welcome home, Your Majesty.

JAMES. Will I get a pony now?

JOAN *laughs.*

JOAN. If you're good. Run and play now. You can run anywhere you like now.

She exits with JOHN STEWART *as* JAMES *and*
ANNABELLA *run off and play, chasing each other, hiding,*
laughing.

MEG. No! You need your beds.

(*Quiet.*) I need my bed.

Jamie? Annabella? Come on. That's enough. You can play
tomorrow. It's time for bed.

JAMES *and* ANNABELLA *are hiding.* ANNABELLA
comes out.

Good girl. Jamie! Come out now. Meg will make you a
posset and sing you to sleep.

(*To* ANNABELLA.) Oh where is he? Isn't your brother the
naughtiest King of Scotland there's ever been?

ANNABELLA. Yes.

MEG. I'll be back to find you, King James.

MEG *and* ANNABELLA *exit.*

Then JOAN *and* JOHN STEWART *enter, they start to make*
love as JAMES *peeks out of hiding and watches.*

JOAN. I knew we'd do it. I knew we'd get safe away. And
they'll never break through your walls.

JOHN STEWART. No.

JOAN. They all hate me. They always hated me. They never
wanted me to be Queen.

JOHN STEWART. You're my Queen.

They kiss again.

JAMES. Mum.

They see him.

JOHN STEWART. Jesus Christ! What the fuck's he doing here!?

JOAN. Jamie… Jamie, why aren't you in bed?

JAMES. Who is he?

JOAN. How many times! Listen. Listen to me, John is your new father. Say it. Say hullo to your new father, James.

JOHN STEWART. Hullo... Hullo, King James.

JAMES. My father's dead.

My father was a hero.

A flicker of nightmare.

JOAN. Where's Meg gone? She was supposed to have sent you to bed.

Meg!

She exits. JOHN STEWART *comes close to* JAMES. *The nightmare is also closing in on* JAMES, *a memory of his father's death.*

JOHN STEWART. You look like him. Like your father.

He died in a drain. Did they tell you that? They caught the 'brave King' in his nightshirt. He climbed under the floorboards to hide. He left his women to fight for him. He robbed the wealth of half of Scotland, so that every man with a sword wanted him dead, and then he tried to hide safe behind his wife's skirts. They cut her arm to the bone. Have you seen that? Have you seen what those bastards did to her, what he left her to face? I curse your father's name every time I look at what was done to her skin. He was a coward and they killed him like a sewer rat.

JAMES. If my father was here he'd kill you with a big sword. And the worms would eat your eyes.

JOHN STEWART *moves closer still, confiding.*

JOHN STEWART. If your father was here I'd cut his legs and leave him sitting in his blood watching me give your mother what he never could. And I'll do the same to you if you don't shut up.

JAMES. No! *No!!!*

Nightmare, thunderous knocking, off. Splintering wood, shouting. Distorted voices calling, off.

VOICES. The King! We want the King!

JOAN *runs on, followed by* ANNABELLA. JOAN *goes to* JOHN STEWART, *who's drawn his sword.*

JOHN STEWART. Oh Christ.

JOAN. There's hundreds of them, riding at the gate! They're breaking in.

JOHN STEWART. Aw Jesus.

JOAN. You promised me! You promised me we'd be safe!

JOHN STEWART. Bar the door!

JOAN. With what!? There's no time!

Hide, Jamie! Quick! Quick!

JAMES *climbs into the box.* LIVINGSTON, CRICHTON, BALVENIE *and armed* MEN *surround* JOHN STEWART, JOAN, ANNABELLA *and* JAMES. WILLIAM *is there too, standing behind his father, watching.* LIVINGSTON *advances on* JOAN.

LIVINGSTON. Where's the King?

JOAN. He's not here. I don't know where he is.

LIVINGSTON. Well, what kind of mother are you? Lost him, have you? I don't think so. You can't rob Scotland of her ruler, Lady Joan.

JOAN. I am the Queen Regent, I rule Scotland and this is treason, Lord Livingston.

LIVINGSTON. You're queen of nothing.

JOAN *is pulling everything together. She squares up to them all.*

JOAN. Do you know what I do to traitors? Do you think I'll spare any of you?

CRICHTON. Do you really think you can threaten us today, Lady Joan?

JOAN. Queen Joan. I'm your Queen, Lord Crichton.

She's looking at BALVENIE.

You know it. You still see it. Tell them, Balvenie.

BALVENIE. Oh, Joan… I still see a bonny white flower. I do. But you've made your choice. And you're no queen when you lie in your sweat with John Stewart.

LIVINGSTON. Where's the King?

JOAN. He's my son. Mine. You'll never have him. Never.

LIVINGSTON. Well, I think he might turn up once we've torn this place to rubble and looked under every stone, but you've wasted enough of our time. (*To* GUARDS.) Hold him.

The GUARDS *grab* JOHN STEWART *as he struggles.*

JOHN STEWART. Get off me!

LIVINGSTON *puts a sword to* JOHN STEWART's *neck.*

LIVINGSTON. Tell me where the King is or I'll slice his throat.

JOHN STEWART. Joan, for Christ's sake!

JOAN. He's my son…

JOHN STEWART. He'll always be your son! We can have more sons. You and me.

MEG. Joan! You can't trust either of them! No!

JOHN STEWART. Joan! Please!

LIVINGSTON *readies his sword.*

JOAN. Don't!

He waits, looking at her, waiting for her answer.

How do I know you'll let us go?

How do I know we'll be safe?

LIVINGSTON. Because you're nothing without the King. Give the royal children to me and I'll let you run away and be nothing.

JOAN *walks to the chest.*

MEG. Joan, no!

JOAN *opens it.*

LIVINGSTON *walks to the chest and looks in.* JAMES *cowers.*

LIVINGSTON. Well. Good to see you, Your Majesty. Up you come.

He pulls JAMES *out.*

JAMES (*quiet*). Go away, don't look at me. Mum! Mummy!

LIVINGSTON. Mummy's got to go away, Your Majesty, she's got to run away fast before I slice her pretty lord into bacon.

JOHN STEWART. Joan, come on!

JOAN. Leave me my daughter.

LIVINGSTON. We would have done. But it seems you're a very careless mother, Lady Joan.

ANNABELLA. Mummy?

JOAN *is leaving.*

LIVINGSTON. Wait!

He grabs JOAN.

That's no yours, that's the King's ring.

He wrenches it from her finger as JOAN *cries out in pain.* JOHN STEWART *moves to defend her but is stopped.*

You don't get to keep Scotland's treasure now.

He pushes her away from him and puts the ring on his own finger.

Run away then. Run away and hide in some wee hole, Lady Joan. You're done.

JOAN *hesitates a beat longer then she starts to leave.*

MEG. You can't leave them! You can't!

JOAN (*to* MEG). Stay with them. Look after them.

(*To* JAMES.) You'll be safe, James, we'll both be safe. That's all that matters.

ANNABELLA. *Mummy!*

JOAN. Stay with your brother, Annabella.

JAMES. Mum, no! Don't leave me with the bad man!

She's gone. MEG *gathers* ANNABELLA *to her.*

MEG. It's alright. It's alright, pet, I've got you.

(*Reaching for him.*) Jamie, I've got you.

LIVINGSTON *stops* JAMES *as he tries to get to* MEG *and* ANNABELLA.

LIVINGSTON (*gentle*). Little red face. Know this. I'm your loyal subject and I'll be like a father to you. Don't be frightened. You're with friends now. Just answer me one question, we're all just curious, one wee question, Your Majesty. Can you do that?

JAMES. Yes.

LIVINGSTON. Was she shagging John Stewart before your dad got cut to collops or did she wait till she'd buried him?

Do you know? Come on. You have to know that. She was, wasn't she?

Everyone starts to laugh, louder and louder. JAMES *tries to run but he's caught and blocked wherever he runs.*

MEG. Leave him, you bastards! He's your King!

There's a moment where JAMES *bumps into* WILLIAM *and the two boys stare at each other, then* JAMES *is pushed away again, spun as if in a game. In the end he dives back in the kist.*

LIVINGSTON. Look at that, he's packing himself! I have the King!

Boxes are starting to move, packing and bustle accelerates. WILLIAM *looks at the kist with* JAMES *inside it a moment longer than everyone else and then we are in a rush of nightmare transition. Then we hear* ISABELLA, *a whisper out of the dark.*

ISABELLA. I can see you.

As the kist sits in –

King's Rooms / Tower Room

JAMES *climbs out of the kist.* LIVINGSTON, CRICHTON, BALVENIE *and* WILLIAM *are there, just watching* JAMES. JAMES *looks back.*

LIVINGSTON. Do you know where you are?

JAMES. Stirling Castle.

LIVINGSTON. You're home, Your Majesty. And you've nothing to fear as long as I can see you. Understand?

CRICHTON. The council hasn't agreed he'll remain with you permanently, Lord Livingston.

LIVINGSTON. Oh aye, aye. You want to witter away about all that don't you, Crichton? Fine, you can do your wee speech and then we'll all carry on. Or you can stop bleating and wasting our time. *I'm* the King's guardian. Never step outside the gate, King James. Never again.

Balvenie?

LIVINGSTON *and* BALVENIE *leave.* CRICHTON *ducks a bow, angry.*

CRICHTON. I'll see you soon, Your Majesty.

He exits. WILLIAM *still watches* JAMES.

JAMES. What're you looking at?

WILLIAM. You're no a real king. You're just a wee laddie.

JAMES *runs at him.*

JAMES. I'm the King! I'm the King! And I'll kill you! I will!

WILLIAM (*laughing*). Aye, if you could catch me you would.

WILLIAM *runs off as* JAMES *hears –*

ISABELLA. I can see you.

JAMES. Who's there?

There's no answer. JAMES *is moving through the castle, searching.*

ISABELLA. I see you.

JAMES (*searching*). Hullo? Are you here?

He finds his way to the tower room, he finds ISABELLA.

ISABELLA. What are you doing in here? You're not allowed.

ISABELLA *sits looking out. She never turns her head from the window, watching the sky.*

JAMES. Can you really see me?

ISABELLA (*without turning her head*). Yes.

JAMES. You can't.

ISABELLA. I can.

Standing there with that mark on your face, how did you get it?

JAMES. I don't know.

ISABELLA. Tell me.

JAMES. It was my twin brother Alexander. He died when we were born. He held onto my head because he didn't want to go to heaven. He wanted to stay and play with me.

ISABELLA. I think the Devil slapped you to mark you as his own. That's how it looks to me.

JAMES *moves closer.*

Stay back or I'll stab you.

JAMES. You haven't got a knife.

ISABELLA. I'll rip an eye tooth from my head and stab you with that.

I'll tear you like a wolf.

JAMES. I killed a wolf.

ISABELLA. Did you now?

JAMES. On my own.

ISABELLA. On your own?

JAMES. I wasn't supposed to. I was supposed to stay back, but I didn't. We'd driven them against the rocks and I saw this

big, big, BIG wolf so I ran at it and I made a HUGE noise…
RAAAAAAAAAAAWR! Like that, and the wolf was going
snip snap snip snap and his teeth were nipping and nipping
the air to bits and he was hurling himself all over like a big
eel you've stuck a fork in and teeth teeth TEETH coming at
me. So I chucked out my coat like this… and he snapped up
at it and there's his throat and there's my sword and I opened
him up. HA!

And he fell down and lay in all his blood like a… like… a…
a big hairy drunk.

ISABELLA *laughs*.

That's true. I did that. You have to kill the wolves or else
they eat all the sheep.

ISABELLA. Why would they not? Don't they need to eat? You
carry your father's blood. You'll grow to be the worse than
any wolf. Your father was a murderer, a tyrant. A grasping
corpse robber with a winter stone where his heart should be.
All Scotland's glad he's dead.

JAMES. Why do you never get up?

ISABELLA. Did you hear me?

JAMES. Yes. Why do you never get up?

ISABELLA. I have to watch them.

JAMES. The birds.

ISABELLA. My sons. The souls of my dead sons are in those
white birds. I've seen them. Two died in blood. One died on
the other side of the sea and couldny fly home till now. They
live in the air. They live in the sky. They're landless and lost.
I can't ever stop watching them.

JAMES. Why not?

ISABELLA. How else will they know how they were loved?

Your father destroyed them. But he wouldn't kill me. He was
a cruel man. He died in a drain. Did they tell you that?

JAMES *says nothing*.

Aye they did. May she soon lie over him as he rots. Your mother was colder than he was. Did they tell you how your father's killers died? She planned it, the whole thing. Did she tell you?

JAMES. No.

ISABELLA. I heard she made it last three days. Watching them die a piece at a time. Did you see their blood on her?

JAMES. No.

ISABELLA. Yes you did. Where is she now?

JAMES. I don't know.

ISABELLA. Yes you do.

JAMES. She married John Stewart.

ISABELLA (*laughs*). Tart.

Faithless and cruel.

Aye, that's the blood that's in you, like black snakes creeping their way down your veins, your father's cursed blood, your mother's cruel blood. You'll be a monster, just like them.

A monster with a child's face.

JAMES. I won't.

ISABELLA. You will. The Dark Ones will come to you in the night and put their bloody knives in your hands and you'll use them. You'll do their work. You're cursed.

JAMES shouts at her.

JAMES. I'm not! I'm not!

He runs. The nightmare is around him, ISABELLA*'s shout pursues him.*

ISABELLA. I see you! I see what you are! You can't hide!

JAMES runs, looking for his box, as the nightmare swirls round him.

King's Room

He finds the kist and climbs in.

MEG (*off*). Where's King James?

> MEG *enters.*

> Where are you? Where's my boy? Where's my wee cub?

> JAMES *peeks out of the kist.*

> Where can he be? Where can he be?

> I know, I'll sit here… and close my eyes… and when I open them he'll be here in front of me.

> *She sits down, closes her eyes.* JAMES *peeks out at her then hides again.* MEG *opens her eyes and looks round, sighs in some irritation.*

> (*Louder.*) Oh, what am I to do? And me with cakes in my pocket spoiling because there's no one to eat them…

> *She waits, no response.*

> …I'll have to eat them *all* myself, we can't have them wasted…

> MEG *takes a package of cakes out of her pocket and starts to unwrap it.* JAMES *sticks his head out of hiding and watches,* MEG *ignores him.*

> Have to eat them all up, can't have this honey making my pockets sticky…

> JAMES *starts to creep out of hiding, creeping towards her. Obviously she can see him really easily but pretends she can't.*

> (*Eating.*) Mmmmmm… lovely honey cakes… delicious… better eat them up before the bears get them.

> JAMES *runs at her with a roar.* MEG *pretends to startle and scream.*

> It's a bear! It's a bear! Give him the cakes!

> JAMES *grabs the cakes and starts to eat them hungrily.*

Oh thank goodness, it's not the bears, it's just His Majesty King James. That's a relief, I thought I was going to be torn limb from limb.

JAMES *makes bear growls as he eats. She wipes at his face.*

King of Scotland? King of Scotland? You're just a messy wee bairn, that's what you are, a happy, messy wee bairn.

ANNABELLA *enters wearing a beautiful white wedding dress.*

ANNABELLA. It's my special special day.

JAMES. Oh *naw*! I'm no playing that game again!

MEG. You need to play it today, darling.

You need to help your sister on her wedding day.

JAMES. It's *boring*!

ANNABELLA. It's not boring! It's my wedding!

MEG *is upset, hiding it.*

MEG. And you have to be ready to give her away, King James, so we need to clean these sticky hands.

JAMES (*to* MEG). Why're you upset?

MEG. I'm not, darling. Now hurry up. You can't make Annabella late on her special day.

ANNABELLA. *My* special day.

JAMES. It's just a game though, isn't it? I don't want Annabella to go away.

ANNABELLA. I won't, silly. I live here.

MEG (*faltering*). She'll come back… to visit. She'll…

JAMES. What?

MEG. Just… do everything like we did the other times, Jamie, like the game. Just like that.

ANNABELLA. I'm going to be married lots of times and get lots of dresses. Like Mummy.

JAMES. Did Mum cut the bad men in pieces?

MEG. What?

JAMES. The men who murdered my father. Did she…

MEG (*cutting him off, sharp*). Who have you been talking to!

(*Calms herself.*) She was just frightened, James. She was drowning in fear.

JAMES. Was she… faithless?

MEG. We don't have time for this! We need to clean you up.

She's helping him.

She was frightened. She was all alone.

Who's been talking at you?

JAMES. Did my father murder people? Was he cruel?

A pause.

MEG. It wasn't murder. Listen to me, listen now, Jamie, I'll tell you a story about your father. Your father, King James, knew the birthday of the boy that helped the man who had the dogs that kept his sheep. He sent that boy a gold coin on his birthday and asked after the dogs by name. That's a king. Now he'd want you to hold your sister's hand on her wedding day. Come on, darling, you have to. It'll be alright.

JAMES. Promise?

MEG. I promise, but we're *late*, Jamie, come on.

JAMES *takes* ANNABELLA*'s hand and* MEG *takes the other as they move into –*

The Royal Chapel

MEG *is talking quietly to* ANNABELLA *as they approach the altar, where a* BISHOP *stands waiting with the* FRENCH AMBASSADOR. LORDS *and* LADIES *of the court watch.*

MEG. Right, Annabella… see that lovely man there, the French Ambassador, remember him? You like him, he pulled honey biscuits out of your ear, remember? Well, he's going to pretend to be the Duke of Savoy and all you have to do is take his hand when King James gives you to him. And then you'll be a married lady like your sisters.

LIVINGSTON *is there, glaring at* MEG.

LIVINGSTON. He better know what he's doing or you'll answer for it.

MEG. He's fine, they're fine, we've practised…

(*Pulling him on.*) Come *on*, James!

JAMES. But it's just a game, isn't it? She's not to go away. I don't want that.

MEG. Shhh, James! Act like a king for once, will you!

BISHOP. *Qui dat nuptum huic mulieri?*

As there's no reaction, he repeats it in English.

Who gives this woman to be married?

MEG *whispers in* JAMES*'s ear, prompting him.*

JAMES. I do.

MEG *whispers again.*

I, King James the Second, King of Scots.

He steps forward, offering ANNABELLA*'s hand. The* FRENCH AMBASSADOR *gathers her up and the procession moves away from* JAMES *and* MEG. LIVINGSTON *is beside the* FRENCH AMBASSADOR.

MEG. You can wait here, King James. You did it. Well done.

JAMES *hesitates, then follows as the procession moves into –*

Castle Courtyard

The procession is nearly gone. MEG *is crying.* JAMES *is standing bereft, calling after them all.*

JAMES. No! I said didn't want to give her away! She lives with me.

She's my sister. Annabella! Annabella, don't leave me!

ANNABELLA *looks back then, her face crumpling.*

ANNABELLA. Jamie!

The nightmare seems to swallow ANNABELLA *up, snatching her away from him.*

JAMES. No!

He's alone with MEG. *He turns on her.*

You promised me!

MEG. James…

JAMES. You *promised*!

She runs from him. JAMES *gets into the kist.* WILLIAM *is suddenly there, he throws a football at the kist.* JAMES *opens the lid and sees him.*

Who are you?

WILLIAM. William Douglas. My father's in your council.

Do you want a game of ball?

JAMES. I can't. I have to wait here till they call me.

WILLIAM. Later then?

JAMES. No.

WILLIAM. Why not?

JAMES. I don't know you.

YOUNG DOUGLAS *and* DAVEY *enter.*

YOUNG DOUGLAS. Aye you do, that's my wee cousin.

Do you know who *I* am, King James, do you remember me?

JAMES. Yes.

YOUNG DOUGLAS. Who am I?

JAMES. You're the Earl of Douglas.

YOUNG DOUGLAS. Look what we've got you. Give him it, Davey.

DAVEY takes out a little wooden horse. JAMES reaches out for it.

DAVEY. Aye, he's a beauty, eh?

JAMES. As beautiful as your horse.

YOUNG DOUGLAS. He is, nearly.

JAMES. Can I ride your horse?

BALVENIE and LIVINGSTON enter.

BALVENIE. William! Leave the King alone.

LIVINGSTON. King James! You're needed.

The council is forming. YOUNG DOUGLAS is already moving away.

You're called to council, Earl Douglas.

YOUNG DOUGLAS. No, I'm going hunting.

Go and tell the boys I'm coming, Davey.

DAVEY hurries off as YOUNG DOUGLAS speaks quietly to JAMES.

See what I've decided, King James, is that you and me need to keep away from all the old men, they'll have us talked to death. I've had a friendly talk with every man here…

CRICHTON. You have indeed, Earl Douglas.

YOUNG DOUGLAS. …and now I'm going hunting.

LIVINGSTON. I need to hear you tell me where the Douglas family stands.

YOUNG DOUGLAS. So ask my old uncle. That's why we keep him. Every family needs an old uncle who's fit for nothing but talk to do the talking. Eh, Balvenie? Do him a favour, make him feel useful again. See you next time, wee King.

YOUNG DOUGLAS *exits*.

The King's Council

A small group of LORDS. *They stand silently round* JAMES *as he takes his place, looking round at them all, bemused and a little frightened*.

LIVINGSTON. We can keep this short. Your council has already agreed, Your Majesty.

All the LORDS *chorus together*.

LORDS. Aye.

JAMES. What? What have you agreed?

LIVINGSTON. All the matters of state that required your royal approval today. That's all we need now. Your assent. You know what to say.

A brief pause then LIVINGSTON *slaps at* JAMES, *prompting him*.

JAMES. As I will it done let it be so.

LORDS (*chorusing*). In the King's name, in the King's name, in the King's name.

The council is dispersing.

LIVINGSTON (*to* JAMES). Get back to your rooms. Get back to your studies.

Balvenie? A word.

CRICHTON *is suddenly next to* JAMES *as* LIVINGSTON *and* BALVENIE *exit*.

CRICHTON. He can't give you orders. You're the King.

JAMES *just looks at him.*

A few of us have been watching Livingston, King James. I don't think he's your loyal subject, do you? I think Scotland's King should stay with men that are loyal, don't you? Give me an order. Command me.

JAMES *still says nothing.*

Anything you like. Tell me to dance a jig, stand on my head…

Still nothing.

(*The wooden horse.*) That's a lovely horse. Would you like a real one?

JAMES. She said I'd get a pony.

CRICHTON. Who did?

JAMES. Mum. She said I'd get a pony, but I never did.

CRICHTON. There's a beautiful wee wee piebald pony just outside the gate. That's yours.

He's pointing, they're both looking out through the castle gate.

JAMES. It's not.

CRICHTON. It is if you command me. Just say 'Lord Crichton, loyal subject, I command you to give me that pony so that I can ride with you to your fortress and from there begin my independent rule of Scotland.'

JAMES. I'm not allowed to go beyond the gate.

CRICHTON. But Livingston's not watching, little King, and once you go beyond the gate you're allowed to do anything you like.

JAMES *hesitates.*

Come on, King James. You're King of Scotland. You can walk out into your kingdom.

JAMES *hesitates*.

You'll be safe with me, King James, I promise you.

JAMES *still hesitates*.

Lord Livingston will never touch you again. I promise you.

JAMES *takes his hand and lets* CRICHTON *lead him forward. Light grows on him as he approaches escape, sunlight beyond the gate.* JAMES *is overwhelmed*.

JAMES. The sun's so bright out there…

CRICHTON. Just a few steps more and we're safe. You'll be on your pony and we'll be galloping away. You need to go a few more steps, King James. We're not safe yet.

JAMES. I can't see where you're taking me.

CRICHTON. Into sunlight! Look, there's the view your father loved, the great plain, the high hills, the tall blue skies of your kingdom… you'll be free in your own kingdom at last, King James, but you need to come *now*!

He pulls at JAMES. *It's too late,* LIVINGSTON *and* BALVENIE *are behind them.* JAMES *and* CRICHTON *are pulled back and the sunlight dies*.

LIVINGSTON. I think we've stopped a robbery, Balvenie. What do you think?

BALVENIE. Lord Crichton?

CRICHTON (*faltering*). I… we…

JAMES. I'm going to get a pony. I'm going to get my own pony and no one's going to stop me.

CRICHTON. Don't think I stand alone, Livingston. You heard the young Earl Douglas, he's ready to be the King's friend.

LIVINGSTON. The King's friend, mebbe, but yours? Let the King go or I'll take your head off myself.

BALVENIE. There's no need for this, Livingston. Lord Crichton has just misunderstood the situation.

CRICHTON. Have I? Earl Douglas has the lands and the men and the power. When the Douglases speak no one will stand against them. They decide who holds the King.

BALVENIE. But the Earl asked me to speak for the Douglas family, and I'm telling you we stand with Lord Livingston.

CRICHTON. What!?

LIVINGSTON. There's your decision.

CRICHTON (*faltering*). But the Earl… He told me…

BALVENIE. Yes the young Earl is every man's friend. But he makes no promises and he doesn't want to be troubled with old men like you and me, Lord Crichton. I think you heard him say that too.

CRICHTON. May he rot and burn in hell!

LIVINGSTON *is taking hold of* JAMES. CRICHTON *holds on and for a moment* JAMES *is pulled between them.*

LIVINGSTON. Poor wee Crichton. Maybe if you'd made it out the gate it would have been a different story, eh?

CRICHTON. You're the robber here, Livingston!

LIVINGSTON. I should have you executed, for treason.

BALVENIE. Speaking for the Douglas family, we feel the peace and prosperity of Scotland is best served when her lords agree. Lord Crichton will apologise for the misunderstanding and offer you a hand in friendship, Livingston. Won't you, Crichton?

CRICHTON *hesitates then he kneels, bowing his head.*

CRICHTON (*furious but resigned*). Forgive me, Lord Livingston. I stand with you.

LIVINGSTON. Aye. You better.

JAMES. No. We're going away out the gate and I'm getting my own pony.

CRICHTON. Grow up, son, he's got half of Scotland at his back.

JAMES (*to* CRICHTON). You promised! You promised!

LIVINGSTON *pulls* JAMES.

LIVINGSTON. And you stay inside this gate like I told you.

A nightmare transition pursues JAMES *into the castle till he is left, entirely alone, beside the kist.*

King's Room, Stirling Castle

After a moment, JAMES *climbs inside.* WILLIAM *comes on and pulls the lid up, talking into the box.*

WILLIAM. Why are you always hiding in there?

JAMES climbs out.

JAMES. I'm not hiding.

WILLIAM. Yes you are.

JAMES. I like resting in there. It's comfy.

WILLIAM. You're weird.

JAMES. You're not allowed in here. These are the King's rooms.

WILLIAM. Do you want me to go away?

JAMES. Yes.

WILLIAM. No you don't.

JAMES. I'm busy.

WILLIAM. You're not doing anything.

JAMES. I am.

WILLIAM. What?

JAMES. King's business.

WILLIAM. You're just sitting about on a box looking glaikit. How old are you?

JAMES. Nine.

WILLIAM. I'm eleven. Why are you always by yourself?

JAMES. I'm not. Why aren't you with the other boys, doing weapons training?

WILLIAM. They won't let me any more.

JAMES. Why not?

WILLIAM. I don't know. It's no like I killed anyone. He was just bleeding a wee bit.

JAMES. Who?

WILLIAM. The sergeant-at-arms. Come on and play ball with me.

JAMES. They won't let me do that.

WILLIAM. No one's watching. Come on.

JAMES *follows* WILLIAM *as he kicks the ball out into the courtyard.*

We should be friends, you and me.

JAMES. Why?

WILLIAM. Because… I can look after you 'cause I'm older than you are. We can do stuff together, it'll be great.

JAMES. Have you got brothers and sisters?

WILLIAM. Aye, hunners of them. But I always have to be with Dad because I'm the eldest. How did you get that mark on your face?

JAMES. It's my father's blood. He put his hand there when he was dying. He was a hero. He fought eight men with a little knife. They had swords. They stabbed him fifteen times. All the wounds were on his front. He wouldn't run.

WILLIAM. That's a good death.

WILLIAM *does a trick with the ball.*

See that? The Earl of Douglas taught me that.

The Earl of Douglas is my cousin.

JAMES. He's my cousin too.

WILLIAM. But the Earl of Douglas is better than you. You know he is.

He's a Douglas, like me. The Douglases are higher than the King.

BALVENIE *is there, watching them.*

BALVENIE. What do you think you're doing?

WILLIAM. Playing ball with the King.

BALVENIE. Did I tell you to do that? No. What did I tell you? Come on!

WILLIAM. To play quiet and stay out of your way.

BALVENIE. No one can be looking at my family tonight! Do you understand? No one!

You get more meat off the table if folk don't see you coming to get it. Yes? Yes? You say it.

WILLIAM. I'm just playing ball.

BALVENIE *goes to hit him.* WILLIAM *flinches.* JAMES *calls over.*

JAMES. He's my friend.

BALVENIE. Is he? Is he now?

JAMES. Can he not be my friend?

BALVENIE *is thinking hard.*

BALVENIE. We'll see. We'll see.

(*To* WILLIAM.) Go back to our room and stay there until you're called for dinner.

Your council wants you, King James.

JAMES. I want to play ball.

BALVENIE. You can play ball later.

The council is gathering, LIVINGSTON *and* CRICHTON. WILLIAM *is gone.*

JAMES *senses the nightmare rising again. He stops, resisting* BALVENIE, *fearful as he feels the nightmare overtaking memory again.*

JAMES. No… no… I don't want to. I want to play the ball…

LIVINGSTON (*to* JAMES). Hurry up, you idiot boy. Your council is trying to do its work.

He turns to CRICHTON *and* BALVENIE.

The three of us are the council of Scotland here today. We agree. This must be done. I have messages from the other lords. Those that needed to know. This will be allowed.

CRICHTON. What makes you think I'll allow it?

LIVINGSTON. Because you want a seat at the table. Don't you?

CRICHTON *hesitates.*

Don't pretend you don't want this too. The boy can't be trusted. You know that better than anyone.

CRICHTON. Is this what you want, Balvenie? At the end of the day this is still your own nephew we're talking about.

LIVINGSTON (*cutting him off*). Balvenie, there's only one question you need to answer, who do you think should be Earl of Douglas?

BALVENIE. How could I stand against every other family? What can I do? I'm just an old uncle that's fit for nothing but talk, after all.

LIVINGSTON. There you go. He's happy. We'll tell the Earl to leave his army at home and send him a promise of safe conduct.

CRICHTON. We're going to become oath-breakers?

LIVINGSTON (*indicating* JAMES). No. He is.

(*To* JAMES.) Your council is agreed, Your Majesty.

LIVINGSTON/BALVENIE/CRICHTON. Aye!

An edge of nightmare is close to JAMES. *He's sensing it.*

So what do you say? Come on! You know what to say.

JAMES (*faltering*). As I will it done let it be so.

LIVINGSTON/BALVENIE/CRICHTON. In the King's name. In the King's name. In the King's name.

LIVINGSTON. And what's the only other thing a king needs to do at dinner?

JAMES. I...

LIVINGSTON. Come on, come on!

JAMES. I must call for the meat.

LIVINGSTON. Like a good wee king. Yes. Call for the meat when we're ready.

YOUNG DOUGLAS appears, triumphant.

YOUNG DOUGLAS. I am the sword of Scotland!

A burst of music and cheering.

A procession thunders into the courtyard surrounding YOUNG DOUGLAS *and his brother,* DAVEY. *An impression of a rowdy, victorious armed band. Everyone crowds to take their places as* YOUNG DOUGLAS *sits at the head of the table.* JAMES *and* WILLIAM *are competing to sit next to him.*

DAVEY *shouts at the crowd.*

DAVEY. Here he is! Here's my brother! Do you see him?!

Cheers.

Who holds the border?

The crowd call back to him.

ALL. Douglas!

DAVEY. Who keeps Scotland?

ALL. Douglas!

DAVEY. Who stops the English?

ALL. Douglas!

DAVEY. Who do you want?

ALL. Douglas!

DAVEY. I said who do you want?

ALL. Douglas! Douglas!

A squabble for position between WILLIAM *and* JAMES *to sit beside* YOUNG DOUGLAS *has continued through this. Now* BALVENIE *shouts over all the other noise.*

BALVENIE. William!

Get away from there! That's the King's place!

YOUNG DOUGLAS. It's my brother's place but the King can have it today – on you go, Davey.

DAVEY *makes room and* JAMES *crows as* WILLIAM *slinks off. At the same time everyone raises their cups and shouts. Everyone remains standing.* YOUNG DOUGLAS *whispers in* JAMES'*s ear.*

JAMES. Oh! Eh… Be seated.

They sit as JAMES *is straight on* YOUNG DOUGLAS.

Can I ride your horse this time? Can I see all your horses?

Can I gallop with you and a thousand horsemen!?

YOUNG DOUGLAS. Oh, I've only a few horses with me this time, wee King, remember, I had to leave the rest at home.

A shred of nightmare, the voice of ISABELLA.

ISABELLA. You carry your father's blood.

JAMES. I don't know why they made me do that. I don't.

YOUNG DOUGLAS. Never mind, wee King, I know, it's fine. It's 'cause they're frightened of me.

JAMES. I'm not frightened of you.

YOUNG DOUGLAS. Why would you be? Aren't we family?

He raises his glass to the table, smiling provocatively at LIVINGSTON.

The blood of the Bruce!

ISABELLA. That's the blood that's in you. Like black snakes creeping their way down your veins.

JAMES. I want you to live here.

YOUNG DOUGLAS. With you?

JAMES. Yes, I want you and Davey here with me.

YOUNG DOUGLAS. So we can terrify the old men together?

JAMES. Yes!

YOUNG DOUGLAS. That would terrify them, James, believe me, they think I want to take your crown.

JAMES. You can if you like, I don't mind.

YOUNG DOUGLAS. No, you keep your crown and I'll keep my horses and we'll both live happy. Tell them that from me, stop them shaking.

ISABELLA. Your mother's cruel blood…

YOUNG DOUGLAS. What's the matter, King James, has someone been frightening you?

JAMES. It's just… It's just… I don't know what to do. I don't know what to do next.

ISABELLA. You'll be a monster, just like them…

YOUNG DOUGLAS. I do. That's easy. You're head of the hall, you need to call for the meat.

ISABELLA. A monster with a child's face.

YOUNG DOUGLAS. Come on. Douglas is hungry. Bring out the meat.

ISABELLA. The Dark Ones will put their bloody knives in your hands and you'll do their work…

YOUNG DOUGLAS. You need to shout, wee man! Go on.

JAMES. Bring out the meat!

In a chorus of cheers, a covered dish is brought in and put on the table in front of YOUNG DOUGLAS. *The cover is taken off to reveal a bull's head.*

YOUNG DOUGLAS. What's this?

LIVINGSTON. Douglas is hungry. Douglas is greedy. You've taken enough, Earl Douglas. Now the young bulls must have their heads parted from their bodies. In the name of King James, you and your brother are sentenced to death, my lord, for treason.

A MAN, *naked to the waist, erupts through the table. He's wearing the bull's head and carrying an axe. Half the guests draw swords, the others are running, screaming.*

YOUNG DOUGLAS *shouts to his brother.*

YOUNG DOUGLAS. Run, Davey! Run!

DAVEY *tries to run but is grabbed by* LIVINGSTON *and others.* YOUNG DOUGLAS *is seized by the* BULL-HEADED MAN *and dragged off.* JAMES *watching, distraught, helpless.*

JAMES. No! Stop it, leave them! They're my friends! Leave them!

The table is knocked over, everything smashed and broken.

YOUNG DOUGLAS. Jamie! Help me!

JAMES. Stop it!

The two DOUGLAS *boys are dragged onto a kist. The* BULL-HEADED MAN *stands over them with a knife. There's screaming.* DAVEY *is killed.*

YOUNG DOUGLAS. Jesus no! Davey! Davey!

YOUNG DOUGLAS *screams and screams again.* YOUNG DOUGLAS *is killed. Silence.*

The BULL-HEADED MAN *turns and looks at* JAMES *for a moment, then walks on, ignoring him.*

LIVINGSTON. In the King's name! In the King's name! In the King's name!

JAMES *runs. He climbs into the kist and pulls the lid down.* ISABELLA*'s whisper echoes round the hall.*

ISABELLA. Your blood is poison, your name is death. That's the nightmare that'll eat you from the inside out. It lives inside you.

MEG *comes into the broken and bloody hall. She's shaking, terrified. She calls out in a broken whisper.*

MEG. Where are you? Where's my boy? Where's my wee cub? Oh God… Oh God help me… Jamie? Come out, pet. Come out, it's just Meg come to find you.

She's looking under tumbled chairs and tables, crying quietly, desperate.

It's just Meg… it's just your Meg… there's nothing to hurt you now… come out, darling… oh please come out…

Nothing, no movement. MEG *is searching frantically then, shouting, accusing the shadows.*

JAMIE!!! Where is he? Where is he? What have you done to him!? He was a bairn! Just a bairn and you ruined him, you bastards! You ruined him! May you rot in hell! All of you should bleed and char in hell for what you've done to that wee boy! You've thrown him into your stews of death! You've drowned that bairn in blood!

(*Breaks down, talking to God.*) Sweet Jesus. Sweet Mary mother please, please, let me keep him safe. Jamie!

She exits, calling him.

Jamie!

In Bedchamber, Stirling Castle.

The closed chest sits in the centre of the room. Offstage, MEG *is calling for* JAMES. WILLIAM *enters. He crosses to the chest and opens it, looking inside.*

WILLIAM. I knew you'd be here. I won't tell them. They won't find you. I won't let them come in.

Slowly JAMES *climbs out of the box.*

Did they kill them both?

JAMES. Yes.

WILLIAM. It'll be fine. Just stay here with me a while. No one's after you. They never kill the wee bairns. Well, they might kill you because you're King but you'll be fine here with me. They won't find you. There's no one here but me. Look.

JAMES. There was all blood… on the floor.

WILLIAM. Did you see how they killed them? Did you not look? We need to look. A fighting man needs to be fit for that.

JAMES. I've dark blood, like snakes, under my skin.

WILLIAM. No you don't.

JAMES. It'll come out. I'll kill people.

WILLIAM. You might. But not with snakes.

When we're grown we can learn killing.

I'm nearly grown. Till then we need to learn how to bear looking at it. I'll teach you.

It's like when you take a beating. You think you can't stand it but if you just get used to what it feels like to get clouted round the heid, you can. Makes you stronger. I'll help you. I'm going to be the greatest warrior in Scotland. See when my father finds out what I can do? We'll be warriors, wee Jamie. We'll rule this country like roaring lions.

JAMES. I don't want to do that.

WILLIAM. Aye you do. I'll help you.

See if anything bad's happening all you need to do is call for me. Just…

WILLIAM *is suddenly wrenched away from* JAMES, *before he can finish the sentence, he's just gone, whipped away into the dark.*

JAMES *cries out, sitting up, looking round wildly for* WILLIAM.

WILLIAM *is gone.* JAMES *is sucked further into the nightmare.*

JAMES. Will!

JOAN *enters. She is bloodstained. She looks feral and haggard. She's trying to coax* JAMES *to her.*

JOAN. Jamie?

JAMES. No.

JOAN. I need you to be a brave boy now, Jamie. A brave, brave little boy.

JAMES. You're hurt. You're bleeding.

JOAN. It's not my blood, Jamie. It's from the men who killed your father.

ISABELLA. I heard she made it last three days. Watching them die a piece at a time.

The BULL-HEADED MAN *enters behind* JOAN.

JOAN. Say hullo to your new father.

JAMES. My father's dead, my father was a hero.

ISABELLA. Your father was a murderer, a tyrant.

The BULL-HEADED MAN *embraces* JOAN, *they kiss.*

LIVINGSTON. I have the King!

ISABELLA. Aye, that's the blood that's in you, like black snakes creeping their way down your veins.

ANNABELLA. It's my special special day.

She is picked up.

JAMIE!!

JAMES. No! Annabella! Annabella, don't leave me!

LIVINGSTON *and* LORDS *are chorusing*.

BALVENIE/LIVINGSTON/CRICHTON. In the King's name. In the King's name. In the King's name.

CRICHTON. The blood of the Bruce.

YOUNG DOUGLAS. I am the sword of Scotland!

DAVEY. Here he is! Here's my brother! Do you see him?!

JAMES. No! Stop it, leave them! They're my friends! Leave them!

YOUNG DOUGLAS. Jamie! Help me!

LIVINGSTON. In the King's name.

ISABELLA. I see you, I see what you are, you can't hide.

JOAN. Jamie, I need you to be a brave boy now, Jamie. A brave, brave little boy.

JAMES. You're hurt. You're bleeding.

JOAN. It's not my blood, Jamie. It's from the men who killed your father.

She kisses him.

JAMES. NO!!

He pushes her violently away and gets back in the kist. The adult ANNABELLA is staring at the kist. JAMES's young bride, MARY, picks herself up from where he threw her. The two young women exchange a terrified look.

ANNABELLA. James...?

JAMES. Leave me! Will! William!

WILLIAM *runs on, breathless*.

WILLIAM. Aw Jesus.

He raps gently on the box.

James? It's Will. Time to get up. It's morning.

The lid of the kist opens, JAMES stares out at him.

See? It's me.

JAMES. William…

WILLIAM. That's right. Are you awake?

JAMES. Yes.

WILLIAM. Are you sure? How can you be sure?

Slowly JAMES *holds up his hand,* WILLIAM *takes it gently and makes a tiny cut with his knife.*

JAMES. Because I felt that.

WILLIAM. There you go. Are you awake now?

JAMES. Yes.

WILLIAM. So you need to get out of the box.

JAMES *climbs out.*

There you are, I'll go and get you a drink.

WILLIAM *leaves.* JAMES *looks round, seeing* ANNABELLA *and* MARY *properly.*

JAMES. Who are you?

ANNABELLA. It's me, Annabella, your sister.

JAMES. No you're not.

ANNABELLA. James, it's me! You know it's me! We talked last night and…

JAMES (*cutting her off*). Alright… alright… so what are you doing here?

ANNABELLA. I came back.

JAMES. What for?

ANNABELLA. Your wedding. You married Mary of Guelders. Today.

Yesterday.

JAMES. I know that. Where is she?

ANNABELLA (*looking uncertainly at* MARY). She's…

JAMES *realises who* MARY *is.*

JAMES. Jesus, Jesus… (*Tries to pull himself together*.) Did I hurt you?

MARY *shakes her head*.

Christ. I… eh… I have nightmares sometimes. Did they warn you?

MARY. Yes. But I did not know it was so bad.

JAMES. No.

MARY. This is very bad.

JAMES. Yes. Sorry. No much of a wedding night for you.

MARY. No. You were… drunk. You sleep. Then this.

JAMES. I said sorry!

He turns back to ANNABELLA.

What are you doing in my rooms? Where's your husband?

ANNABELLA. We talked about this yesterday. I never met him. I waited in Grenoble for years but he never came to marry me. You sent an ambassador asking for my dowry back.

JAMES. Did I?

Livingston probably took care of that.

ANNABELLA. So I've come back to live here. Do you remember that?

JAMES. Of course I remember that! I'm not crazy! I'm just… half-asleep… I didn't recognise you.

ANNABELLA. No. I didn't recognise you either when I saw you again. Just the mark, on your face.

JAMES. No mistaking that.

MARY *is getting herself together. Edging out*.

(*To* MARY.) I just have nightmares sometimes. You don't need to be scared.

MARY. I am not scared. I am… very brave.

JAMES. You're nearly crying. Look at you.

MEG *has come back on*.

MEG. Jamie, she's hundreds of miles from everyone who loves her. She barely speaks the language and she doesn't know who you are.

JAMES. Well, I don't know who they are! Either of them!

WILLIAM *comes back with wine*.

Are we all ready for the hunt, Will?

WILLIAM. Aye, the rest of us are. You're not though, are you?

JAMES. Well, help me then!

He's looking for his clothes, pulling them on.

Meg, take those two out of here and… get them fed or something.

MEG. James… they're preparing the wedding breakfast… your bride needs to be with you.

JAMES. Well, she can be with me after the hunt, can't she? Come on, get them out of here.

MARY *is already going*.

MARY. C'est trop dur. C'est trop dur…

ANNABELLA *follows* MARY. MEG *gives* JAMES *a look and follows*. JAMES, *helped by* WILLIAM, *is nearly dressed for the hunt. After the women leave he looks back at the bed, remembering*.

WILLIAM. Was it a bad one?

JAMES *nods*.

JAMES. Jesus, Will… she saw me climb in the kist, like a frightened bairn.

WILLIAM. Aye, well… Tell her you were looking for your wedding ring.

JAMES. Look at me, I'm still shaking with it.

WILLIAM. You're fine. Are you…? Are you still seeing anything?

JAMES. No. No one here but you and me.

WILLIAM. Good. Hurry up then.

JAMES. Give me a chance.

WILLIAM. Everyone's waiting, they want to know.

JAMES. Know what?

WILLIAM. What she was like.

JAMES. Jesus. I'll think of something.

WILLIAM. You look fine, man. No one could tell.

JAMES. Thanks.

WILLIAM. Now, let's go hunting.

In Balvenie's Room

BALVENIE *is carefully sorting deeds and paperwork. There's the sound of drinking and cheering, off.* WILLIAM *enters.*

WILLIAM *is happy.*

WILLIAM. Come out and have one with me, Dad. I've not even seen you since I got here. Come on.

BALVENIE. You're drunk.

WILLIAM. We're just in from the hunt. The first hunt after the King's wedding. Of course I'm drunk.

BALVENIE. I didn't ask you here to watch you puke ale all over the place. I want news of my family. Is the baby strong?

WILLIAM. It's got strong lungs, that's all I know.

BALVENIE. That's good. That's very, very good.

WILLIAM. I brought you a present. Wait till you hear how I got it… It was for the hunt. Why did you not come out with us?

BALVENIE *is not listening properly. He interrupts.*

BALVENIE. How old are you now?

WILLIAM. Nearly twenty.

BALVENIE. Twenty. Twenty. A man in his young prime. I was twice your age before I had any children at all, how many living have I now?

WILLIAM. I'm bored tripping over them. I've no patience for counting them.

BALVENIE. Ten living. Ten.

The crop came late but, man, did it come strong!

What lands have I given you?

WILLIAM. Avoch and Aberdour.

BALVENIE. And what have you found for yourself?

I had no lands at your age. I'll give you that but I had strong blood. Strong strong blood. I had time on my side. First I learned wisdom, then I grew.

I don't know if you have time on your side. Your mother's soft stuff. She falling apart like wet wood.

WILLIAM. The bairns you put in her are killing her.

BALVENIE. Do you think so? That might be it. You might be right. If you put hard metal through a rotten log it will split apart, eh?

Is your sister married yet?

WILLIAM. Which one?

BALVENIE. To Hamilton, we're marrying her to Hamilton.

WILLIAM. Yes. She left last month.

BALVENIE. And the dowry?

WILLIAM. Sent.

BALVENIE. I think I was too generous there. Far too generous… still… Hamilton is good land to seed with grandchildren. And how is Moray?

WILLIAM. Archie's fine.

BALVENIE. Strathaven? Craigie?

WILLIAM. I don't… Craigie?

BALVENIE. The dear little lady of Strathaven and Craigie?

WILLIAM. Oh Bella! She died. In March. Didn't they tell you?

BALVENIE. Hmmmm.

He thinks a moment

Then we have to marry your younger sister to Craigie at once unless… unless I can betrothe her to Errol… yes… that's a better catch.

You don't look as if you're following this at all, Aberdour. Christ. That's her look, that same glaikit look.

WILLIAM. She never failed you. Never.

BALVENIE. What are you talking about? She fails me every time I climb on top of her. Her guts are falling out her arse. Nothing but my duty and her bleating. If my first wife had lived I might have known happiness, cunt like a tight wee nut. Christ I wish you'd her blood.

WILLIAM. I'm strong as you are.

BALVENIE. Come back and tell me that when you've had two lives. Two. One full of fear and longing and stretching for love out of my reach, that's you, Avoch and Aberdour, that's youth, but I'm past all that. Past all that and still strong. Who'd've believed it. No one would have believed it when I was your age, you know. I wouldn't have. Another life.

Twenty? You've milk on your chin and your balls are still buried in your pelvis…

The girl I married to Duffy, dead? Where does that leave us though? Where does that leave us on the map.

He's looking at a map, checking places in relation to each other.

Banff, Avoch, Aberdour, Moray, Strathaven, Stonehouse…

So if you've not found your own wealth what have you been up to?

WILLIAM. I won a fight…

Well, it was a… I led a raid, into Northumbria.

BALVENIE. Did you though.

(*Absorbed in his map*.) Dunkeld... Eskdale, Lauderdale... bethrothed to Errol and Biggar... have I missed a daughter? God, I can't count for the wine...

WILLIAM. Only a dozen of us... we broke into the field, drove out the cattle but... we couldn't get them moving ahead of us... Need to bring drove boys with you on ponies, don't you? I'll know next time... but, Father, I stole the best horse... black as December and breathing like a rick fire...

BALVENIE. Shoosh a minute, will you? What have I forgotten?

WILLIAM. I brought the horse to you. It's a present. It was a great raid... And we all got home, all twelve of us, galloping back over the border, well, we thought we were over the border... man, that's some thrill, eh? Galloping blind on a rocky sea road in the dark... but the thing was... the thing is...

BALVENIE (*finding it on map*). Galloway! How could I forget we were getting Galloway?

WILLIAM. Aye, it was Galloway. We'd missed the border. Turned out we'd never made it into England at all so... I ended up stealing Galloway's horse.

BALVENIE *is just staring at him.*

Some laugh, eh?

BALVENIE. We are already in negotiations for your wedding with Galloway. We're sending betrothal gifts!

WILLIAM. Aye well, that's a Galloway horse outside. Do you think we could call it a swap?

Without warning, BALVENIE *hits him. He hits him with something heavy – a candlestick, a stone bottle – clubs him so that* WILLIAM *is felled at once, shocked and bleeding.*

BALVENIE. Do you know... do you have any idea how long we've been waiting to get Galloway?

WILLIAM *can't answer, he's blind with pain, struggling to get up.*

Have you not been listening? Do you not understand
anything? Listen, Banff, Avoch, Aberdour, Moray,
Strathaven, Stonehouse… Come on, you say it…

WILLIAM *can't speak,* BALVENIE *kicks him viciously.*

Menteith, yes? Dunkeld, yes?

He kicks WILLIAM *again.*

Say it! Tell me you understand your inheritance…

WILLIAM (*mouth full of blood*). Dun… keld…

BALVENIE. Eskdale, Lauderdale, Douglasdale, Wigton… and
Galloway and Galloway and *Galloway*… would close the
border with a wall of our land.

My son and heir. My fucking son and heir?! I'll send
Galloway your head as a wedding gift.

Can we still save the deal? Do they know it was you?

WILLIAM. They didn't… catch… any of us…

BALVENIE. Alright… alright… kill the horse and have it
burned before anyone else sees it…

WILLIAM. Dad, it was a present for you…

BALVENIE *kicks him again.*

BALVENIE. Shut up, you stupid… to think you came from me.
Aye well, my turds come from me but I don't have to love
them, eh?

We'll wait it out. We'll give it a month or so, then we'll send
the first of the betrothal gifts, see if she throws them back at
us. If she keeps them we'll know we've got away with it.

She won't make war anyway. She wouldn't dare.

Now listen… Banff, Avoch, Aberdour, Moray, Strathaven,
Stonehouse…

(*Kicks at* WILLIAM.) Come on…

WILLIAM (*halting, in pain*)….Eskdale, Lauderdale, Wigton…
and Galloway.

BALVENIE. Better.

WILLIAM *starts to cry.*

Don't do that, it always gets you more beating... I learnt that
far younger than you. Why have you not learned that yet?

WILLIAM. I wanted you to have the horse.

The horse is so beautiful... I thought you'd love him...

BALVENIE *hits him.*

BALVENIE. A beautiful ring of land, all around the kingdom of
Scotland. All our land. Douglas land... Jedburgh...
Dumfries, Inverlochy, Ruthven, Dingwall, Elgin, Huntly,
Brechin... What lands are they?

WILLIAM. Ours.

BALVENIE. The Douglas lands. The Earl of Douglas's lands.
Mine. What else gives a man worth on this earth? A good life
is invisible unless you own the land they bury you under. I
own half of Scotland.

WILLIAM *says nothing.*

And you're my eldest. The son and heir.

Thank God I'll probably outlive you. You've got that melting
look round your face. You're the spit of her really, aren't
you? Soft meat. Soon rotten.

BALVENIE *exits.*

JAMES *enters. He's startled to see* WILLIAM *on the floor,
bleeding.* WILLIAM *scrambles up quickly, getting himself
together.*

JAMES. I was looking for your father.

WILLIAM. He just left.

JAMES. Christ. The room's full out there. The whole hunt's
back home. We're just starting the drinking properly.

The sound of raucous voices, off. Someone calls.

LORD. King James! Come on through!

JAMES (*calling off*). Give me a moment here.

　　That was some day out, eh? Three stags. Can you believe it? Three. Was that a fourteen-pointer, you brought down? I know it was. You were the man today.

WILLIAM. If I hear you talking about seeing me like this I'll cut your throat. I will.

JAMES. Christ, man, that'd be treason. They'd have your head.

　　You missed a bit.

WILLIAM. What?

　　JAMES *cleans a last bit of blood off him*.

JAMES. There you go. No one could tell.

WILLIAM (*quiet*). Thanks. You go on out. I'm fine now.

JAMES. Shut up. I'm not leaving you like this.

WILLIAM. I'm fine.

JAMES. Would you leave me? No. So shut up. You know what the deal is. We stand by each other. Always.

　　WILLIAM *takes his hand*.

WILLIAM. Always.

　　There's another roar from the drinkers, off. BALVENIE *enters and watches them secretly.*

　　Christ, listen to them out there. Drunken bastards.

　　They're all bastards, James. There's just you and me.

JAMES. That's enough. We'll be fine. Just you and me.

　　Let's just get drunk, man.

　　They run off.

　　BALVENIE *has been watching this – he enters the room and snatches up his 'Earl of Douglas' ceremonial robe.*

　　End of Act One.

ACT TWO

Royal Bedroom

The room is just lit by candles on the desk where JAMES *is signing documents, with* LIVINGSTON *standing over him.* MARY *is in bed, asleep.* JAMES *is dressed for bed.*

LIVINGSTON (*showing him*). Just a few more. Sign here on this one.

> CRICHTON *enters. Again, he seems just to observe the scene for a moment.*

CRICHTON. I didn't know we had a council tonight.

LIVINGSTON. We don't. You're not needed here, Crichton. Go to bed.

> CRICHTON *just stands, watching.*

Now… the grants of the abbeys, Your Majesty…

(*Showing him where to sign.*) Here… and here…

CRICHTON. Sounds like Privy Council business to me.

LIVINGSTON. That is at the King's pleasure.

CRICHTON. Oh, the King's pleasure, is it?

LIVINGSTON (*advancing on him*). When did you get so bold, wee man? So now you think you can just walk into the King's bedroom without an invitation and not lose your head for it?

CRICHTON. I'm just thinking the rest of the Privy Council might like to know we're doing business by moonlight now.

LIVINGSTON. You stay out of my business, Crichton, and I'll let you scuttle about doing yours till I'm ready…

JAMES (*cutting over them both*). Mother of Christ! Can we finish this? Come on! I just…

I just want to be done with this, Crichton. Enough.

A stand-off.

LIVINGSTON. You heard him. You heard your King.

A beat.

In the bed MARY *has been woken. She turns over angrily, muttering in French.*

CRICHTON. Excuse me for disturbing you, Your Majesty.

CRICHTON *exits.* JAMES *is reading the document.*

LIVINGSTON. That was well done, Your Majesty.

Come on, we all want our beds now. Sign it.

JAMES. But… why am I giving land to…?

LIVINGSTON. If you read everything, James, we'll be here till dawn. Sign, stop messing about.

JAMES. Is this your brother-in-law I'm granting the abbey to…?

LIVINGSTON. He is your *loyal* servant and if that wee display of Crichton's didn't remind you let me tell you you'd have precious few of those without me and mine. It's for the good of the realm! Sign and shut up!

JAMES *signs.*

They're coming for us. Don't think they're not.

JAMES. Who?

LIVINGSTON. I don't know… no him alane. He's too sleekit to jump till he sees the shore. But he's bold enough for threats again, is he? Well, we'll hold them off. Just do what I tell you when I tell you and we'll see them all off. Never you fear, wee Majesty. I'll keep us safe. There.

(*Gathering up papers.*) That's us done.

(*Bowing, more formal.*) It's well done, Your Majesty, and done in your name. Sleep well, Your Majesty.

LIVINGSTON *exits.* JAMES *gets into bed by* MARY.

After a moment, JAMES *becomes aware of noise and movement at his writing table. Someone is sitting there.*

JAMES *gets up and moves closer to see.*

It's YOUNG DOUGLAS. *He's covered in blood. He holds up bloodstained papers.*

YOUNG DOUGLAS. In the King's name.

JAMES *is panicking, he tries to get to his kist.* YOUNG DOUGLAS *and* DAVEY *are blocking his way.* JAMES *pulls a knife from under his pillow.*

MARY *wakes up abruptly.*

JAMES (*trying to get past* YOUNG DOUGLAS *and* DAVEY). No! Please! I'm sorry, please!

ISABELLA. The dark ones will put their bloody knives in your hand and you'll do their work.

MARY *goes to him.*

MARY. James? James?

ANNABELLA *hurries in.*

(*Looks round for help.*) It is happening again. Someone help!

ANNABELLA. Oh God, look at his eyes!

YOUNG DOUGLAS. Why are you frightened, aren't we family?

DAVEY. Cousin James.

MARY. What is it? James?

ANNABELLA *crosses herself.*

What is he looking at? What is he seeing?

ANNABELLA. I don't know!

JAMES. They made me do it, they made me... it wasn't my fault...

MEG *hurries on.*

MEG. Oh Christ save us.

(*To* MARY.) Leave him, pet, you can't reach him.

(*Calling off.*) Is William Douglas out there? Fetch him in, the King needs him!

MARY. Why does he do this!? *Il est fou ou quoi?* Is he possessed?

MEG hurries off. JAMES cries out again.

JAMES (*gabbling to himself, still trying to pass*). Get in the box get in the box get in the box…

YOUNG DOUGLAS. What's the matter, King James, has someone been frightening you?

MARY is suddenly between JAMES and the ghosts.

MARY. What does he look at? What is there?

MARY puts herself in JAMES's eyeline.

ANNABELLA (*terrified*). No, Mary! He'll hurt you! Leave him!

MARY. Stop looking there! Look at me! I am your wife! Look at me.

The DOUGLAS ghosts vanish.

Allors ça suffit!

(*To JAMES.*) Stop it! Stop being mad! I will not be married to a madman!

She hits at him. JAMES grabs her. He wakes, lost, staring at her.

No more nightmares. Enough.

So. Are you awake?

JAMES. Yes.

MARY. How do you know?

She kisses him.

JAMES. Because I felt that.

MARY. You were crazy. You were seeing things that weren't there. Stop it.

JAMES (*shaky*). Sorry.

MARY. And you're holding me too tight.

JAMES. Sorry.

He lets her go.

MARY. I did not say to let me go.

She holds on to him.

MEG *enters with* WILLIAM. *They take in the scene.*

MEG. My God… how did she manage it?

MARY *takes* JAMES*'s face in her hands.*

MARY. Now listen to me. Everything here is strange for me. I
    still understand almost nothing. So you must stop being
    frightening.

JAMES. Yes.

MARY. I am your wife now.

JAMES. Yes.

MARY. There is months of this. It is making me miserable. I do
    not want to be miserable. I want to be happy. So we will be
    happy.

JAMES. Yes.

MARY. We will love each other.

JAMES. Yes.

MARY. I can love you very easily because I like the way you
    look. But no more screaming.

JAMES. No. Sorry.

She kisses him.

ANNABELLA (*moved*). Oh.

WILLIAM *turns to* MEG.

WILLIAM. So where's the problem?

JAMES *notices him at last.*

JAMES. Will! What are you doing here?

WILLIAM. That's what I'm asking.

JAMES. This is my Queen.

WILLIAM. I know. We met. At your wedding?

JAMES (*to* MARY). This is William Douglas, the dearest friend I have.

MARY goes to WILLIAM.

MARY. You love my James?

WILLIAM. She doesny do small talk, eh?

(*To* MARY.) Aye, he's alright, as kings go.

MARY. Good. So you are my dear friend as well. *Comme ça tout va bien marcher.*

She kisses him formally on both cheeks.

Enchanté.

(*Turns to* MEG.) Now please we need sun.

MEG. Come and help me let the morning in.

They pull back the shutters and let pale winter pre-dawn light into the room.

A clean morning.

A wee dust of snow and a hard frost on it.

It's a good day. This bright weather will hold for a week now.

It's the Feast of the Holy Innocents.

MARY pulls away from JAMES *and bounces with delight.*

MARY. *Games!*

Oh at home I love the games! We play chasing games and kissing games...

WILLIAM. Well, here we play the ball.

MARY. What's that?

JAMES. The best game there is. I'll win it for you. Watch me.

WILLIAM. Aye, dream on.

MARY. This is going to be a good day, a good, good, *good* day!

(*Hugs* ANNABELLA, *speaking just to her*.) You see? We have to stop being frightened, *chérie*. That is how we will live here. No fear. You try.

ANNABELLA *hugs her back*.

ANNABELLA. I'm cold.

MARY. So we go to the kitchen and get wine and steal the cakes while they are hot!

ANNABELLA. Aye, we'll get the party wine today if we're quick.

MARY *and* ANNABELLA *hurry off*. MEG *following*.

MEG. Christ save us! You can't start the drinking before church!

JAMES *and* WILLIAM *look at each other for a moment*.

JAMES. It was another nightmare.

WILLIAM. Aye. But you're alright. She sorted you, eh?

JAMES. She must have.

WILLIAM. Good. They'll maybe leave me in my kip next time.

Right, I'm going to lay out the field for football.

JAMES. I am going to beat you, you know.

WILLIAM. Do you think? I don't think so, Jamie. I don't think I love you enough to let you win.

JAMES. Let me?

WILLIAM. Only way you will win.

They exit, laughing and chasing each other.

The Castle Courtyard

MARY *and* ANNABELLA *enter, eating.* MARY *has a little bag or basket of cakes.*

MARY. I dare you… to… roar like a lion.

ANNABELLA. No.

MARY. You have to.

ANNABELLA. I don't want to.

MARY. You have to. Today we play games. And you are a Stewart lion.

ANNABELLA *does a half-hearted roar,* MARY *laughs.*

Qu'est que ce?!

ANNABELLA. I don't want to, I'm not a Stewart lion! I don't even feel Scottish! I hate it here!

MARY. You speak Scottish…

ANNABELLA. I hate it! The skies are too high and the folk talk right at you and it's cold and they keep feeding you oily herring and telling you it's lovely! It's not! It's bogging! I want…

MARY. What?

ANNABELLA. To go back… don't you want to go back?

MARY (*ignoring her, still playing*). I dare you…

ANNABELLA. Don't you want to be home again?

MARY. This is home now… I dare you…

ANNABELLA. No, it's my turn. I dare you…

MARY. *Quoi?*

ANNABELLA. To tell me the truth.

MARY. This is my home now.

I dare you… to… smile.

ANNABELLA. Oh, Mary…

MARY. Please.

> ANNABELLA *smiles*. LIVINGSTON *enters, as* MARY *spins* ANNABELLA.

> Yes. *Yes*. Now dare me! Dare me.

LIVINGSTON. Games.

ANNABELLA. Yes.

LIVINGSTON. Lovely. Carry on.

MARY. Will you play?

LIVINGSTON. No.

> LIVINGSTON *is waiting*. ANNABELLA *whispers to* MARY. MARY *resists the dare*. ANNABELLA *pushes at her, laughing now*.

> BALVENIE *enters under this*.

> So? Have you talked to him?

BALVENIE. You're imagining things.

LIVINGSTON. I doubt that.

> MARY *is moving closer on* LIVINGSTON, *looking for a chance to tickle him*.

> Crichton is smirking. He's got some plan to meddle with me… or murder me.

BALVENIE. What do you care what Crichton thinks? When did you get so jumpy?

LIVINGSTON. You wait, he'll be creeping up behind me, first chance he gets.

> MARY *is behind him. She tickles him*. LIVINGSTON *whirls on her. She drops the cakes*.

BALVENIE. Christ, Livingston, don't kill the Queen.

LIVINGSTON. Your Highness…

MARY. It is… a game.

LIVINGSTON. Aye… sorry.

MARY. Just a game.

BALVENIE. Day of the Innocents, Livingston, tricks, football… games all day.

BALVENIE *is close to* LIVINGSTON.

And Douglas stands beside you, Livingston. You know that. Stop worrying.

LIVINGSTON. Aye. Right enough. I can rely on you, can't I?

BALVENIE. I've got your back. You can trust me. Don't you know that by now?

LIVINGSTON. Aye, I trust you to stay fat, eh, Balvenie?

(*To women*.) What do you think, Your Highness, Princess Annabella, he looks like a man who knows how to stay fat, eh? The abbey at Coldingham was it, Balvenie? I think the crown will be giving you that gift, I've got a feeling about it… Crichton can plot all he wants as long as I keep feeding you up, eh, Balvenie?

LIVINGSTON *exits*.

BALVENIE (*to* MARY). Did he scare you?

MARY. No.

BALVENIE. No. Don't let him scare you. No one here means you harm, Queen Mary.

MARY *is now gathering up the broken cakes, he helps her, tastes one*.

Apple cakes. Wonderful. You see I'd still eat that.

ANNABELLA. You can't eat them off the *ground*!

BALVENIE. If I don't, the dogs will.

ANNABELLA. Who are you? I should know you, I'm sure, but…

MARY. This is Balvenie, Annabella, the Earl of Douglas. The father of *William* Douglas…

MARY *has gone to* ANNABELLA.

I dare you… to kiss William Douglas.

ANNABELLA *gasps*.

ANNABELLA. Be *quiet*, Mary!

MARY. I dare you! I dare you!

> WILLIAM *enters under this*. MARY *screams in excitement when she sees him, pushing* ANNABELLA *towards him.* ANNABELLA *is pushing her back, chasing her off.*

ANNABELLA. Stop it! Be *quiet*!

They run off, giggling. BALVENIE *has started to laugh.*

WILLIAM. What's the joke?

BALVENIE. It's on me, William, it's on me.

> Look at you. You could win a war and you could marry a princess, couldn't you? It's that easy.

> It's in your blood, isn't it? The blood of Robert the Bruce.

WILLIAM. What about it?

BALVENIE. I shouldn't forget that's in you, should I?

> WILLIAM *is absorbed in marking out the football pitch.*

WILLIAM. Whoever plays from this side will have the sun in their eyes. I'll make him play this end.

BALVENIE. Maybe I haven't made the best of you, William. I might be guilty here. I may have overlooked one of my strongest resources, my best assets. What are you doing?

WILLIAM. Laying out the field, for the football.

BALVENIE. No. Events are moving on, as we hoped. So there must be no football today. That's not in the best interests of the Douglas family.

WILLIAM. Aye it is! The Douglas family can beat anyone else on this field! I'm telling you! Me and the King are battling the day and Douglas will *win*!

BALVENIE. William... William... William... It's energy, isn't it? It's not stupidity. You understand what's happening, I know you do.

Douglas can't seem so powerful, William, until it is, until there's nothing that can stop us. Do you see?

WILLIAM. Aye.

BALVENIE. I know you do. And I know you understand why.

WILLIAM. So, one day, when no one's looking, you can slip onto the Scottish throne and make a Douglas King of Scots.

A beat.

BALVENIE. That wasn't said, that is never said.

William, the day you were born, my legacy began to form, I just want to see that when I look at you.

WILLIAM. No football today.

BALVENIE. There you go!

Come on then, come and sit by me in the church.

The Chapel Stirling Castle, an hour later

The music continues as MARY *and* JAMES *sit side by side in the church. They look solemn and pious as paintings.*

ANNABELLA *sits close enough to half-hear what they are saying.*

Then MARY *coughs, racking and wet. She spits delicately in a lace hanky and looks at it. She pulls a face. She looks front again, formal.*

JAMES *doesn't react to any of this.*

MARY. That is the cough that is killing people.

I think this cough may kill me.

JAMES *is keeping his formal pose. He shushes her. She lowers her voice.*

I have spoken to the Bishop. I asked him to make me ready, he said, 'Are you frightened of death?' I said '*Non!*'

She thinks it's a mad question.

Do you believe he asked me that? I cannot believe he asked me that. Why should I be frightened? I am good enough for heaven. This is sure.

JAMES. What are you talking about?

MARY. I am telling you I am not afraid to die. And I am telling you I have reason to be afraid. Many reasons. But I am not. Afraid. Ever.

One day I will run through the fields of heaven. We both will.

I hope we get there when we are still young. I think we will.

Most people do, after all. But not yet. I must not die yet. We have important things first. I know my part but do you?

JAMES. Why are you talking about dying?

MARY. Because it is the moment. I do not think *this* will kill me. The people who die of this die before the sun sets, so quick.

So, I think I am carrying the sickness but I do not think I will die of that.

JAMES. Stop talking about dying!

MARY. If I *do* die I will wait for you at the gate of heaven. But of course you will miss me. Your heart will break. *Ça c'est sur.* So you should think of that. Of what it means to be my King.

JAMES. Shhhh!

The Bishop's frowning at us.

ANNABELLA *is now listening intently.*

MARY. I did not talk while he prayed. *Et en plus...* I am his Queen you are his King.

JAMES. He's one of my advisers. I don't want to...

MARY (*interrupting*). What? Why are you so afraid of all these old men who order you about?

JAMES. I'm not afraid of them, I just…

MARY. This is your kingdom! You do not need advisers to be
King. You *are* King.

JAMES. Aye but…

I'm young yet. I don't need to be bothered with all that…

MARY (*mutters*). *Mon Dieu*.

JAMES. What? No, what?

She shrugs.

I'll come into my power soon. You'll see. One day soon.

MARY. Well, I hope this day comes before the baby.

JAMES. What baby?

MARY. *Nom de Dieu*, are *you* a baby still?

JAMES. You're…

Are you…?

MARY. What did you expect?

JAMES. Oh my God!

Everyone turns to look.

MARY. Careful. All your *advisers* will scold you for being so
noisy.

JAMES. But… Mary, that's…

MARY (*cutting him off again*). So when the day comes that you
are *really* the King, tell me. My son will be a prince. His
father should be a king. I do not want to die before I see this.

A huge surge of music, triumphant.

Castle Courtyard

LIVINGSTON. Your King's coming in! The King's coming in!

The chant and reprise as in James I. *The* MUSICIANS *have got closer and closer to* LIVINGSTON *on this chant, at the final shout, as if they're doing a trick, they suddenly have weapons in their hands, pointing at* LIVINGSTON*'s throat.*

A silence.

CRICHTON *moves slowly in on* LIVINGSTON.

Aye, very funny, very funny. Enough of the jokes, the King needs...

CRICHTON. This is no joke. We're arresting you.

LIVINGSTON. *Arresting me!* For what?

CRICHTON. You've stolen the King's wealth long enough.

LIVINGSTON. Crichton, the King has seen all the tricks and jokes he needs to for Holy Innocents' Day. Balvenie! Tell them!

BALVENIE. This is no trick. I can't help you, Livingston, sorry. Not my place to meddle in the King's business.

LIVINGSTON. The King's business!? The King's business!? What does any man here know about that if I don't?

CRICHTON. Out of his own mouth.

LIVINGSTON. Balvenie! Get the crown officers!

CRICHTON. What makes you think Douglas would stand with you? You're a dusty wee owl trying to roost wi peacocks, Livingston, but we're plucking your feathers the day.

LIVINGSTON. Balvenie!?

BALVENIE. The thing is... no one likes you, Livingston. You made too many enemies. And now you stand alone.

LIVINGSTON. You two-faced, lying, treasonous bastard, Balvenie! I'll burn your guts before your face for this!

BALVENIE. It'd be a brave man who stood at your back now, Livingston, and you never thought I was a brave man, did you?

CRICHTON (*pitching over* LIVINGSTON). Your Majesty, King James, by your orders and in your name we arrest Livingston for crimes against Your Royal Majesty, to whit, the appropriation and mismanagement of the royal revenue for his own benefit and the benefit of his family…

As CRICHTON *is talking,* LIVINGSTON *is seized. He struggles, trying to shout over* CRICHTON.

LIVINGSTON. I took nothing that wasn't mine. I worked for the King. I worked for Scotland. Who'd've have ruled this country if I hadn't. A child! A clueless half-grown boy who knows more about falling off horses and playing ball games than he'll ever be able to learn about running a country. A snot-faced bairn greitin for his ma! You want him to rule you? Good luck!

CRICHTON (*pitching over* LIVINGSTON). You are arrested by order of the King!

JAMES. I haven't given any orders!

They're still pulling at LIVINGSTON.

I haven't given any orders!

What are you doing in my name! In my name? In my name? I don't even know what you're fucking doing!

Everyone stops. Everyone looks at JAMES.

(*Looking at* MARY.) Yes. Yes it is that day.

LIVINGSTON. Thank you. Thank you, Your Majesty, I like to think I always did teach you good sense.

JAMES *moves closer to* LIVINGSTON.

JAMES. Where did you get that ring?

LIVINGSTON. What?

JAMES *lifts* LIVINGSTON*'s hand, showing the ring.*

JAMES. That's the King's ring. My father's ring, where did you get it?

LIVINGSTON. It was… I don't know exactly…

What has that to do with anything! Can you not see what's happening here!?

JAMES. I remember where you got this ring! I remember and I've *never* forgotten!

JAMES *takes the ring from* LIVINGSTON.

(*Quiet.*) Arrest him.

(*Louder.*) This is your King talking! Arrest him! Lock him up!

LIVINGSTON *is dragged off through the small crowd. He's yelling back at* JAMES.

LIVINGSTON. Aye, play their game and see what happens! They'll have you! They'll finish you! I'm all that stands between you and their knives! You're dead now, you idiot boy! Dead!

BALVENIE *addresses the crowd.*

BALVENIE. There'll be no more games now. The King needs a new Chancellor!

With your permission, Your Majesty, my lords… Crichton… I offer my service, my experience, my… wisdom to you all. (*A pause.*) Crichton?

CRICHTON. Aye… that'll do for today.

BALVENIE. Your King must consult his council.

There's work to be done today.

JAMES. No, we'll have the football first, surely.

BALVENIE. Your Majesty, that would be very unwise.

JAMES. I promised my Queen. I want to play football.

BALVENIE. Well, you can't. You've work to do now.

JAMES. But…

BALVENIE (*cutting him off*). No! Let your elders guide you, Your Majesty. We know what we're about.

(*To the crowd.*) Clear the courtyard! There'll be no more games! Go and make ready to welcome your King to his new council!

WILLIAM. What are you talking about, old man? Jamie? Are we here to play or not!?

BALVENIE (*hissing*). What are you... Be quiet!

WILLIAM. The Douglas family is ready! The Douglas family is ready to play! I'm here to take on the King! I say the Douglas family can take down any other family in this country!

Aye, wee King James can give orders but can he stand against the Douglas family!? I say he can't. What do you say, Jamie?

Everyone is looking at JAMES. JAMES *hesitates.*
BALVENIE *moves in.*

BALVENIE. King James... I'm not sure you appreciate the... volatility of the situation we're in now.

CRICHTON. Your Majesty, he's right, Livingston still has his allies...

BALVENIE. Half the council are here, we need to plan...

JAMES. I don't know what you're talking about. We'll plan when I know what you're talking about.

BALVENIE. That's why you have to hear our counsel now and...

JAMES. Well, if it was that important you should have explained it before this.

No?

(*As they're at a loss.*) Well, you can explain yourselves tomorrow. This is Holy Innocents' Day. The day we play games.

BALVENIE. Yes but...

JAMES (*cutting him off*). Then I say we'll still have our game! I'm the King and I say we're playing the ball on Holy

Innocents' Day like we're meant to! Who's with me!?
Stewart! Stewart!

A shout as other voices join him. WILLIAM *starts the
counter-shout throwing the defiance straight at his father.*

WILLIAM. Douglas! Douglas! Douglas!

CRICHTON. And where do you stand, Chancellor Balvenie?
With the King or with the Douglas family?

BALVENIE. King James, you still needs a man to stand father
to you, to advise you, to guard you from the rash, dangerous
acts of madness your youth might lead you in to.

Abruptly, MARY *seems to be choking. She flaps her hands,
trying to swallow a coughing-sneezing fit.* MARY *turns from
them, sneezing explosively, several times. She has sneezed
right over* BALVENIE.

He wipes off his face.

MARY. Oh, I am so sorry.

BALVENIE says nothing. He's groping for a handkerchief.
WILLIAM *is trying not to laugh, as is* JAMES.

MARY *hands him a hanky.*

Here it is… it is… quite clean.

*BALVENIE waves her away. He finds a hanky of his own
and wipes off his face.*

JAMES. We can have a council tomorrow, man, alright? Today
is for the games.

*WILLIAM has produced a ball, a ragged bundle of leather
and rags. Cheers as he throws it up then kicks it to* JAMES.

*There's a sudden scramble for sides, the mood changed,
laughing and jostling.*

CRICHTON exits. BALVENIE *watches the game for a
second, furious, then he follows.*

MEN and WOMEN *have been lining up behind* JAMES *or*
WILLIAM. *The* MEN *pulling off coats, the* WOMEN
tucking up their skirts.

Give me the ball! Give me the ball now!

It's thrown to him.

(*To* WILLIAM.) I'll show you what I've learned since you last saw me, William Douglas.

WILLIAM. Go on then.

With an ear-splitting yell, JAMES kicks the ball up in the air and then everyone runs for it. MARY watches.
ANNABELLA hesitates for a moment but as the game gets going she gives a yell and runs to join them.

The rules of medieval football are pretty obscure and open to interpretation.

Basically there's no goal. One side of the courtyard is JAMES's 'goal' and if the ball hits anywhere on that wall it's a score for the other side and vice versa.

The ball has to be hit with feet.

Apart from that there are no rules as we'd understand them and the main aim is to stop the opposing players getting or moving the ball by any means possible – kicking, punching, biting gouging… It's basically a screaming, rowdy street fight with occasional contact with the ball. MEN and WOMEN are going for it with enormous enthusiasm but rapidly everyone is beaten to the point of collapse. Only WILLIAM and JAMES are left standing, limping, battered, utterly exhausted but refusing to give up.

They are each staggering after the ball. As one of them reaches it, the other knocks them over and they wrestle for a minute until one of them breaks free and struggles for the ball again.

WILLIAM seems to be injured. JAMES relaxes his hold. WILLIAM springs up and kicks the ball hard against the wall.

JAMES goes at WILLIAM with a sword. WILLIAM just faces him down.

Everyone is watching. No one speaks or moves.

WILLIAM. Game over. DOUGLAS!

JAMES. You bastard.

A moment. It really looks like JAMES *might kill* WILLIAM. *Then he starts to laugh.*

You fucking cheating Douglas bastard! You win!

JAMES *pulls* WILLIAM *into an embrace.*

The two teams start to pick themselves up properly, handshakes and embraces, laughter.

MARY *makes her way to* JAMES.

MARY. That was a game!

JAMES. Were you scared I'd be hurt?

MARY. No! Of course not!

JAMES. Listen to her! Look at me, woman! I am hurt! He nearly murdered me!

WILLIAM. Aye and you bit me!

MARY. That was a game.

JAMES. I love it.

WILLIAM. Me too.

ANNABELLA has joined them. She's covered in dirt and blood, grinning. The other players are moving on and off, preparing for a party outside, building fires in the courtyard, bringing food and drink.

ANNABELLA. We play it differently here. I'd forgotten. That was mad! I love it! I'm happy! I'm happy!

JAMES. Christ, Annabella, look at the state of you!

WILLIAM. She bit me too!

ANNABELLA rounds on him, elated and ferocious.

ANNABELLA. I am not afraid of you, William Douglas!

He holds his hands up, backing off, laughing.

WILLIAM. Christ, call her off, Jamie!

Hours have passed.

WILLIAM, JAMES, MARY *and* ANNABELLA *are sitting close round a small fire, passing wine between them. It's hours later. They've been talking and drinking for some time.*

WILLIAM *yawns.*

Man, I'm getting too old for this.

ANNABELLA. You are. You're twenty. You've had a whole life.

WILLIAM. No. I've not been let at it. It's all nearly gone and I can't make it mine. I still answer to others. Always.

MARY. Maybe you have all the time you need. Maybe you will live to be older than a tree, like your father.

WILLIAM. Maybe I'll die in a war but never lead an army.

I tell you though, I want to die fighting. No time to worry. Just think, 'Shite I messed that up, I shouldn't have picked that fight' and feel the blade go in. That'll be it. Pray it's quick. That's the only way to die.

That's another thing you ladies can't know. You'll die in bed, every one of you. One way or another.

ANNABELLA (*suddenly furious*). You don't understand anything!

My best friend in Grenoble died. They had to cut the baby out of her. They said it wouldn't kill her but of course they were just lying. She held my hand and it drove my rings into my fingers. Look.

(*Holds up her hand.*) I'll keep the marks for ever.

We kiss death every day, William Douglas, and we smile at him.

WILLIAM. Fine. Alright. Just saying…

ANNABELLA. You know nothing.

MARY (*to* ANNABELLA). *Mais pourquoi tu es si fâché mon ami, qu'est ce qu'il y à?*

ANNABELLA. Nothing… just… (*Can't go on.*)

JAMES. Annabella? What's wrong?

ANNABELLA (*to* JAMES). I know. I heard.

WILLIAM. Know what?

ANNABELLA. The cough won't kill you, no, it's not the cough you need to be frightened of. I just want to keep one friend!

MARY. *Ah mais tais toi!* If I am not frightened you cannot be frightened. No fear. Remember? It is forbidden.

WILLIAM. What's going on?

MEG *enters.*

MEG. Are you bairns going to stay out in this much longer? You'll catch your deaths. Come on, come on inside.

JAMES. We're not bairns, Meg. None of us, stop fussing.

MEG. Well, you're my bairn, always. Don't be long, I've got your posset warming.

She exits. WILLIAM *is falling about.*

WILLIAM. She's got your posset warming!

JAMES. Aye alright, alright.

WILLIAM. Hold the wine! The King's away to sook on a warm posset!

JAMES. Shut up! I never drink the stuff, she just makes it! She's right though. It's cold, Mary. We should go in.

WILLIAM. Why? Is she too French and fragile to stand a wee bit of Scottish December?

JAMES *and* MARY *say nothing, looking at each other conspiratorially.*

ANNABELLA. Haven't you been listening, William Douglas? She's going to have a baby!

He gets it.

WILLIAM. Oh it's like that, is it? Fine then you should go in but we'll have another drink, eh, James?

JAMES. No, man, come on, it's late.

WILLIAM. Get tae fuck! It's nowhere near daylight. Come on, Jamie! I'll get another bottle.

JAMES. Nah, Will, come on, it's time to get inside.

WILLIAM. What's inside that you canny have out here?

JAMES. My Queen!

WILLIAM. Aw fuck that, you already got her up the duff, plenty more lassies out here...

JAMES *is instantly furious*.

JAMES. Right! You say sorry! You say sorry for that!

WILLIAM. It was a joke, man! Come on! Sense of humour. Sit down.

JAMES. No. We're going in. Come on, Mary.

WILLIAM. You won't even finish drinking with me? After what I did for you?

JAMES. What did you do? Cheat me out of the match, drink my wine and insult my wife?

MARY (*stopping him*). James. It is alright.

WILLIAM. You don't know what I did for you. He's going to beat me bloody for what I did and you won't even...

JAMES. Who? Who's going to beat you?

WILLIAM. My father!

JAMES. Aw for Christ's sake, William, listen to yourself. You're a grown man! Stand up to him!

ANNABELLA. James, stop it.

WILLIAM. A grown man, eh? A family man like you, all cosy with your wife and your bairn and your wee crown?

JAMES. Aye. Just like that. What's wrong with that!?

WILLIAM*'s mood switches abruptly. He's frozen, bereft.*

WILLIAM. Nothing. Nothing's wrong with that.

You're…

Congratulations, man. I'm… I'm happy for you. God save the King, eh?

JAMES. William…

WILLIAM (*moving away*). No really. Well done. I'm…

I'm sorry. I'm sorry, Mary.

MARY. William, come inside with us.

WILLIAM. No no, I'll finish the bottle first.

JAMES *and* MARY *hesitate.* JAMES *turns to* MARY.

JAMES. I'll no be long. Annabella, take her in.

MARY *exits.*

ANNABELLA *goes to* WILLIAM *and kisses him.*

WILLIAM. What was that for?

ANNABELLA. To show you. I'm not afraid of you, William Douglas.

ANNABELLA *exits.* JAMES *goes to* WILLIAM.

JAMES. Be happy for me.

WILLIAM. I just said I was.

He reaches out and touches the mark on JAMES*'s face.*

It feels just like the rest of your face. No different at all.

JAMES. It's all just me.

WILLIAM. Aye.

JAMES. Come inside with us.

WILLIAM. No. No, I can't be with your family tonight, James. I'll have family business of my own to deal with.

The moment holds a beat longer, then JAMES *exits.* WILLIAM *swigs from the bottle.*

An armed MAN *enters on one side of the stage.* WILLIAM
sees him and turns to run the other way, but another MAN
blocks his exit. They fight but the MEN *quickly overpower*
WILLIAM *and pin him. During the fight* BALVENIE *enters*
and watches. He holds a heavy stick.

BALVENIE. Hold him still.

He whacks WILLIAM.

I don't even understand why you did that.

He hits him again, coughs, recovers, hits him again.

I knew you were stupid but I didn't know you were mad.
Why did you do that?

WILLIAM. Because I'm no wanting Jamie's crown… old man.

BALVENIE *hits him again. A terrible fit of coughing seizes*
him. He tries to raise the stick again. He collapses.
WILLIAM *struggles.*

Dad?

(*To the* MEN.) Help him! Let me go! Let me help him!

They let him go. WILLIAM *runs to* BALVENIE.

Dad?

It's alright, it's alright. I've got you. Can you walk?

He tries to raise BALVENIE. *Shouts at the* MEN.

Help us!

The MEN *help* WILLIAM *half-carry* BALVENIE *off.*

It's alright. It's alright. I'm here, Dad. I'm here.

They exit.

King's Room, Later the Same Night

MARY *and* JAMES *are on the bed.* MEG *enters with a cup of posset.*

MEG. Now, I know what you're going to say, but it's a cold night, I'm going to stand here till I see you drink this.

JAMES (*gentle*). No. I need to talk to you.

He takes the posset from her. Gives it to MARY.

MEG. What? What is it?

JAMES. Meg, sweetheart, I'm giving you an orchard.

MEG. What? James…

JAMES. I'm too old for mothering now, Meg. I'm giving you a hill full of apples and fields full of fat sheep, enough so you can get the best man that has the sense to love you and make some prettier babies to love than me.

Pause. She takes this in.

MEG. Oh, darling… no… no… don't send me away. Never send me away.

JAMES. No. Never. You'll be just outside the wall. I'll look down to see you every day and if you're not happy I'll ride down and carry you off again.

MARY. And I will need you, Meg, when it is time.

MEG *is nearly in tears.* JAMES *is close to her.*

JAMES. I'm your bairn if I'm anyone's, Meg, but I'm no bairn any more.

MEG. No. You're my King. God bless you. God bless you, King James.

She clings to him for a moment then exits. JAMES *takes the posset from* MARY *and drinks it.*

JAMES. Don't tell William.

MARY. Sometimes I do not like him.

JAMES. What?

MARY. I know you love him but sometimes I do not like the way he talks to you.

JAMES. Listen, Mary, you need to understand the way it is with me and William. We might look like we're away to kill each other sometimes but that's how we are. Never interfere.

MARY. Of course not. But sometimes he scares me a little.

JAMES. Well… I won't let him do that again.

He kisses her. He moves away.

MARY. Will you sleep now?

JAMES. Soon.

MARY. Where do you go? When you walk in the night?

JAMES. I'll be back soon.

He exits.

Isabella's Room, Night

JAMES *enters.* ISABELLA *startles awake.*

ISABELLA. I wasn't asleep!

(*Looking out the window.*) Oh, my brave boys, where are you?

JAMES. My father died a hero.

ISABELLA. Your father died in a drain.

JAMES. You wanted to kill my father and all his blood.

ISABELLA. If my wishing could do it you'd be dead.

JAMES. Who else wants us dead?

ISABELLA. Walter… Alisdair… Oh, my bairns… there you are… there you are… oh look at their white wings and their dark eyes… My boys. I see you. I do.

JAMES. I've had Livingston executed.

ISABELLA. Jumped-up wee nyaff. You're well rid.

JAMES. What happens now? Will someone try to take his place? Who should I fear most?

ISABELLA. How should I know?

Why do you always come back to bother me?

JAMES. Because you're the oldest thing I know that talks.

Tell me what you know. Livingston said they'd come for me. Tell me which family I should fear most now.

ISABELLA. I won't tell you. I'll watch death eat you and laugh. How would I know? I've seen nothing but this room and my son's souls on the wind for longer than you've lived.

How would I know what's going to happen now?

I can make a guess though.

JAMES. Tell me and I'll set you free.

ISABELLA. If you set me free I'll kill you. *I'll* be your death if you ever set me free.

JAMES *moves to exit*.

JAMES. I'll get them to sweeten the air in here for you. They can bring you roast chicken.

ISABELLA. I'll eat it but I'll never thank you. Look around you. Who makes the little lords bob and rustle like sparrows when the hawk's shadow passes over. Who has the smell of blood on his breath when he smiles in your face?

JAMES. Who?

ISABELLA. How should I know? I've seen nothing but this room and my sons' souls on the wind for longer than you've lived.

I can make a guess though. You'll see it soon… if you're looking.

JAMES *moves to exit again*.

JAMES. Your door's open. You can come out any time you like.

ISABELLA. I'll come out to watch death eat you and I'll laugh.

JAMES *exits*.

A Room in the Douglas Castle

BALVENIE *is lying in bed, dying*. WILLIAM *sits staring at him. Occasionally he wipes tears from his face*.

BALVENIE. What are you crying for?

WILLIAM. You've got the fever. They think you're dying.

BALVENIE. I'm not.

WILLIAM. It's alright, it's alright, the priest's here.

BALVENIE. Send him away. He's not needed.

WILLIAM *is close to breaking down*.

WILLIAM. Alright. But I'm with you, alright? I'm here.

BALVENIE. I don't want you here. Go away.

(*Coughing*.) I'll die... when I'm ready to die...

WILLIAM. My heart will burst like an egg dropped on stone. Christ, you're my father. When you're gone age will just drop on me like winter rain. I won't be able to stand up with the weight of grief on me.

BALVENIE. Well... you don't need to worry about that yet.

WILLIAM. Oh listen, Dad, listen... you are really sick. Hear that noise you're making? That's blood in your breath.

BALVENIE *coughs rackingly*.

See what I mean. You've caught the cough, the fever, it's killing everyone.

BALVENIE. Help me sit up.

WILLIAM. No, you're best staying peaceful now.

BALVENIE. Help... me... sit... up!

> WILLIAM *moves reluctantly to help him*. BALVENIE *is groaning with effort*.

WILLIAM. You're the colour of oatmeal. Aw Jesus...

> (*Wipes at his face again*.) I never thought I'd see you like this. I need to get you the priest.

BALVENIE. I'm not... dying...

WILLIAM. Dad, I think you are. But I'm here. I'll help you. It'll be a good death. Brave.

BALVENIE. Cold...

WILLIAM. What?

BALVENIE. I'm cold.

WILLIAM. That'll be the start of it.

> The fire's dying. Turn your back on it and walk into the dark. Time to go.
>
> Oh Dad, what'll I do? I can't feed you to the worms. They want you though, they're going to have you.
>
> I'm going to stay with you. I won't leave you alone.

BALVENIE. Do you think I want you pawing round me then? You even sound like her. Never stopped crying.

> BALVENIE *groans and coughs*.

WILLIAM. I'm here to say goodbye. You're my father. I'm your son. These are the last words we'll have. Give me your blessing at least.

BALVENIE. I never gave you anything you didn't waste or lose. A thick-headed turnip with your mother's glaikit face. Be quiet now.

> Listen... you must do nothing... *nothing*... you'll lose it all... just sit still till I'm walking again...

WILLIAM. Dad, you'll never be walking again.

BALVENIE. No! You'll bring... *everything*... to ruin... just *wait*...

WILLIAM. You smell of ruin... and rot... Just make it a good death. Come on.

BALVENIE. Ah Christ... it hurts... my breath... it hurts...

WILLIAM. Listen... if you held your breath you'd just go. Stop bleating, Dad. Hold your breath and imagine you're dying like a fighting man... like a man on a spring battlefield. The sun blinding him as he shuts his eyes and takes his last breath...

Just shut your eyes...

Feel the sun...

Shut your eyes...

BALVENIE. You're not... ready... you'll lose everything I got for you...

WILLIAM. It's mine to lose.

BALVENIE. You're not fit for the name Douglas!

WILLIAM. I'll be the Earl of Douglas by morning. It'll be my land.

BALVENIE. Oh Christ... listen to me...

WILLIAM. No. I can't hear you. Even your voice is leaving you. The dark's coming now... you can feel it, eh?

BALVENIE. Patience, just... Oh Christ I'm cold...

He coughs.

I'm cold...

WILLIAM. What's that? You need the cold air? I'll fetch you some cold air.

WILLIAM *wrenches a window open.*

BALVENIE. So cold... help me... I'm too cold...

WILLIAM *roughly pulls the covers off him.*

WILLIAM. I'll help you to the cold. There.

Now hurry up, will you?

This is breaking me in pieces. My heart's shattered. Get on with it, will you!

The new Earl needs to be busy.

The new Earl needs to be about his work.

BALVENIE *is choking.* WILLIAM *watches.*

Elgin, Huntly, Brechin, all mine...

Melrose, Dunbar and Galloway... all mine...

Mine...

Mine...

BALVENIE *is dead.* WILLIAM *covers him.*

The scene transforms to BALVENIE*'s funeral.*

Castle Courtyard

Funeral music. BALVENIE*'s body is draped in rich coverings and carried to rest in the chapel.* WILLIAM *follows it. A group of* MUSICIANS *gather round him.*

CRICHTON, HUME, ANNABELLA, MEG *and other* LORDS *and* LADIES *of the Scottish court gather.* JAMES *and* MARY *enter last.* MARY *is now heavily pregnant.*

WILLIAM. Thank you all for coming here.

Thank you for honouring the name of Douglas.

WILLIAM *goes to kneel by his father's coffin.*

The court processes past him, each one crossing themselves and bowing to the coffin, then acknowledging WILLIAM.

They all pass in silence, CRICHTON *and* HUME *are last.*
CRICHTON *steps up, he speaks quietly as he bows his head*
close to WILLIAM.

HUME. My lord, Earl Douglas, we share your grief.

WILLIAM. Do you?

CRICHTON. May I express the sorrow of the whole council,
we will meet soon to discuss your own place among us, I
hope we may help you understand your role as one of the
King's advisers...

WILLIAM (*cutting him off*). Have I asked you to do that?

HUME. No but...

WILLIAM. Then why are you still talking to me!? I don't need
to talk to either of you. There's only one family in this
country with power worth spit. Douglas. Maybe Crawford to
the north-east, Lord MacDonald in the Isles, they might get
close, but you two? Why are you even talking to me? Get
away from me.

As they don't move.

I said, get away from me!

They back off, alarmed.

HUME (*calling after him*). We came to offer respect, my lord!
We came to honour your father and offer you respect! You
owe us the courtesy of your attention...

CRICHTON (*shushing* HUME). Leave it! Don't provoke him
now. Look at him!

WILLIAM *is trying to rally the crowd, calling out as*
DAVEY *did before.*

WILLIAM. Who holds the border?

Most are just standing, watching, but others group round
WILLIAM, *a loud, aggressive little army.*

DOUGLAS SUPPORTERS. Douglas!

WILLIAM. Who keeps Scotland?

DOUGLAS SUPPORTERS. Douglas!

WILLIAM. Who keeps wee James safe!

DOUGLAS SUPPORTERS. Douglas!

WILLIAM. I said who does the King need!?

DOUGLAS SUPPORTERS. Douglas!

WILLIAM is moving closer to JAMES.

WILLIAM. Just you and me, James. Just you and me at last. Oh man, we can rule Scotland now.

MARY. King James rules Scotland.

WILLIAM. Aye. He does, wee Mary. He does. But I help him, see. I'm his right-hand man. Amn't I, James?

JAMES. You're drunk.

WILLIAM. Do you know what? I haven't had a drop! Amazing, eh? I think this is shock. Or grief. We should drink though, eh?

JAMES. You should calm down, man. Let me do this, alright? Then we'll have that drink.

He addresses the watching crowd.

The head of the Douglas family deserves the highest honour.

The DOUGLAS SUPPORTERS *whoop and cheer.*

And I extend the highest honour to my cousin, my friend, William Earl of Douglas, I hereby appoint him my papal envoy.

There's a cheer from the DOUGLAS SUPPORTERS. *Limp applause from everyone else.*

This is news to WILLIAM, *he's completely thrown.*

WILLIAM. What?

No, no, no… That's not what you promised me! No. I'm not leaving the country.

JAMES *indicating the watching* LORDS.

JAMES (*quieter*). Look at them, William! They're like frightened dogs that don't know whether to bite or run. You need to calm down. You need to stop stirring things up. You need to step away from the crown. It's making the whole world nervous.

WILLIAM. Step away. From you?

JAMES. From the court.

WILLIAM. You're sending me away!?

JAMES. It's an honour! You'll make a fortune out of it!

WILLIAM. No.

No.

Jamie, don't do this. Please. Please don't do this.

JAMES. Come on, Will…

WILLIAM. This is the moment! This is the time! This is the day! You and me, Jamie, you and me!

JAMES. It's done, Will. It's done. I need you to go.

A beat. WILLIAM *looks at* MARY.

WILLIAM. This was your idea, wasn't it?

ANNABELLA. William, you're frightening everyone.

A beat.

WILLIAM. Aw well, Jesus, we can't have that, can we?

He starts to move off.

JAMES. William…

WILLIAM *has turned on* HUME.

WILLIAM. What are you looking at, Hume, eh? What are you looking at? Don't you know who I am?

When HUME *doesn't answer,* WILLIAM *shouts in his face.*

I'm the King's fucking papal envoy.

How scary is that? Eh?

WILLIAM *exits*.

JAMES. My lords… ladies… We will still…

We'll have the funeral feast.

The feast is in the Great Hall.

Everyone starts to move away.

MARY. I liked him but he has no control. I think he may be mad.

JAMES. He's not mad he's just…

MARY. Mad.

She moves away. ANNABELLA *is looking at* JAMES.

JAMES. It's alright, he'll be in a better mood when he gets back. He will.

They exit.

Great Hall – Six Months Later

WILLIAM *and* JAMES *are sitting close together. They've eaten, now they're just drinking. The dancing and music recede into the distance.*

WILLIAM. Everyone loves you, don't they?

JAMES. Oh, you don't?

WILLIAM. I don't mind you. I'll take a drink with you.

JAMES. Thanks. You want some more of *my* wine?

WILLIAM. Call this wine? I've had nearly a year in Rome, remember. I know good red wine from ditch water now, Jamie. But I'll drink it because I like you.

JAMES. Glad to hear it.

WILLIAM. Everyone likes you, that's what I'm saying. You make folk smile. They think you're a good man.

JAMES. I try to be a good man.

WILLIAM. And they believe that's what you are.

It can't just be the smile, though you've got a great smile...

JAMES. I do?

WILLIAM. A boy's smile.

JAMES. A *boy's* smile?

WILLIAM. Aye. Friendly... but cheeky... a great wee boy, grinning at us all.

JAMES. Aye, well I'm full grown, William.

WILLIAM. No, no... I'm just saying... You'll have that smile when you're sixty, man... I'm not getting at you... I'm just saying it helps folk like you.

See I'm actually better looking than you.

JAMES. Is that right?

WILLIAM. Aye well, you've got the... the thing there, haven't you...?

(*Indicating birthmark.*) Proof that your mother got you in a raspberry bush.

JAMES (*sarcastic*). No, the angels slapped me for leaving heaven.

WILLIAM. Ha!

Well, scrub that stain off you and you're still not a looker next to me but it does me no good. It makes folk hate me.

JAMES. Oh is that what does it?

WILLIAM. Aye, the women hate me because they don't want to love me but they can't help themselves. The men hate me because once they've seen me their women never get wet again unless they're whispering my name. Everyone hates me.

JAMES. Because you're so good-looking?

WILLIAM. It's the main reason, I'm sure of it.

See, what I'm saying is, half the badness that's said about me, half the wickedness I'm supposed to have done is no wickedness at all. It's just folk saying, 'Look at that William Douglas, I hate him, he's so good-looking.'

(*Starts to laugh.*) I'm joking, man, can't you tell?

This wine is shite, why are you insulting me with the shite wine?

JAMES. That's the best we've got.

WILLIAM. It's shite. You're trying to poison me.

JAMES. I'm drinking it.

WILLIAM. Because you don't know it's shite.

JAMES. I like it.

WILLIAM. Because you're too stupid to know it's shite.

JAMES. Everyone else likes it.

WILLIAM. Because they're all feart to tell you your wine's shite. Well, I'm no feart.

JAMES. Clearly.

WILLIAM. Christ Almighty, what does it take to make you lose your temper, Jamie?

You used to have a great temper.

Used to be all you had to do was hold something up where you couldn't reach it.

Holds up food above JAMES*'s head.*

Come on, Jamie, come on, little Jamie…

JAMES. I grew up, William.

WILLIAM. You're no fun any more.

JAMES. And you're an arse.

WILLIAM. You used to like me though.

JAMES. I did. I thought you were great.

So what badness do you think folk are saying about you?

WILLIAM. I don't know.

The usual.

JAMES. What might they be saying?

WILLIAM. I don't know! You tell me!

That I'm not doing what our lovely wee King wants me to do.

JAMES. You're not sending me your taxes.

WILLIAM. Oh listen to you. All grown up and counting money.

What do you care. You've got enough, haven't you? Maybe I just can't be bothered to gather your money in for you. Maybe I've got better things to do.

JAMES. Like killing the men I send to ask after my taxes.

WILLIAM. Oh I only killed one of them!

Like you've never murdered a tax collector!?

JAMES. No.

WILLIAM. No, because they're your tax collectors, but take it from me, Jamie, everyone *wants* to murder a tax collector.

WILLIAM *helps himself to wine.*

I'm sorry, Jamie. I'm sorry. I never meant to fall out with you.

JAMES. Then don't. Let's fix this. Come on.

A beat.

WILLIAM. You've done as bad as me and no one hates you for it.

JAMES. How are you working that out?

WILLIAM. No look, I'm here to apologise, alright? It's understood. It's the right thing to do, you'll hammer even more of my money off me if I don't... greedy wee shite that you are... No but... fair enough... that aside... it's the right thing to do plus we were always friends, we were *good* friends... I love the ghost of that wee boy grinning at me from your face there... so I do, sincerely... apologise for the wrong I've done you. Alright?

JAMES. Yes.

WILLIAM. All I'm saying is that it's not so much wrong. You've done worse. You've just got the face to get away with it.

JAMES. Well… thanks for the apology, William.

WILLIAM. I don't mean a word of it. I'm as good as you. Any day.

Can we stop this and go and get a better drink or something?

JAMES. Stop what?

WILLIAM. We're done here, aren't we? Apology on the table, you've picked it up…

I'm not going to *kneel* to you, man, so don't hold your breath waiting on that.

JAMES. What were you apologising for?

WILLIAM. Sorry?

JAMES. What were you apologising for?

WILLIAM. You don't *know*?

JAMES. I'd just be interested to know what you think you're apologising for?

WILLIAM *stares at him for a moment*.

WILLIAM. Killing your tax collector.

JAMES. You are such a piece of dog filth, man.

No you are.

You've turned nasty. It's not funny.

WILLIAM. You heard the story then?

JAMES. Yes.

WILLIAM. Oh man, it was brilliant. See I'd only *locked up* the first tax collector you sent but, when lord what's-'is-face, tax collector number two turns up, I was annoyed for a *wee* minute, can't deny it – but I made as nice as anything.

'Of course, so sorry for the wait, will you take some dinner while I fetch the money and the first tax collector you're missing?'

He's sitting waiting on his dinner. We bring it in under a cover.

(*Mimes lifting a cover.*) There's his pal's head!

WILLIAM *falls about*.

JAMES. How is that funny?

WILLIAM. It a bit funny though, eh?

JAMES. No.

WILLIAM. Come on, it was a bit funny. The man's face…

JAMES. No. That's not a joke.

WILLIAM. Aw man, if you'd been there you'd've laughed, on Christ's blood I *swear* you'd have laughed…

JAMES. No.

WILLIAM (*imitates lord*). 'So where's my tax-collector pal Lord What's-'is-doodle?'

(*Imitates servant.*) 'Oh he'll be here directly, sir.'

(*Uncovers a dish of food.*) 'Here he is!'

WILLIAM *falls about*. JAMES *is just staring at him*.

Aw come *on*, Jamie!

Alright, alright… I'm sorry, I won't kill any tax collectors ever again.

Where's the wine?

You shouldn't have sent two of them. That was just aggravation. Asking for it. You had your answer when the first boy never came home.

He's grabbed the wine and poured it.

Are you not drinking?

JAMES *says nothing, he's just studying him.*

Fuck that, if you're not drinking I'm off home, either you've poisoned the stuff or you're planning on staying sober enough to stab me. Safe conduct my arse, I'm not safe unless you're as pissed as I am, *drink*, will you!

JAMES *lets him fill his glass.*

And why are you looking at me like that?

He pushes away from the table.

Come on then. Come on.

JAMES. Will, what are you doing?

WILLIAM. You're after a fight. Come on then.

JAMES. Do I look like I'm after a fight?

WILLIAM. Course you're after a fight, what's wrong with you?

JAMES. Man, you came in here under safe conduct! What do you th–

WILLIAM (*cuts him off*). Aye, so did my big cousins. Remember?

The nightmare is just coming back at the edge of JAMES*'s vision. It is only there for him.*

JAMES. You're my friend. You were a friend to me that night, William, I'll never forget that.

WILLIAM. Oh I think you will. I think you did, Jamie. You forgot all about it. Didn't you?

ANNABELLA *enters at the other side of the room.*

JAMES. Annabella, I told you we needed some peace.

WILLIAM. She can't keep away from me, can you, Annabella?

ANNABELLA *sits down quite a distance from them, watching them.*

Crazy as a drunken goose. Who's going to marry that?

(*Calling over.*) Sorry, Annabella. I won't marry you but you can still have a fuck if you like, I know you want it.

JAMES. Alright, shut up, man.

WILLIAM. You ready to fight?

JAMES. No, I'm not ready to fight! What's wrong with you? Just shut up. Keep your nasty mouth shut.

WILLIAM. Looks to me like you might be thinking of starting that fight.

JAMES. What's wrong with you!? What's *wrong* with you?! Suppose we did fight, you're in my castle, my men, my family all round me… how do you think that would end?

WILLIAM. You threatening me, Jamie?

JAMES. I'm *not* threatening you! That's the bloody point.

I'm making up with you! Trying to. Have you noticed that yet!?

WILLIAM. You think I'm frightened of falling out with you? You think I care about that?

JAMES. No! You don't! It's fucking obvious. You're a defiant fucking hero or whatever you think you are. Why are you here, Will?

WILLIAM. You asked me here.

JAMES. And why did you come?

A beat.

WILLIAM. To let you know.

JAMES. Let me know what?

WILLIAM. That you're no better than me. And I won't be doing anything on your say-so any time soon. I just wanted to look you in the eye and say that. I think we both need to be clear about that.

JAMES. Aw man.

Aw man, you're a nightmare, you're a dark and stormy nightmare. What am I supposed to do with that?

WILLIAM. I don't care what you do, little Jamie.

I'm just telling you how it is.

JAMES. You've got to know I'm likely to have to execute you for saying things like that!

WILLIAM. So why am I not dead?

JAMES. I don't want to kill you, Will.

WILLIAM. Well... I got to see what dying in bed looked like, Jamie, and I'm no going like that.

No I am not.

He gets another drink.

My dad took me round all our land a few years back. He'd got it all, all the Douglas land and more, damp patch by damp patch. Banff, Avoch, Aberdour, Moray, Strathaven, Stonehouse... Jesus... He took me over every wet, thistle-sprouting, rocky inch of it. He poked sheep and cattle he'd inherited from all my dead cousins and uncles and he laughed like a crow eating eyeballs at the fat arses on those beasts. This was him showing me how to be a rich man. Proving to me that we were rich men.

And you know what gets me?

He'd *been* to Rome. Have you been to Rome, Jamie?

JAMES. No.

WILLIAM. No.

Neither had I till you sent me. I suppose you thought you were doing me a favour?

There's a house, not a rich man's house, a wine merchant's house, an ordinary shop man's house you ride past on your way into town.

It has paintings of angels on its walls that look like a window into the next world.

It has *peacocks* in its yard. I'm not joking. The *wine merchant's* kids are kicking peacocks' eggs around his garden in Rome.

With angels watching them.

And I come home and I'm supposed to feel like a rich man because I've got another hundred wet sheep?

What's the point? Tell me? What's the point of that?

Seems to me that round here there's no point in any of it if you've got to do what another man tells you to do. Is there?

You can take my land, take all my money, have my property, go on... I'm a rich man, apparently, take the lot. Take the head off my shoulders, Jamie.

But you're never going to tell me what to do. Alright?

That's what it means to be a rich man in this country.

JAMES. So you'd like to be King.

WILLIAM. I don't want to be fucking King.

JAMES. You're a great-great-great-grandson of the Bruce. Like me. You could be King. Or would your friends not like that?

WILLIAM. What friends?

JAMES. Crawford, up Aberdeen way, remember him? MacDonald Lord of the Isles.

I heard you were quite friendly.

WILLIAM. I don't even like them. I'm not even *talking* about that...

MARY *comes in with a baby.*

JAMES. Mary, get out of here.

MARY. I am not in the way. I am just walking the baby. We will stay over here.

JAMES *moves to her.*

JAMES. No. You need to stay out of here. I told you.

WILLIIAM. Christ, man, your women have you where they want you, don't they?

ANNABELLA (*quiet*). We're not afraid of you, William Douglas.

WILLIAM. *Well, you fucking should be!*

There's no human soul tells me what to do now. And there never will be again.

JAMES *turns back to* WILLIAM.

JAMES. Well, that's funny because I heard you were dancing to Tiger Crawford's tune these days, or maybe John MacDonald's.

WILLIAM. That's still preying on your mind, is it, wee Jamie? That's got you all of a quiver, has it?

JAMES. I heard you'd made a deal with them.

WILLIAM. A deal?

JAMES. A pact then. Do you want to call it a pact? Fine, we'll call it a pact.

WILLIAM. To do what?

JAMES. Kill me. First chance you get.

A beat.

WILLIAM. You think I'd murder you?

JAMES. Oh aye right, push me off the throne then. And I suppose then you'll just let me run around Stirling playing football and singing songs, that's likely, eh?

WILLIAM. I never talked about murder. To anyone.

JAMES. Christ, man! Stop *lying* to me!

WILLIAM. I'm not lying to you.

JAMES. See, I thought that was maybe what you came to apologise about. Your little deal with Crawford and MacDonald.

Crawford to the north-east, MacDonald to the north-west, fearless wee Douglas with his radiant good looks blazing his way up from the borders… I'm a sad little hazelnut in your jaws, amn't I? You thought I didn't know?

WILLIAM. I didn't know you listened to what they're blethering about in the kitchen, Jamie…

JAMES. So it's not true?

WILLIAM. I don't know what's in another man's head. Crawford and MacDonald can think what they like. Doesn't mean I'll dance to their tune any more than yours. And I never talked about murder. All the rest… you brought on yourself when you decided to show the world you were master of me, Jamie. You're not. You never will be.

JAMES. So it's true.

What's in it for you, Will, a *thousand* more wet sheep? I thought you were above all that grubbing about for land and money. Isn't that what you were just telling me? So why do you want my crown, Will?

WILLIAM. I don't. I've my own power, wee King. Better than yours. All you need to know is that you don't tell Douglas what to do. Ever.

JAMES. You've made a deal with my enemies. You've killed my servants. You're plotting to kill me.

WILLIAM. Are you asking me now or telling me?

JAMES. *Why?*

A beat.

WILLIAM. Fight me.

JAMES. What?

WILLIAM. Just… Come on… *fuck* you, James… come on then! If that's what you think… Come on! We'll fix this then. Fight me!

Look, I'll make it easy for you, no blades, eh?

WILLIAM *slams his knife into the table.*

Just have a go at beating my brains out. We'll do it that way.

Come on!!! You and me! You and me!

JAMES. *There's no 'you and me', William!* You killed it! Understand?!

That's gone now.

Done.

A stand-off for a moment.

WILLIAM. Aw Jesus…

The BULL-HEADED MAN *moves through the shadows in the room, streaked with blood.* JAMES *can see him, no one else can.*

Well, you better have me executed then, James, eh? Since I'm that fucking dangerous, since I'm in here, a king-killer, in here, with his King. Better call for some help, James, eh? Because if that's who I am there's no hope, is there? No hope for any of us.

If I'd wanted to murder you I could've strangled you in your sleep, Jamie, couldn't I? You always slept deep when I was keeping watch over you, after all. Keeping the nightmares away from you.

JAMES. You murdered my men! You're planning war against me!

WILLIAM. Aye, right enough, right enough, what was I thinking, I don't even know why I came to talk to you.

You're right. We're done now.

You still have nightmares, James?

I think you still have nightmares.

You're right, I'm your nightmare.

How are you going to send me away? Eh? How are you going to do that, wee Jamie?

WILLIAM *goes to get himself another drink.*

JAMES. You said you were my friend.

WILLIAM. Oh the *bairn*. Listen to him!

I am your friend. It's good we're having this talk. You need to know what you're up against. I won't be ruled. Everyone needs to know. Douglas has made his mind up. He's made his mind up to do whatever Douglas pleases till he dies.

Aye, if you try and tell me what to do I will bring you war, Jamie.

If *anyone* tries to tell me what to do I'll bring war, Jamie. I can raise an army any time I want.

But maybe I won't. I like you. Live quiet and I'll maybe leave you alone, little red face.

(*Moving closer to him.*) As long as we *both* know that any time I liked... *any* time I liked I could just walk in here, stamp on your bairn's head, slice your wife's throat and fuck your sister on the floor in front of you and you couldn't raise a finger to stop me. As long as we both know that.

Actually, that sounds like a plan. Shall I do that? Or maybe I'll slice your bairn, stamp on your sister's head and fuck your wife? She looks like a better shag to me. Is she?

JAMES *is half-seeing the nightmare, half-seeing* WILLIAM, *looking for an escape.*

JAMES (*quiet*). Stop it... stop it... get away from me...

WILLIAM (*laughs*). Look at you... look at the state of you... are you scared of me, wee boy? Are you looking for a box to hide in?

(*Points.*) Shall we use that one? Aye, why don't we do that? You get in the box and put your fingers in your ears and I'll shag your pretty wee wife. Is that a plan? Just get in the box, Jamie, you like that, don't you? You feel safe in your wee box, eh? Get in the box.

He's blocking JAMES*'s path – however* JAMES *moves,* WILLIAM *is blocking him.*

What's the matter, Jamie? Just get in your box.

Where's your box, wee man?

Get in the box!

Get in...

Before he can finish the sentence JAMES *has knocked him down. He grabs the knife and stabs* WILLIAM *twice.*

WILLIAM *screams.*

JAMES *steps back.*

WILLIAM *is struggling on the floor, shocked and bleeding. He's not quite dead. It's all been horribly quick.*

WILLIAM *makes a horrible, blood-choked noise and struggles to get up.* JAMES *instantly rushes at him again kicking, punching stabbing him to death.*

ANNABELLA (*screaming*). Stop it! You've killed him! Stop it!

MARY *is screaming.*

MARY. Murder! Murder! Help us!

JAMES *is collapsed near* WILLIAM*'s body.*

ANNABELLA *is frozen with shock.* MARY *is soothing the baby.*

ANNABELLA. We should have… we should have…

MARY (*rubbing at it*). There's blood… they put blood on the baby…

ANNABELLA. Why didn't we stop him? Why couldn't we…?

MARY. There's *blood*!

ANNABELLA. Mary, what do we do? Mary?

MARY. *Laise mon fils!*

(*Quieter.*) No one touches my son! No one.

MARY *and* ANNABELLA *exit.*

WILLIAM*'s body lies broken on the ground.* JAMES *just sits, staring at it. There is a ragging sound approaching from the shadows, rasping breathing.*

ISABELLA *crawls out of the darkness. She stops as she sees* JAMES, *taking in the scene.*

ISABELLA. Is that your work? Clever wolf-killer. That was my guess.

They were always trouble, the Douglases. I hate them too.

JAMES. He's my friend.

ISABELLA. A king has no friends. You're strong, little King. I came out to watch you die but you've beaten my cursing.

What will I do now?

JAMES. Go away.

Go and do whatever you like.

ISABELLA. Whatever I like?

JAMES. Yes.

ISABELLA. Have you a knife about you then?

Without standing up, JAMES *holds up a knife for her. She comes and takes it. She's about to stab him. She hesitates.*

Aw Christ, you look like Walter. Oh my darling...

JAMES. I've her dark blood. It got out. It got out. I killed him.

ISABELLA. What can you do? You're the King. You've done what you had to. You did well.

Oh I'm tired, son. I'm tired of all of this. I'm weak but my body's too strong, it wouldn't let me die. I can't even remember their faces. But there's Walter looking at me, there you are, darling... look at the state of you... let's clean you up, eh?

She takes her sleeve or cloth and starts cleaning the blood off him.

We hear MEG *singing off, a lullaby.*

That's a brave wolf-killer. King of Scotland? King of Scotland? You're just a messy wee bairn, that's what you are, A happy, messy wee bairn.

JAMES *cradles* WILLIAM *as she wipes the blood.*

End.

JAMES III
THE TRUE MIRROR

Characters

JAMES III, *King of Scots*
MARGARET, *Queen of Scots, originally Danish*
JAMIE, *the eldest Prince, future James IV, thirteen to fifteen years old*
ROSS, *the middle Prince, eleven to thirteen years old*
JOHN, *Head of the Privy Council*
COCHRANE, *a lord of the court, twenties*
RAMSAY, *the King's personal servant, twenties*
DAISY, *a laundress, twenties*
SANDY, *the King's younger brother*
ANNABELLA, *the King's paternal aunt*
PHEMY, *a younger lady of the court, fifteen years old*
TAM, *a member of the household, sixteen years old*

A CHOIR, MEMBERS OF THE COURT *and* PARLIAMENT, SOLDIERS, GUARDS, *etc.*

ACT ONE

The Great Hall, Stirling Castle

A dance. Various members of the Scottish court whirling on the dance floor. JAMES III *and* DAISY *are sitting out of the dance watching* MARGARET *dancing.* MARGARET *is very lavishly dressed with a lot of jewellery.*

DAISY. She's really well dressed, isn't she?

JAMES. Who?

DAISY. The Queen.

JAMES. Yes.

DAISY. Maybe too many jewels… but that's beautiful on her, isn't it? That colour.

JAMES. Wonderful with her eyes.

DAISY. Aye. The King still goes to her room, you know. You can see why.

JAMES. Yes.

DAISY. That's who I'm waiting to see. The King. They say he's beyond gorgeous.

JAMES. Do they?

DAISY. My friends do.

JAMES. You've got friends here?

DAISY. Aye. They got me a place here. It's fine, you know, it's like a proper appointment. Lady of the wardrobe. I mean, I do the clothes. I love clothes.

JAMES. They're what distinguish us from animals.

DAISY *sucks in her breath.*

DAISY. Oh, that's clever. You're clever.

JAMES. Thank you.

DAISY. My name's Daisy by the way.

JAMES. Pleased to meet you, Daisy.

DAISY. So do you know the King?

JAMES. Very well.

DAISY. What's he like. Is he gorgeous?

JAMES. Well, you see… the thing is… I *am* the King!

DAISY laughs.

DAISY. Aye, sure.

JAMES. No, really.

COCHRANE sweeps past, joining the dance.

COCHRANE. Not dancing, Your Majesty? Come on!

JAMES. In a minute.

DAISY is horrified.

DAISY. Oh, sweet Mary Mother of God!

JAMES. I'm so sorry, Daisy… I should have let you know
but…

DAISY. But… no one told me and you weren't announced or…

JAMES. No, no, I didn't do the coming-in-with-the-trumpets
thing or…

You see it just seems a bit… showy, all that. Don't you
think? I just feel… well, all that pomp. It kills conversation,
doesn't it?

She stares at him for a moment.

DAISY. Oh God.

JAMES. What?

DAISY. It's really you and you're here.

JAMES. Yes.

DAISY. Talking to me!

JAMES. Well, I hope I'm not a disappointment.

DAISY. Oh my *God*. *No!*

Sorry. I can't believe I'm actually talking to you.

JAMES. I'll dance with you if you like.

DAISY. Oh my…!

Yes!

JAMES. Why don't you wait over there and I'll find you for the next dance.

DAISY *hurries off as the dance finishes*. MARGARET *joins* JAMES.

And how is the French Ambassador?

MARGARET. I think I've reassured him you're committed to the alliance. Next time don't make fun of his shoes, not to his face anyway. Who was that?

JAMES. I think she works in the laundry.

MARGARET. Were you doing the 'I'm just a shy, bashful common man' routine?

JAMES. That's a very malicious description.

MARGARET. It's what it looked like.

JAMES. It always works.

MARGARET. For a day or two, then the real you sort of shoulders its way out, doesn't it?

JAMES. I had you in love with me for at least a year.

MARGARET. Oh, I'm still in love with you, dearest. It's an affliction, like a club foot. I just drag it around after me and carry on.

JAMES. That's sweet.

JOHN *shouts through the room*.

JOHN. As we are summoned by our King and by God, the Three Estates of Scotland are hereby called to service!

JAMES. And here we go.

He kisses MARGARET *swiftly and follows* JOHN *as all the men present process into and take their place in the Three Estates.*

The Great Hall, Stirling

JAMES *has put on formal robes and sat himself on a throne facing his parliament. A sense of a great crowd of men around him, individual voices will shout out of this.*

JOHN *steps forward and starts to read out the agenda of the parliament.*

JOHN. May it please Your Majesty, your graces, my lords and all here present. His Majesty's Parliament will this day debate the following matters.

One: The request of His Royal Majesty that taxes shall be raised to fund his pilgrimage to the holy site of Amiens.

SANDY, *the King's brother, is the first to mutter from the parliament.*

SANDY. Och, not this again...

JOHN. Two: The pressing matter of renewed aggression by the English Navy on our merchant shipping disrupting our trade and causing great deprivation amongst the people of the country...

SANDY *shouts again.*

SANDY. They can have war if they like! Bloody pirates!

Some assent.

JOHN. Three: The matter of the promise made, at our last parliament, by His Royal Majesty when he vowed to us that he would, in future, be bound by the counsel and advice of the Three Estates of Scotland. He also promised us that he would resume the operation of the crown courts and pay the crown officers that administer them. His failure to do so is creating violence and anarchy throughout the realm! Which forces us, my lords, your graces, forces us...

There is growing uproar under this speech. JOHN *is trying to shout over it...*

One LORD *and* COCHRANE *are shouting in support of the King.* SANDY, *another* LORD *and a* BISHOP *are shouting against them. All these shouts cut over each other and are repeated (and embellished upon).*

COCHRANE. Where's your respect, eh? Where's your loyalty? You're bloody traitors, the lot of you!

SANDY (*trying to get his attention*). James, James, James... Can you see what we're coming to here!? Can you not just put a stop to this?

BISHOP. You made a promise before God, before God, King James!

JOHN (*shouting over the hubbub*)....which forces us to bring the matter *again* before this parliament in the hope that it may finally be resolved... Quiet! QUIET! Let the King speak!

Everyone falls silent, waiting on JAMES. *He has remained unmoved throughout this.*

JAMES. That wasn't on the agenda I approved.

JOHN. What?

JAMES. That last bit, promises and that, I never said that was to go on the agenda.

JOHN. It seems wise to your Privy Council...

JAMES. You're supposed to advise me what to put on the agenda, aren't you? Not stick things on there because you're all in love with the sound of your own voices...

SANDY. You made a promise, James...

JAMES (*cutting over him*). No. Not doing that. Take that one off and we'll talk about taxes.

LORD ONE. You tell them!

JAMES. My pilgrimage, my *holy* pilgrimage, bishop, to the shrine at Amiens, for which I require sixty thousand pounds…

SANDY (*cutting over him*). Aw, come on, James, no one's that holy…

JAMES stares him down for a moment, then he gets up and exits.

JOHN. Your Majesty…

LORD. Where's he going?

Uproar again, lines shouted over each other.

COCHRANE. There's the answer you deserve.

LORD ONE. He's not your dog, you know! Don't you try keeping him on a lead!

LORD TWO. You are breaking your covenant with the Estates!

SANDY. Oh, get back here, you arse!

In the sudden silence one LORD's *shout rings out clear.*

LORD THREE. Sandy, what are you going to do about this? What are you going to do? Because I'm ready!

A few cries of assent. SANDY *is just shaking his head. Not engaging with this.*

JOHN. Quiet!

Parliament is adjourned until this afternoon at the King's pleasure!

A bell sounds. They all exit.

The Garden

ROSS *and* JAMIE *are play-fighting.* PHEMY *seems to be doing her nails.* ANNABELLA *seems to be sunbathing.* MARGARET *sits with a sleeping baby in her lap.* JAMES *collapses next to her, exaggerated exhaustion.*

JAMES. God, I loathe parliament.

MARGARET. I like it.

JAMES. You would.

She looks down at her sleeping son. JAMES *watches her. She looks up and sees him watching. She smiles.*

MARGARET. What?

JAMES. Just…

He doesn't know how to finish the sentence.

MARGARET. What?

JAMES. You surprise me. You do.

MARGARET. Yes?

JAMES. Let's go inside.

MARGARET. James… I've just got him off to sleep.

JAMES. Leave him on the grass, he'll sleep fine on the grass.

(*Indicating* ANNABELLA.) She'll watch him.

(*To* ANNABELLA.) You'll watch him, won't you, Aunt Annabella?

ANNABELLA *looks up and stares at him but says nothing.*

JAMES *pulls at* MARGARET.

Come on.

MARGARET. Family time!

JAMES. What?

MARGARET. You promised me family time.

We can find each other later.

JAMES. I might not want to later. Who knows?

(*As she reacts*.) Oh, don't look like that! I'm being honest. I said I was being honest. You said you *wanted* me to be honest!

MARGARET. And now I don't want you at all.

JAMES. Yes, you do.

MARGARET. Someone should say no to you, James. Someone should start. You'll thank them in the end.

JAMES. Do you think? Doesn't seem likely.

Leave the baby. Come on. It's a baby. It's not going to run off anywhere, is it?

MARGARET. Jamie has a present for you.

Jamie?

JAMIE *stops fighting with* ROSS, *reluctant*.

JAMIE. I didn't bring it.

MARGARET. Yes, you did. It's in your bag, go and find it to show your father.

JAMIE *exits*. ROSS *trails after him*.

JAMES. Did you know that the skin there, between your breasts, has tiny tiny hairs on it, like the bloom on a pink rose…

MARGARET. I can't say I've ever studied it that closely.

JAMES. Well, you should. When were we last together?

MARGARET. Two months ago. Nice to know it was memorable.

JAMES. Two months is an eternity. It's been so long I've forgotten. It'll be like the first time all over again.

MARGARET. You're a bastard, James.

JAMES. But you missed me.

MARGARET. I don't even like you.

JAMES. I don't care.

He kisses her.

JAMIE and ROSS *are back.* JAMIE *is holding a piece of paper.*

MARGARET *gently pushes* JAMES *off her, indicating the boys.*

MARGARET. Jamie's written a poem for you.

JAMES (*surprised*). Has he?

MARGARET. It's beautiful.

(*Coaxing* JAMIE.) Show him, Jamie! Go on.

Shyly JAMIE *offers the poem to his father.* JAMES *looks at it.*

JAMES. You wrote this yourself?

JAMIE. Yes.

MARGARET. It took him weeks.

JAMES (*reading*). This isn't for me. It's about your mother.

(*To* MARGARET.) It's for you.

MARGARET. Yes, but…

You inspired him.

JAMES. How do you make that out?

MARGARET. You…

But you love poetry. That's why he wrote a poem! To please you! You're always talking about the poets you love, the work you're sponsoring…

JAMES (*interrupting*). Aye, but I don't make an arse of myself writing the stuff, do I? And I tell you, if I did, I'd do better than this adolescent pap.

(*Showing her line.*) Look at that! Look! Doesn't even scan.

He throws the poem back at JAMIE.

You leave poetry alone till your balls have dropped or till you can buy some decent lines.

JAMIE *picks up his poem and exits.*

(*To* ROSS.) Well, what are you hanging about for? Have you got a sonnet you want to assault me with as well?

ROSS. No.

JAMES. No. Good boy. I like you. Go and find yourself something sticky and indigestible.

JAMES *gives* ROSS *a coin.* ROSS *takes it and exits.*

MARGARET *is settling the baby by* ANNABELLA *and getting up.*

I'll see you upstairs in a minute.

MARGARET. I'm not coming with you, James, I'm going after Jamie. You've upset him.

JAMES. How can you make me wait after two months apart? Margaret, I need you.

A pause. JAMES *kisses* MARGARET.

Good, I'll see you up there.

He exits. MARGARET *looks at* ANNABELLA *and* PHEMY.

ANNABELLA. The wee man's safe with us.

PHEMY. If it's the way you're feeling, it's the way you're feeling.

MARGARET. I hate the way I'm feeling. I hate it.

ANNABELLA. Oh, I've been there. I have.

MARGARET *exits.*

PHEMY *starts to sing.*

Robin sat on a good green hill
His sheep all he could see
Merry Makyne said him till
'Robin please pity me
For I hae loved you loud and still
These years two or three,
I've loved in secret noo if you will
Touch me or see me dee.'

ANNABELLA *gathers up the sleeping baby and carries him off.* PHEMY *exits with* ANNABELLA.

MARGARET *enters, she is a wee bit dishevelled and is very happy. She's surprised to see* JOHN.

MARGARET. Lord John… Did the King ask to see you?

JOHN. I need a word.

MARGARET. I don't think he's expecting you.

JOHN *says nothing.*

Well, he'll be here shortly. Drink?

JOHN. I'm no thirsty.

MARGARET. That's alright. It's very good wine.

JOHN. I'm fine.

MARGARET *is getting herself a drink.*

MARGARET. It sounds as if you had a rather turbulent session in parliament this morning.

JOHN. That's one way of putting it.

MARGARET. Word of advice?

Don't patronise him. I know he's annoying sometimes but it's because he cares. He gets passionate about his ideas, he's a remarkable man. Just… give him that respect. Before you open your mouth and start scolding him.

JOHN. He was behaving like an arse.

A beat.

MARGARET. Well. That was blunt.

You're quite right then, we shouldn't waste any of the King's wine on you.

SANDY *enters under this,* MARGARET *turns to him, delighted with the distraction.*

Sandy!

He kisses her on the cheek.

SANDY. Look at you, you look fantastic!

MARGARET. I don't, I was running so late today. James is on his way.

She pulls a face, indicating JOHN, *drops her voice.*

(*Quiet.*) Do you know what he wants?

SANDY (*quiet*). I can think of a few things.

MARGARET. He's *rude*!

SANDY. Aye, he's definitely that.

JAMES *enters with* COCHRANE. RAMSAY *trailing behind.* COCHRANE *is carrying a bottle.*

COCHRANE. It's the real thing, I'm telling you, from Graves. Here…

COCHRANE *pours for him.*

MARGARET. James? Your Majesty? Your Privy Counsellor is waiting.

JAMES *tastes the wine.*

JAMES. Man, that's good.

COCHRANE. Listen, I can get you any amount. Whatever you want.

JOHN *moves closer to them.*

JOHN. Your Majesty…

JAMES. Yes, yes, John, in a minute…

COCHRANE (*placating*). Just give us a minute.

(*To* JAMES.) I think that's better than the 1474.

JAMES. I think this might be a great wine. Do you think? You know what I mean by a great wine? One that evokes memory…

COCHRANE. That's it! That's it! You close your eyes and you can see the weather on the day the grape was picked. You can smell the sun on the wet earth and feel the breeze.

JOHN. Your Majesty, we need to discuss the afternoon session of parliament…

JAMES. Mother of Christ, I'll be with you in a moment! Just make a start will you!

JOHN. So how do you want me to do that?

JAMES. Do what?

JOHN. Make a start on parliament business without the King's attention?

MARGARET. Does this look like a Privy Council chamber? What were you thinking of anyway, bringing your business here?

JAMES (*to* COCHRANE). Let me taste the first one again.

MARGARET. Is anyone else allowed an opinion or is this a private wine tasting?

COCHRANE. Sorry, Queen Margaret, here you go.

He pours her some.

JOHN. There are urgent matters that require…

JAMES (*cutting him off*). This is urgent. This is urgent. My wine merchant has to send word to Leith today before the next high tide or this whole vintage might go south to the King of Spain. Do you want the King of Spain to get better wine than me, John?

MARGARET. We all know what Lord John wants, don't we? We all know his opinions. He's so open with them. I think he wants to learn a bit of patience and a few manners.

JOHN exits. JAMES and COCHRANE are delighted, COCHRANE clinking his glass off MARGARET's.

JAMES. This is why I got them to send me a Viking.

MARGARET. This wine tastes muddy.

COCHRANE (*tasting*). She's right, I'm definitely not liking the first one so much.

JAMES. Earthy? I thought earthy.

MARGARET *and* COCHRANE *speak together.*

MARGARET/COCHRANE. Muddy.

JAMES. Let Ramsay have a taste, he's drooling on his boots there.

COCHRANE fills RAMSAY's *glass and* SANDY's.

SANDY. Just tastes like red wine to me. I'll have a drop more though.

COCHRANE. I think we can get them down to four for a barrel for the Graves vintage.

JAMES. Ramsay, run down and tell them I'll buy the shipload… Off you go! Quick!

RAMSAY exits as JAMIE *enters.*

What's he doing here?

JAMIE stops dead, mortified.

MARGARET (*rebuking him*). *James!*

She guides JAMIE *over.*

Come on, sweetheart, it's alright.

He needs to spend time with you, James.

SANDY. And I need to see my nephew! My God, look at the size of you!

He claps JAMIE *in a hug.*

How're you doing, Jamie?

JAMIE. Great, thanks.

JAMIE is beaming, delighted to see his uncle.

SANDY. Have you been practising?

JAMIE. A bit.

SANDY. Wait, I brought you something… hang on…

SANDY produces a football.

We can have a kick about later, see how you're getting on.

COCHRANE. Let's see? Oh, I can still do this, give it here.

COCHRANE, SANDY *and* JAMIE *start playing with the ball, moving it between them using hands and feet.*

RAMSAY *is back on, breathless.*

RAMSAY. I've done it. You'll have the wine by tonight. Do you need anything else, Your Majesty?

JAMES. Probably, just wait, don't pester me.

(*Quiet, to* MARGARET, *indicating* JAMIE.) I don't want him here.

MARGARET. How can he understand the business of being a king if he never sees you with your court? This will all be his work one day.

JAMES. Anticipating my death. Nice.

MARGARET. I just meant…

JAMES. Well, there's not a lot of work going on, is there? Ball games. That's what we've got going on.

RAMSAY. I could find the musicians.

MARGARET. You could find the Privy Counsellors.

JAMES. Oh, funny.

(*Calling.*) Cochrane, Sandy! Stop that, my party, my games. Come over here.

They do so.

Make yourself comfortable, come on. You need to help me out. There's an awful lot of talking going on in that parliament of mine.

SANDY. Well, whose fault's that?

JAMES. Sorry?

SANDY. Can I just ask you something? What the hell is so special about Amiens? That's the third time you've been banging away at us, trying to get money for that expedition. (Won't happen, by the way.) What's at Amiens?

JAMES. You've been.

SANDY. Aye, that's why I'm asking!

COCHRANE (*as if it's obvious*). The cathedral, man!

SANDY. You want to go and look at the cathedral? What for?

COCHRANE. Inspiration.

JAMES. Cochrane and I are planning a cathedral for Scotland.

SANDY. Sixty thousand pounds' worth of inspiration, eh?
    Great.

JAMES. *Anyway*, I thought we could have our own debate.

MARGARET. James, it's too hot for arguments.

JAMES. Not argument. Debate. About love.

SANDY. What?

JAMES. You'll have heard of it, Sandy, I'm sure.

    What is the highest form of love?

SANDY. We know that. We're taught that…

JAMES. Leaving God out of it. Just this once. The highest form
    of earthly love. Is it the love required by duty? A child's love
    for its father, maybe.

    The love you can't help. Slicing through you like lightning.

RAMSAY (*abrupt*). Yes.

    The love that…

    When you can't help it. It takes you over.

    RAMSAY *is instantly deeply embarrassed*.

JAMES. Well, Ramsay has voted.

    Cochrane?

COCHRANE. I'm not playing your games, King James. I know
    your games.

JAMES. Going to have to press you, Cochrane.

COCHRANE. I love my work. What can I tell you?

JAMES. So, the King's service? Is that work?

COCHRANE. Never that.

MARGARET *is getting up*.

JAMES. Margaret? Where are you going?

MARGARET. I'm bored with this game.

JAMES. You haven't played it yet.

If you had to choose, Margaret. The love of a mother for a child or a woman for her lover, which is best?

MARGARET. The one that doesn't ask you to choose.

JAMES. Oh! Good answer! Jamie? Same question.

JAMIE. I... I don't understand the question.

JAMES. And I thought we were buying you a decent education. Brother Sandy!

SANDY. Yes?

JAMES. Do we believe in brotherly love, Sandy? Brother Alexander?

SANDY. Well, I hope we do!

JAMES. So do I. So do I.

Where are we putting it? Above the love for a father?

SANDY. Ooooh... Same?

JAMES. Alright... above the love for a child?

SANDY. Eh... same again, maybe a wee bit lower.

JAMES. A man for his lover?

SANDY. Oh, higher than that. For sure.

JAMES. Higher than you'd put your love for any creature that gripped you under the sheets. You love me more than that?

SANDY. You know I do!

JAMES. So have you betrayed many of your lovers?

SANDY. Eh?

JAMES. Cheated them? Lied to them? Conspired to have them killed, maybe?

SANDY. What…

JAMES (*driving over him*). Because I've got a strong suspicion you might be plotting all that against me, Sandy.

SANDY. *No!*

JAMES. No? You speak against me in parliament. You've got a very cosy little gang there with all your neighbours. What else are you all talking about when you're not shouting me down?

SANDY. What lies have you been listening to?

JAMES. You know what? I don't even *like* you, Sandy, never did.

COCHRANE. James… this isn't the time.

SANDY (*to* COCHRANE). Oh, so this is your doing, is it?

(*To* JAMES.) If you've let the likes of him fill your head with poison there's nothing more to say, is there? You think I'm a traitor.

JAMES. I know you are, Sandy. And what's more, I bet I'll have the proof of it soon.

SANDY. Well… once you get an idea in your head there's no shifting it, is there? I'll need to go…

(*To* MARGARET.) Sorry, Margaret.

MARGARET. No, Sandy, just wait…

James! Come on! What has he done?

JAMES. You think I don't know my own brother?

SANDY. See you next time, Jamie.

SANDY *exits*. JAMES *shouts after him*.

JAMES. Traitor!

JAMIE. It's not true!

MARGARET. Jamie!

JAMIE. He's not a traitor!

> JAMES *goes to hit him.* MARGARET *restrains* JAMES, *furious.*

MARGARET. Stop it! Don't you dare hit him!

> JAMES *turns on her, terrifyingly angry.*

JAMES. *Get your hands off me!!*

> *Everyone is shocked,* JAMES *is lost in himself, trying to hold it together, breathless with rage.*

COCHRANE (*to* MARGARET, *gentle*). Leave him. It's alright. You just need to know how to handle him.

> JAMES *is still really agitated, holding it in.* COCHRANE *goes to him, speaking quietly.*

That's enough, you've done enough, just… let it cool down now.

JAMES. Fuck off, Cochrane.

COCHRANE. So I will if you don't look me in the eye and remember yourself. Come on. You don't want to let this out. You want to keep yourself together.

JAMES. I'm fine.

COCHRANE. You're great. You said your piece. You've told him you know what he's up to.

JAMIE. Don't kill him! You can't kill him!

JAMES. Actually, you know I can. Being the King.

MARGARET. Stop it, James!

> MARGARET *has pulled* JAMIE *to her.*

JAMES. Choices, Margaret. It's all about choices.

> (*To* COCHRANE.) Let's go and see if there's any of the good stuff left up in our room, shall we?

Ramsay, find the musicians.

JAMES *and* COCHRANE *exit*.

A sound starts in the Three Estates, the stamping of many feet. It grows louder and louder.

MARGARET. What's that?

RAMSAY. The parliament. They want him to come to them. They're waiting for him.

MARGARET. Tell them the King is busy.

Tell them to be quiet!

Tell them to go home!

RAMSAY *exits*. MARGARET *is comforting* JAMIE. ROSS *enters and stands watching*.

(*To* JAMIE.) He isn't angry with you, he's angry with his parliament, you understand that, don't you?

ROSS. Mum?

MARGARET (*ignoring* ROSS). Jamie?

ROSS. Mum? Jamie's taken my horse, it's not fair.

MARGARET. Not now, Ross. Jamie, look at me...

JAMIE *pulls away and exits*.

ROSS. Mum?

MARGARET. Oh, for God's sake, Ross! Will you never learn to see when you're not wanted!

ROSS *runs off in the opposite direction to* JAMIE.

The Queen's Room, Stirling Castle / The Tower Room, Night

MARGARET *is reading documents, sitting at a table strewn with paperwork.*

At the same time we see JAMIE *sitting looking out at the night sky in a bare room.*

ANNABELLA *enters, carrying a drink.*

She's surprised to see him.

ANNABELLA. What are you doing here? This is my place.

JAMIE *doesn't answer her.*

JAMIE. I just…

ANNABELLA. Have you been crying?

JAMIE. No.

ANNABELLA. No. You don't want to be doing that.

It does you no good.

JAMIE *is starting to leave.*

JAMIE. I'm sorry. I didn't know it was your place.

ANNABELLA. Oh, stay, stay if you like. It's no my place really, is it? Whole castle will be yours one day.

JAMIE. I just wanted somewhere quiet.

ANNABELLA. Me too. I should've known better. There's no place in Scotland you can get away from conversation.

JAMIE. You could go up on top of the mountains.

ANNABELLA. Aye, but with my luck I'd still hear someone talking at me.

JAMIE. Who?

She doesn't answer, just taking a drink.

God?

ANNABELLA. Maybe.

JAMIE. Ghosts?

ANNABELLA. More than likely.

Are you hearing anything?

JAMIE. No. Just you.

ANNABELLA. Good. Let's just sit quiet then.

They watch the sky.

In MARGARET's *space* JAMES *enters, in a hurry, restless.*

JAMES. I want a choir.

MARGARET (*absorbed in figures*). Yes?

JAMES. I want a choir to follow me everywhere.

MARGARET. Doing what?

JAMES. Well, the way I see it, but tell me what you think, there are elements of… discomfort, in almost every waking moment.

Reminders of human frailty.

Moments of… bestial vulgarity.

I'd like to… cushion… every moment with something beautiful. With music.

A pause. MARGARET *writes.*

MARGARET. So are you going to take them with you when you have a shit?

JAMES. What?

MARGARET. Because that is a vulgar moment of human frailty, one of the most vulgar.

JAMES. I see… fine, yes, alright…

MARGARET (*cutting him off*). And I don't think they'll fit in there with you. You could get one choirboy in with you maybe, but you know how people would talk…

MARGARET *writes.*

JAMES. I thought we could have them behind a screen in our bedroom, dearest. To distract me during the *most* vulgar, the *most* unpleasant of my royal duties.

MARGARET *says nothing.* JAMES *registers her expression.*

Oh, that wasn't funny, was it? What is it?

Margaret?

Margaret, come on, look at me.

She does so.

What?

MARGARET. What do you think!?

JAMES *realises.*

JAMES. Oh! I was angry.

MARGARET. Yes!

JAMES. Did I frighten you?

MARGARET. Do I look frightened?

JAMES. What then?

MARGARET. You *disappointed* me, James.

JAMES. Oh, no no no no no. Never that.

JAMES *turns away, struggling with his feelings.*

JAMIE. Why does he hate me?

ANNABELLA. It makes him angry to think about you sometimes.

JAMIE. Why?

ANNABELLA. Because you're the end of him. If you live.

JAMIE. But I'd never harm him!

ANNABELLA. No. But you're what's coming next.

JAMES. I'll try and be more patient with the brat. I'll try. Alright?

MARGARET. Thank you.

ANNABELLA. His mother loved him so dearly, you know, like her most precious treasure. It was cruelty. You shouldn't love a child like that unless you can promise to live for ever.

I let all my children run away from me like water. But, here I am. Still alive. What a cruel joke life played on me there.

Just stay away from him, Jamie. As far away as you can.

JAMIE. But Mum's always wanting to be with him.

ANNABELLA. I'll talk to her, alright?

MARGARET. Do you ever think about your father?

JAMES. Sometimes.

He was… energetic. Always kicking something, throwing something… rushing around…

He loved football. Football and fighting.

I think I was too slow for him… too…

Well, you can only run so fast when your legs are just the length of a twig.

He was… noisy… huge voice… huge laugh. That mark on his face.

(*Shows her.*) Didn't scare me. Kids get used to anything, don't they?

My mother… my mother was my whole world… When I think of her face now… Christ, she was so young…

She had me crowned on the battlefield. I didn't really understand that my father was dead. Then I thought… will I have to see him dead?

Mum was shaking when she led me out. I could feel her hand vibrating.

They were all kneeling in this mud and there were puddles… puddles of blood on the muddy ground. They did the coronation right where the fighting had been fiercest so…

I was looking at these pools of blood… I'd heard people saying that a gun had exploded and ripped him apart…

I thought, is that my father's blood?

It might have been. It might have been, of course.

Then they put this heavy metal crown on me and I was King.

MARGARET (*quiet*). Poor little boy.

He looks at her, reads the compassion on her face.

JAMES. Ah, you do still love me, don't you?

MARGARET. You won't settle for less, will you? From anyone.

JAMES. No.

They kiss. After a moment MARGARET goes back to her work.

ANNABELLA. What do you see? What can you see out there?

She's indicating the window.

JAMIE. Just the dark.

ANNABELLA. Me too. Why do we need to see more of that? Here, try this.

She offers him her drink.

JAMIE (*drinks*). What is it?

ANNABELLA. It's *uisghe beatha*, a wee bit of sweet wine and a rind of orange. Sometimes I drop a bramble in it. Come on, I'll show you how to make it.

She leads him off.

JAMES. Are you sure you're not a bit jealous?

MARGARET. Of whom?

JAMES. The Countess of Atholl, perhaps?

The Duke of Buccleuch?

MARGARET. The Duke of Buccleuch? *Really?*

JAMES. You're surprised?

MARGARET. I'd never have guessed.

JAMES. *He* was surprised too. Astonished. Quite cross with himself.

But there you have it.

A very large, angry moth… and a very, very bright flame. Poor Buccleuch.

MARGARET. Yes indeed.

Poor Buccleuch.

JAMES. It's Cochrane, isn't it?

MARGARET *gives him her full attention again*.

MARGARET. No.

JAMES. Isn't it?

MARGARET (*wanting to mean it*). Cochrane is a brilliant man. You understand the same things. You describe the buildings you want and he can make that stone dream real. There's no one else you can talk to like that. He's a good man.

JAMES. Yes. I think so.

And he gets it, doesn't he? The value of the things that matter… those skinflints in the Estates… sitting on my taxes…

We may have to sell something.

MARGARET. Why?

JAMES. To pay for my choir.

MARGARET. No.

JAMES. What do you mean, no?

MARGARET. We can't afford it.

JAMES. I think you've forgotten who you're speaking to.

MARGARET. I asked to see the treasury papers.

JAMES. Why?

MARGARET. Because someone has to start helping you!

(*The papers*.) Have you looked at these?

JAMES. God, no.

MARGARET. There *is* no money, James.

JAMES. A *choir*, Margaret, a few singers.

MARGARET. How many?

JAMES. A small choir.

MARGARET. How many?

JAMES. Only forty or so…

MARGARET. No.

JAMES. Are you telling me, are you presuming to tell me, I can't afford music? *Scotland* can't afford music?

MARGARET. James, you can't afford to annoy people like this any more.

JAMES. People?

MARGARET. Everyone! The entire nation!

JAMES. They're my subjects.

It doesn't matter how much I annoy them, does it? What are they going to do? Stop me being King?

MARGARET. I imagine it's being discussed!

They look at each other for a moment.

I just…

I worry for you.

That's all.

I worry.

JAMES. Oh, don't do that, never do that.

MARGARET. But…

JAMES (*cutting her off*). Is that new?

MARGARET. What?

JAMES. That…

> (*Waves his hand.*) What do you want to call it? Scarf? That on your shoulders.

MARGARET (*looking*). Oh. Yes, yes, it is.

JAMES. Can I see?

> *She pulls the cloth free and hands it to him.* JAMES *is staggered at the beauty of the colour. It's red.*

> Oh!

MARGARET. I know.

JAMES. *Oh!*

MARGARET (*laughing*). I know!

JAMES. HOW!?

MARGARET. It's just madderwort.

JAMES. It's not!

MARGARET. It is. I found a little man who does something different with the root.

JAMES. What?

MARGARET. He won't tell me, he won't tell anyone. It's his living after all.

JAMES. Bring him here and torture him till he tells you.

MARGARET. No!

JAMES. Look at that. *Look* at that, that's red.

MARGARET. That's red.

JAMES. That's blood and wine and dying suns.

> MARGARET *has pulled more cloth out.*

MARGARET. Look at his yellow.

JAMES. Oh!

MARGARET. I *know*!

JAMES. That is yellow.

MARGARET. Summer broom in flower. Gorse buds.

JAMES. I want it. I want both of them.

MARGARET. I've bought all his stock. There'll be no more till next year.

(*Showing him.*) He has this blue.

JAMES (*grudging*). That's a blue.

MARGARET. Yes.

JAMES. It's not a bad blue. I've seen much worse.

MARGARET. It's a good blue.

JAMES. But it's just a blue. I need the red.

MARGARET. Well, it's mine.

JAMES. You can give me the yellow.

MARGARET. I'm not giving you any of it, James.

JAMES. Half the yellow then… and one length of the red.

MARGARET. You can't have it.

JAMES. No, you have to give it to me.

MARGARET. Alright, alright… but no choir.

JAMES *hesitates for a long moment.*

JAMES. Alright. No choir.

He kisses her again. It gets more passionate. MARGARET *breaks away.*

Tomorrow night, then.

She hesitates, then she smiles.

MARGARET. Tomorrow night.

The Queen's Room, the Next Night

PHEMY *and* ANNABELLA *are helping* MARGARET *get the room ready for a romantic night.*

MARGARET. I want you to stay a while tonight.

PHEMY. Eh?

MARGARET. To eat with us. You're my dearest friends. The King always shares my company with his friends, I want to share mine.

PHEMY *and* ANNABELLA *look at each other.*

PHEMY. Well…

MARGARET. What?

PHEMY. If it's what you want…

ANNABELLA. No.

MARGARET. Annabella…

ANNABELLA. No, I'm not doing that.

MARGARET. But why not?

PHEMY. You know I doubt he'd even want us here.

MARGARET. Yes, he would.

You're his aunt, Annabella! You barely see him.

ANNABELLA. And what does that tell you?

MARGARET. Oh, not you as well!

She busies herself, angry with them.

You know none of you ever consider how difficult it is for him. How lonely he must be.

PHEMY. Oh, Margaret, don't!

MARGARET. Don't what?

PHEMY. Just… you always see things his way… that's not the way we see it.

A beat.

MARGARET. Really? So how do you see it?

PHEMY. Oh, don't make me tell you. We'll fall out.

MARGARET. I want you to tell me.

PHEMY. No, I love you, we're not going to do this.

MARGARET. Annabella. Tell me. How do you see it?

ANNABELLA. You need to break with him. He's dangerous.

MARGARET. *Dangerous?*

ANNABELLA. I've been meaning to say this to you for a while now. It's time. You need to cut him off.

MARGARET. I won't cut him off! I love him!

PHEMY. I loved him too! I did. You're not crazy. He pulls it out of you.

MARGARET. I see him clear. I do.

ANNABELLA. Lassie, he's turned you inside out and made a glove out of you. For years.

A beat.

MARGARET. Well... I suppose you won't be sharing supper with us, Princess Annabella. Don't let me hold you back.

ANNABELLA (*to* PHEMY). I'll see you later.

ANNABELLA *exits.*

PHEMY. My cousin died.

MARGARET. I'm sorry.

PHEMY. The harvest failed and now meal's four shillings a bag and who's got that? Folk are starving. I can't eat dinner with him, Margaret. I can't.

MARGARET. The King can't stop the crops failing.

PHEMY. But he could do more, could he not? He could do something.

MARGARET. This is what I mean. No. How can he? He's a king but he's just a man. Everyone wants him to make the world perfect just because he looks as if he ought to be able to do it.

Think how lonely that is for him, Phemy.

I'm the mother of his children.

I connect him to the world.

I'd never turn away from him.

I'm the only one who can reach him.

A beat.

PHEMY. Aye... mebbe.

I'll tell them to send the dinner up when he comes.

JAMES enters. JAMES and MARGARET start to make love.

It's the next morning. RAMSAY and SERVANTS enter dragging baggage.

MARGARET gets out of bed and looks out the window.

JAMES. What are you looking at?

MARGARET. Ramsay, with your bags.

JAMES. Yes. I thought I was staying longer but... I need a change of air, a different view.

MARGARET. Well... maybe we could travel with you.

JAMES. Maybe.

No.

Wait until I call the next parliament. I'll have to come back then.

You can come to that with me. You might like it.

He kisses her and exits.

MARGARET sits for a while, looking out the window as PHEMY sings again.

Robene, you must have heard them say
In songs and stories old,
The man that would not when he may
Shall have not when he would.
God help the soul that falls for you,
I'd warn her if I could
The first poor lass that goes with you
In field or bank or wood.

MARGARET *exits during the song.*

PHEMY *finishes her song and exits.*

The Great Hall, Stirling, Three Months Later

JAMES *processes in with* MARGARET *as the Estates assemble.*

JOHN. As we are summoned by our King and by our God, the Three Estates of Scotland are hereby called to service.

A small CHOIR *hurries in and groups itself behind* JAMES. JOHN *walks forward. He raises a ceremonial staff.*

May it please Your Majesty, your graces, my...

He is cut off by the CHOIR *bursting into song. The song builds to a dramatic pause/climax.* JOHN *raises his ceremonial staff to speak again,* JAMES *shakes his head, stopping him.*

The CHOIR *sing something like –*

The King, The King, His Majesty, His Majesty
Praise him, Praise him
Fal-la-la la la-la
Fal-la-la la la-la
Fal-la-la la la-la
Fal-la-la la la-la.

The CHOIR *finishes on a crescendo, enthusiastically conducted by* JAMES.

SANDY. Oh, fuck this!

SANDY *exits, followed by the whole parliament. Over this,* JOHN *finally speaks.*

JOHN. Well, as parliament is dissolved, Your Majesty. The council needs to meet today. I will find you later.

JOHN *exits.* MARGARET *goes to* JAMES.

MARGARET. A cathedral is larger than any of us. A cathedral is the closest thing a mortal creature gets to seeing immortality. A cathedral is a great beast we build of stone that carries us inside it like a whale, swimming through the centuries towards the throne of heaven.

JAMES. That's beautiful.

MARGARET. That's how you explained it to me. So why aren't you explaining it like that to them?

You idiot, James! You *idiot*!

These are the men you *need* if you ever want to raise an army! They're your only defence against invasion!

JAMES. Oh, Christ in a bread basket, here we go again. *Let* England invade! I'll be *delighted* to surrender. Save a lot of time and money and all that wasted effort bouncing around waving our fists and kidding on we're not just a wee boy without a catapult facing up to a bear.

Let England *eat* us and get it over with! What's the point! What's the point? Today, tomorrow, a hundred years from now? They'll do it one day, won't they? They're bigger than us! They've got more money! Face the reality, dearest! They're having us! Let's get it over with and get on with something that makes sense of our imminent plummet into an open grave! Like a wee madrigal, maybe. Can you sing one, darling? Can you do anything that's fundamentally *useful*? No. All you can do is tell me what I can't have.

By the bleeding arse of the saviour, I *wish* I'd done the deal with a nice English princess. Then maybe all this carry-on would be by and I'd have some *peace* to *live* to actually *live* a life that makes sense of God's creation.

But what do I get? A fucking Norse coin counter.

Oh… oh… and… sorry, I was forgetting your wedding gift to me, wasn't I?… *and* Orkney and fucking Shetland!

MARGARET. You won't change, will you? Not in the face of threats, not in the face of reason… You just won't change.

JAMES *thinks about it.*

JAMES (*pleased*). That's true. Thank you.

MARGARET. That's very, very dangerous, James.

He exits. MARGARET *moves into –*

The Queen's Room, Stirling

MARGARET *enters.* ANNABELLA *and* PHEMY *are playing cards. She is in a state. They can see she is.*

ANNABELLA. Good day in parliament?

MARGARET. Don't start! Just…

I want the room.

ANNABELLA. We're in the middle of a hand.

MARGARET. This is my room. I want the space.

ANNABELLA. We'll be finished in a moment.

PHEMY. Princess Annabella…

ANNABELLA. I'm not sitting squashed in that wee room through there twiddling my thumbs. And it's raining outside.

MARGARET. Will you give me some peace!

JOHN *enters with a* GUARD.

JOHN. Is he here?

MARGARET (*last straw*). Oh *God*.

ANNABELLA. And what do you think you're doing?

JOHN. I need to speak to the King.

ANNABELLA. You weren't invited here! Get out!

MARGARET. It's alright, Annabella.

JOHN. I've the authority of parliament…

MARGARET. Really? I don't believe you've ever mentioned that before.

JOHN. I have the authority of parliament and I'm looking for the King.

He nods at the GUARD *who tries to move through to look in the adjoining room.* PHEMY *blocks him.*

MARGARET. And you think you'll find him in our bedroom?

JOHN. Why? Whose bedroom should I be looking in? Archie.

The GUARD *tries to move forward again.*

ANNABELLA. Get him, Phemy!

PHEMY *pounces, she's got the man by the balls and the earlobe. She shakes him, he screams.*

GUARD. Get her off me!

JOHN. That's a crown officer.

GUARD. Get her off me!

MARGARET. Phemy, drop him!

JOHN. She just assaulted a crown officer.

ANNABELLA. He just trespassed on his Queen's privacy!

JOHN. We have a duty to find the King.

MARGARET. How does that work if the King doesn't want to be found?

JOHN. The King swore an oath to be loyal to his parliament…

MARGARET. If you say the word parliament one more time I will let Phemy do whatever she likes. I'll help.

The GUARD *that* PHEMY *has captive screams again.*

Phemy, seriously, drop him.

A groan from the imprisoned GUARD.

Phemy!!

PHEMY *drops the* GUARD.

PHEMY. Thing is, Margaret, he'll go for me now, soon as his eyes stop watering. You canny let go of their balls once you've got them. That could get you killed.

The GUARD *is struggling to straighten up and breathe.*

GUARD. Oh, you're getting killed, sweetheart. You're right there.

MARGARET *and* JOHN *are squared up to each other.*

MARGARET. If you want a private conversation with me, Lord John, I will be happy to talk to you.

JOHN. Wait outside, Archie.

GUARD. Aye but…

JOHN (*cutting him off*). Wait outside.

The GUARD *exits.*

MARGARET. Princess Annabella, we need the room.

ANNABELLA. Of course you do, Queen Margaret. Of course you do. I'm truly sorry to be in your way.

ANNABELLA *and* PHEMY *move to exit.*

But we'll just be next door. I'm sorry, Margaret.

MARGARET. It's alright.

They exit.

JOHN. If you know where he is, if there's even a chance of getting him back to talk to his parliament today, he has to do

it. They're leaving. It'll be three months before we can
assemble again.

MARGARET. I don't know where he is.

JOHN. Christ, what a mess.

MARGARET. We have audited the treasury papers and the King
has signed the urgent matters of foreign correspondence.

She looks out papers and hands them to him.

You had no business disturbing us like this. You've no right.

No one cares about the business of parliament. As long as the
rich men keep their land and their money. That's all any of
you really worry about, isn't it?

You don't even show up unless you think he's going to ask
for taxes.

JOHN. I've attended every parliament since I became entitled.

MARGARET. Then you must be seriously starved of other
distractions.

JOHN. Make or change the law and you change the lives of
every human soul in the country. That's what I see happening.

MARGARET. And who cares? Most people don't care about
the law. They want someone else to make it for them and
then they never think about it unless they need something to
complain about apart from the weather.

JOHN. Oh, is that what you think of us?

(*Pointing at the page.*) That's wrong.

MARGARET. No.

JOHN. Yes.

MARGARET. No.

You need to add the figures in from this column here, see?

(*Points.*) And that's the total there.

JOHN. The King never even looked at these, did he? This is
your work. It has to be.

MARGARET. Yes. I'm helping the King.

JOHN. You're happy with that, are you? Doing his work while he… What is he up to anyway?

MARGARET. Oh, I'm sure whatever you're imagining will be far more entertaining than the truth.

JOHN *reads another page.*

JOHN. Well, never mind. As long as he's got someone sorting out his laundry, eh?

MARGARET. What?

JOHN. Oh, I think you know what I'm talking about.

(*Looking round him.*) Have you got anything to drink in here?

ANNABELLA *enters moving fast. She glares at him. She gathers up a bottle and gives him another glare as she exits.*

Water's fine.

As MARGARET *still doesn't respond.*

Or not. I'm fine.

MARGARET. Have you any other business here?

JOHN. Why do you defend him? Why do you help him?

MARGARET. Why don't you? You're a God-fearing man, aren't you? You've kneeled in the church and sworn to protect your King, haven't you? What's your word worth? What's your promise worth, my lord?

JOHN. You tell me. Looks like you're the one juggling all the figures.

MARGARET. I just help where I'm needed.

And there's not much money here to count. So it's easy.

JOHN. Maybe you could sell a necklace or two. Help us out.

MARGARET *touches her throat defensively.*

Not that one. That one suits you too well.

A beat.

What does he say about me?

MARGARET. Who?

JOHN. The King.

MARGARET. He says you've got no sense of humour.

JOHN. He's wrong about that.

MARGARET. So tell me a joke.

JOHN. James Stewart is King of Scotland.

MARGARET. That's not funny.

JOHN. No, it's not.

What else does he say?

MARGARET. Why would I tell you what my husband says?

JOHN. Is he your husband? We're none of us very sure about that.

A beat.

This whole nation is like a house a few of us are trying to hold together with our bare hands. The weather's getting in… the door can't hold its lock… and there's a stormy night coming.

MARGARET. Yes.

JOHN. If he's going to have favourites he needs to pick them better and give them less. It's like he's making a game of us all. Dancing about with some laundry maid in public when he won't even come out to talk to his councillors. Do you know what I mean?

MARGARET. Yes.

JOHN. Can't you do anything about it?

MARGARET. I'm trying.

JOHN. Well… I suppose that's something.

He gets ready to leave.

You look better here, in your own room.

MARGARET. Better than what?

JOHN. You look good.

You look like a queen.

You look like a bonny flower, a Marguerite, turning up to find the sun.

A beat.

MARGARET. Why would you say that?

JOHN. Because it's true.

You should always tell folk what your eyes see, it's important.

See, I can't do jokes but I can do compliments.

JOHN *exits. After a moment*, MARGARET *follows*.

The Garden, Early Morning

A riot of roses. JAMES *stands alone in the garden, looking at the roses in the early light.*

His CHOIR *begin to sing a capella, a haunting and beautiful song.*

JAMES *looks at the singers, looks at the roses and the dawn.* JAMES *is moving and we realise he is directing the singers, conducting them, the song swells,* JAMES *moves amongst them, lost in the music as it builds and builds…*

SANDY *enters.*

The music builds, it seems to stop.

SANDY. What do you think…?

Another burst from the CHOIR. *It stops.*

Have you…?

JAMES *holds up a hand, stopping him. Another drawn-out note from the* CHOIR.

They all wait.

Are you done?

Another note. The song finishes.

JAMES *sighs deeply in satisfaction.*

Silence.

JAMES (*patient*). Look at the roses, look at the sky, let the
memory of the music settle...

SANDY *waits.*

SANDY. Are you done now?

JAMES. Do you see those roses?

SANDY. Aye.

JAMES. Sandy, these were planted by our grandfather. James
the First of Scotland planted them to delight his Queen. But
he'll never have seen this. He planned it. He'll have looked
at the little twigs he nurtured, he'll have looked at the few
brave buds and imagined what we're seeing here, but he
knew he'd die before those little rose trees ever grew into
this garden. He planned it for us. For you and me and all the
Scots coming after. Do you know what that is, Sandy?

SANDY. No.

JAMES. That's the generosity of a king.

Do you see?

SANDY. Have you been here all night?

JAMES. Yes. But do you understand?

SANDY. No one could find you, man, it was bloody chaos.

JAMES. Sandy, do you understand what I'm saying?

SANDY. Aye! Yes, it's a bonny garden.

A beat.

JAMES. There is no point in explaining.

None.

And I knew that. I *knew* that.

Why did I even let that idea in my *head*?

SANDY. Is this why you sent for me?

JAMES. What?

   Aye, you can go, forget about it.

SANDY. I thought you were ready to make a deal.

JAMES. A deal?

SANDY. Aye.

JAMES. A deal? With you?

SANDY. Aye.

JAMES. Why would I do that?

SANDY. Well... you'll have to get yourself some support
   somewhere, sooner or later.

JAMES. Right.

SANDY. You want the truth, James? I've been holding them
   back.

JAMES. Oh that's good of you.

SANDY. There's some of them ready to kill you today.

JAMES. Really? Do I have time to get some breakfast first?

SANDY. But if they see I'm standing by you, if they see we're
   in this together...

JAMES. Together?

SANDY. Sharing the throne.

JAMES. Oh, wouldn't that be cosy? The two brothers cuddled
   up together on one seat?

   No.

   Go away, Sandy, I'm done talking to you.

   JAMES *tries to move off,* SANDY *stops him.*

SANDY. I can't hold them back much longer.

JAMES. Why are you still talking to me?

SANDY. What do I get out of loyalty to you, James? Why
   should I hold them back ?

JAMES. Because the alternative is treason.

SANDY. So arrest me, brother. Call all your loyal friends to defend you.

JAMES turns on him like lightning. Swiftly and efficiently he lays SANDY out.

He holds SANDY pinned.

JAMES. Wereny expecting that were you, little monster?

No, no bugger ever does. Funny that.

(*Turns to the* CHOIR.) Come on! Come on! A song of triumph and manly vigour. Quick now!

The CHOIR exchange panicked looks then launch into something suitable.

Treason! Treason! There's a king killer here! Treason!

JOHN, *the* GUARD, MARGARET, JAMIE, COCHRANE, ANNABELLA, PHEMY, ROSS *and* LORDS *from the Three Estates enter from different directions. They stop, taking in the scene,* JAMES *still holding* SANDY. *No one knows how to react. The* CHOIR *finish on a crescendo.*

(*To the* CHOIR.) Lovely. Thank you.

(*To* JOHN, MARGARET *and the rest.*) So, my brother, Alexander, Duke of Albany, has admitted, in front of these witnesses…

(*Indicates the* CHOIR.)…that he's been plotting against me.

CHOIR *murmurs.*

Well, Lord John, what does my Privy Council want? Are you going to arrest him or shall we just skip straight on to regicide and civil war?

JOHN *hesitates for a moment, then he nods at the* GUARD. *The* GUARD *takes* SANDY *from* JAMES *and holds him.*

JAMES *speaks close to* SANDY's *face.*

I will have your lands. I will have your titles and you will run, *run*, little brother, out of Scotland and never come back. Because if you do come back I am going to tear your own entrails out your soft traitor's stomach and watch you eat them!

JAMIE. No! No, just let him explain, let him...

SANDY. Don't do this

JAMES. And there it is. There it is. More treason.

JAMIE. No, it's not treason...

MARGARET. Jamie, be quiet!

JAMES (*to* JOHN). Take my brother away.

The GUARD *exits with* SANDY.

MARGARET. James... he loves his uncle. We all did, you can't expect...

JAMES (*cutting her off, to* JAMIE). Well, you're never getting this crown, laddie, you can forget about that idea. Do you all hear me? I put this son aside.

MARGARET. Jamie is your *heir.* You can't change the law of God!

JAMES. How do I know he's mine?

I think you always fancied brother Sandy. In fact I'm sure of it.

COCHRANE. James, come on now...

JAMES. Shut the fuck up, Cochrane.

JAMES *turns back on* MARGARET.

(*Indicating* JAMIE.) I don't like him any more. At all. I like the other one.

MARGARET. What 'other one'?

JAMES (*points at* ROSS). Him. He should be King.

MARGARET. He can't be!

JAMIE (*upset, sincere*). I'm sorry, I'm sorry, Dad...

You're my father, I'll obey you. I'll try and be the son you want.

JAMES *studies him, considering a moment.*

JAMES. No… no… no… you see I'm not buying it. I'm not. He's sleekit, this one. Tricksy. Like brother Sandy. I like the other one.

(*Points at* ROSS.) And he's far nicer to look at. I like his face.

MARGARET. But you can't just…

JAMES (*cuts her off*). I'm supposed to be able to make the rules. Amn't I? Or what's the point? What's the point, Margaret?

MARGARET. You simply can't do this. You can't disinherit your own heir.

JAMES (*interrupts*). If you can think a thing you can do it. Try it. Go on, try it.

You're scared to try it.

That's why I'm hated.

Because I can imagine a larger world.

It's why all the saints were persecuted when you think about it.

MARGARET. If you do this. If you really try and do this, I will cut you off, Jamie and Ross and baby John will live with me and you can…

JAMES. Not Ross. Ross wants to come with me. Don't you, Ross?

ROSS (*quiet*). Yes.

MARGARET. Ross… I know you love your father but you'll still see him and…

ROSS. You love Jamie over me.

MARGARET. No. No, I don't love any of you over the others. Whatever your father has told you..

JAMES (*cuts her off*). I didn't have to tell him anything. Everyone can see it.

MARGARET. Jamie is the eldest. He has more responsibilities. He might sometimes get more of my attention but…

ROSS. You gave him my horse.

MARGARET. That was… The horse was too big for you, Ross.

ROSS. It was my horse.

JAMES. And I'll give you a new horse. A bigger horse.

MARGARET. James. Stop this.

ROSS. I want to live with Dad.

MARGARET. Then…

> (*Falters*.) Then we'll talk about that. We can…

> (*Angry to* JAMES.) I will never forgive you for this, James, and I am moving into my own household!

JAMES. Fine. On you go. Hope you're paying for that yourself. Know why I'm skint, everyone? Know why the Scottish crown is skint? Her dad never coughed up what he owed for her dowry.

> You think we're poor.? This one was brought up in a fishbox. King of Norway and Denmark? He's living in a sand castle on an icy beach.

MARGARET. But we were always rich in courtesy, even if I couldn't pass that gift on, dearest. I've tried.

JAMES. You've been very trying, madam. No doubt about it.

MARGARET. And my dowry *was* paid in full.

JAMES. Oh, aye, aye… what did we get? What did we get for you? Orkney and Shetland. Fantastic! Just what I always wanted!

MARGARET. You always bring that up! You always bring that up! Shetland is a *jewel* of an island and if you can't shift your lazy arse up north to see that for yourself, don't…

JAMES (*interrupts*). Oh, aye, right right, next time I want to watch bloody Danish cast-offs shagging their livestock and knitting socks out of herring I'll be *straight* up there!

> MARGARET *goes to* ROSS. *She kisses him.*

MARGARET. It will be alright in the end, sweetheart, I promise, I promise, don't worry.

She turns on JAMES, cold now.

Jamie, baby John and I will live in Stirling. You can have Edinburgh.

JAMES. Stirling's got better ceilings.

MARGARET. Edinburgh is your bloody capital!

JAMES thinks.

JAMES. Yes, but the rooms are cosier here… but then the company is better in Edinburgh… alright you can have Stirling but *I* get the tapestries.

MARGARET. I hope they fall on you and suffocate you!

JAMES. Nothing could be as suffocating as your presence, my angel.

MARGARET. You can visit. Twice a year. When we do the accounts.

JAMES. If I choose to visit.

MARGARET. Naturally.

JAMES. Fine then.

MARGARET. Good.

MARGARET exits in one direction, JAMES in the other. Everyone else just stands stunned, looking at each other. ROSS moves first, hurrying after his father, then JAMIE follows MARGARET.

One by one the characters exit after either MARGARET or JAMES till only ANNABELLA and PHEMY are left.

ANNABELLA. Smell those roses.

It's a bonny day, a bonny, bonny day, let's make the most of this sun, Phemy, I doubt it'll soon be gone for good.

PHEMY exits after MARGARET as ANNABELLA settles herself and turns her face up to the sun.

End of Act One.

ACT TWO

The Queen's Room, Stirling

There is a big bathtub sitting on its own in the middle of the floor.

PHEMY *enters with a bucket of hot water, she is staggering, exhausted.*

ANNABELLA *enters with a tent of cloth, she begins to fix it up on hooks round the bath.* ANNABELLA *is still in her nightdress. She looks at* PHEMY.

ANNABELLA. You never carried that up here yourself!

> PHEMY *nods, too exhausted to speak.*

> Well, what's that boy doing!? Get him up here!

> ANNABELLA *heaves the bucket up and empties it into the tub. She hands it back to* PHEMY, PHEMY *trails out again.*

> MARGARET *enters half-dressed. She's tying her hair up or getting ready to get dressed, getting ready for the day.*

> ANNABELLA *sticks her hand in the water.*

> One more should do it.

MARGARET. You go ahead. I already had a washdown with the first bucket.

ANNABELLA. Oh, Margaret, you never take the time for a soak these days.

MARGARET. I want to get on. The King has sent me messages from the papal ambassador. I need to think how to advise him.

ANNABELLA. You should advise him that if he's not going to treat you like a decent wife he should pay you a wage.

MARGARET. I like being busy.

ANNABELLA *is hidden behind the curtain as she gets in the bath.*

ANNABELLA. A wash in a bucket's likely better for your soul. Do you know, when I was in France when I was a girl, they didn't believe we washed in Scotland.

ANNABELLA *vanishes behind the bath curtain again.* PHEMY *labours in again with a young boy,* TAM, *helping her carry the bucket.*

MARGARET. Oh, the Princess Annabella's already got in.

ANNABELLA (*behind the curtain*). Well, she can pour it in on top of me, can't she?

MARGARET. She's got the boy with her.

ANNABELLA. Which boy?

MARGARET. Wee Tam.

ANNABELLA. I'm sure he's seen a pair of tits. You've seen a pair of tits, haven't you, Tam?

TAM *is too mortified to answer.*

Well, if he's not it's about time he did. Come on, wee Tam. I'll no bite you.

MARGARET. Don't let her tease you, Tam.

ANNABELLA. It's alright, wee Tam, your next pair will be bonnier than these...

It's all uphill from here.

TAM *and* PHEMY *have gone into the bath tent.*

Open your eyes, Tam! I won't blind you!

PHEMY. Watch! Watch, you're pouring it all over the floor!

ANNABELLA. He won't look at me, Margaret!

MARGARET. Leave the boy alone!

PHEMY. Tam, you'll never get a decent shag if you're that feart of a woman's fanny! Come here.

Splashing and then TAM *runs out the tent and straight for the exit.* ANNABELLA *and* PHEMY *are laughing.* MARGARET *is shaking her head.*

MARGARET. You're cruel. Cruel.

PHEMY comes out of the bath tent.

PHEMY (*scorn*). He spilt half the water on the floor! I'll get a mop.

She exits.

ANNABELLA *sticks her head out of the tent so she can talk to* MARGARET.

ANNABELLA. I'm so pale. Too long inside. Am I pale?

MARGARET. You look like a tree.

ANNABELLA (*surprised*). What?

MARGARET. A bonny tree. A bonny birch tree with silver bark.

ANNABELLA. Well… thank you… I think.

MARGARET. It's what I see. People should say what their eyes see, it's important.

I love starting the day like this, with clean water and good conversation. I love it. Do you want flowers in there?

ANNABELLA. Rose petals?

MARGARET *is looking.*

MARGARET. We're out, you could have the pine and birch… I love the smell of that on me…

ANNABELLA. On you go.

As long as I smell sweet.

She ducks back in the tent. PHEMY *comes back in.*

PHEMY. Lord John's come to see you, Margaret. He won't wait.

ANNABELLA. Well, he'll need to.

JOHN *enters as she's speaking.*

JOHN. Well, he can't.

A shocked silence. ANNABELLA *speaks from the bath tent.*

ANNABELLA. Is he out there? Is he standing out there?

JOHN. Morning, Princess Annabella.

ANNABELLA. Mother of God.

She sticks her head out the tent to look.

MARGARET. Lord John, we're not receiving visitors.

JOHN. I won't be in anyone's way. You just carry on.

ANNABELLA. We might alarm you.

JOHN. Princess Annabella, you could never do anything but delight me.

ANNABELLA (*to* MARGARET). Great shoulders and a smooth, smooth liar… you know where we are, just shout. Phemy! Come and get me dry.

ANNABELLA *ducks back into the bath tent.* PHEMY *hurries in beside her.*

MARGARET. The King's not here. He won't arrive until…

JOHN (*cutting her off*). Tomorrow. I know. I came ahead of him.

MARGARET. You…

Why?

JOHN. Cut out the wee man.

MARGARET. What?

JOHN. I give him the papers, he gives you the papers, you do all the work and give them back to him, then he gives them back to me. That's how it works, eh?

MARGARET.…I suppose… Yes.

JOHN. So let's save time. I reckon you and me can sort things out together. Quicker. Better. What do you say? We can do that, can't we? You and me.

She says nothing.

I'll see you in the hall when you're done here.

He moves to exit.

You smell wonderful, ladies, you really do.

A pause, MARGARET *is still stunned.* PHEMY *and* ANNABELLA *come out of the tent,* ANNABELLA *wrapped in towels.*

ANNABELLA. No one would judge you. No one could. No one.

MARGARET. I'm not going to…! (*Breaks off again.*)

ANNABELLA. You're not going to go and work through all the treasury documents with him?

MARGARET. No, I am…!

I will do that.

Why shouldn't I do that?

ANNABELLA. No reason at all.

PHEMY. It'd be stupid not to. He's come all this way.

MARGARET. I have to…

I have to look..

What dress should I wear?

PHEMY. The red. For sure.

MARGARET. No, no! I have to look formal! I have to look…

I need my jewels.

She hurries off. PHEMY *is calling off.*

PHEMY. Tam! Come and get this water!

TAM *enters and sorts out the bath, getting it off.*

ANNABELLA. Should we go down after her?

PHEMY. No. Why?

ANNABELLA. I think he has a hard face.

PHEMY. Aye! And then he smiles!

ANNABELLA. We shouldn't have let him in.

PHEMY. She's a grown-up woman, Princess Annabella. She's safe enough.

ANNABELLA. We should never let anyone in. It's never safe.

PHEMY. But did you see the smile on her when she was running for her jewels.

ANNABELLA. It's never safe.

TAM *is still clearing up*.

TAM. She's right. We shouldny be letting anyone in. There's plague.

ANNABELLA. What?

TAM. There's plague coming. Started in the docks at Berwick and they say it's moving through the town.

PHEMY. Berwick's a long way off.

TAM. This is the worst kind, they say, you don't know it but it's already in the air around you. You breathe it in at breakfast, you're in heaven before you get your dinner. Folk just drop and die where they're walking.

PHEMY. Stop it. You're frightening me.

TAM *exits*.

ANNABELLA. It may never come as far as Stirling. It'll depend on the wind.

PHEMY. You've seen this before.

ANNABELLA. Three times.

I don't think it's too early for a wee drink, do you?

PHEMY. Aye… go on then.

They exit.

The Garden, Day

JOHN *is coaching* JAMIE *in fighting*. MARGARET *watches*.

JOHN. Practise that, you know what you're about now.

JAMIE. Thanks.

MARGARET. Go and get fed, Jamie. Tell them I'll eat later.

JAMIE *exits*. MARGARET *moves closer to* JOHN.

Thank you.

JOHN. Nae bother. I enjoyed it. He's good.

MARGARET. I can see he learns everything he should but he needs this. He really needs this.

JOHN. Course he does. He'll be King one day, eh?

If you like… I could bring some men from my place to be with him, train with him, look out for him, you know? He's maybe ready for that kind of company.

MARGARET. A guard of his own?

JOHN. Aye.

MARGARET. Yes.

Yes.

You're probably right.

JOHN. If the King has no objection.

MARGARET. I doubt he'll ever know.

They're close together now.

He knows very little of what we do.

PHEMY *enters, flustered*.

PHEMY. Margaret, the King's at the gate, he's come today.

MARGARET. Oh.

JOHN. Then I'll be on my road. But I'll see you soon?

MARGARET. Yes.

Yes, I'd be happy to see you.

She watches him exit, then follows.

The Hall at Stirling, Same Day

JAMES *is waiting,* MARGARET *enters.*

MARGARET. Is Ross with you?

JAMES. I expect so, someone usually packs him whether I want them to or not.

That bastard from the Privy Council hasn't even sent me the papers.

MARGARET. Really?

JAMES. No.

They never sent me a thing.

MARGARET (*floundering*). No… he… I… no.

JAMES. What?

MARGARET. Nothing.

He… I have the papers. They're ready for you.

She offers them. He's studying her.

JAMES. You look different.

Have you changed your hair?

MARGARET. No.

JAMES. You've got a lovely colour in your face.

MARGARET. Thank you.

JAMES. All flushed with the excitement of doing your sums, eh? So Lord John was here already, was he?

MARGARET. Yes.

JAMES. Yes, I know he was. What a dull morning you must have had.

Well, never mind.

I've brought you something. A birthday present.

MARGARET. But that's months away.

JAMES. But I won't see you, will I? And I want to be here when you see this.

JAMES *is pulling on a covered mirror.*

MARGARET. Where's Cochrane?

JAMES (*casual*). Oh, he's dead.

MARGARET. *What!?*

JAMES. As a coffin nail.

MARGARET. But… what happened? When?

JAMES. Never mind Cochrane.

JAMES *is pulling* MARGARET *towards the standing mirror. It has been covered with a cloth.*

It's from Venice. The glassworkers of Venice have discovered this extraordinary technique. They can make mirrors that reflect the real world, exactly as it looks, no distortions, no blurred shadows… you see things *exactly* as they are. It's remarkable. No one's *ever* looked in mirrors like this before.

Look at this.

He guides her to stand in front of the mirror. He pulls the cover off.

MARGARET *has stepped back so she can't see her reflection, only his.*

MARGARET. Oh!

JAMES. Yes?

MARGARET. That's you! That's exactly what you look like! That's what my eyes see!

JAMES *grabs her impatiently and pulls her so she is looking at her own reflection.*

MARGARET *gasps in shock. She stares at herself for a moment.*

Is that...?

JAMES. Yes.

MARGARET. That's *me*!

She starts to laugh.

JAMES. What are you laughing about? That's you! That's what you look like. That's what I see, that's what everyone sees.

MARGARET *is laughing even harder, she points at the mirror.*

MARGARET. Look at her!

JAMES. Look at you! That's you!

MARGARET *controls her laughter. She looks at herself, considering.*

MARGARET. James, this is making me so happy.

JAMES. *What!?*

Look at your face. Look how old you are.

MARGARET. Oh, I thought I was *much* older than that!

JAMES. Look at your skin! Look.

He pushes in beside her, pointing at his own face and hers.

Look at the holes! Look, tiny holes in your skin, look at the hairs, look at these lines, look, like the skin on porridge. Look how ugly you are.

MARGARET. I thought I was *much* uglier than that.

I like this woman! Look at her! She's ready for a laugh, isn't she? I'd love to get drinking with this woman. I *really* like the look of her. Is that really me?

JAMES. That's what you've come to. Yes.

When I married you, you had skin like milk and rose petals and a mouth like a fresh berry.

Pause.

MARGARET. But you never told me that. No one ever told me that. That pretty girl is dead and gone and I never knew her.

I *like* this woman.

She notices his state.

You thought this would upset me? That's what you wanted, isn't it? You wanted to taunt me?

JAMES. No! No, I didn't! I wanted…

I thought you would see it too.

I thought you would feel it too. You usually…

I wanted you to understand, you bloody aggravating woman!

JAMES *stares at the mirror for another angry moment, then he turns away from his reflection.*

MARGARET. James… yes, that is what you look like. That is what everyone has been looking at. But you've hardly been short of admirers, have you?

JAMES. They're all idiots! To dote on *that*.

He waves his hand angrily at the covered mirror.

Or worse… *worse*, they've known *exactly* what they're up to, making a fool of me with their smooth skin and shining little faces…

MARGARET. James. *Everyone* thinks you're stunning. You *know* that!

JAMES. No, I don't know that! I don't know that, I think you've all been lying to me. I've long suspected I'm surrounded by liars and now I know!

Jesus. If you don't understand that…

Who am I supposed to talk to!?

A beat.

MARGARET. James? What happened to Cochrane?

JAMES. The imbecile went drinking in the wrong bar.

Maybe there wasn't a safe bar in the whole of Scotland.

Maybe I shouldn't have made him Earl of Lennox. I don't think it was a popular appointment. Do you? And it looks like my critics are getting very confident. Very impudent.

MARGARET. You're not safe.

JAMES. No.

Here's something you never thought you'd hear me say, Sandy was right.

He was holding them back. And now he's gone.

A beat.

MARGARET. This is what you have to do –

JAMES. Yes?

MARGARET. Take back some of the lands and titles you've given to your friends. Give them to men who might support you.

JAMES. No.

MARGARET. Bring new men and women into your court, send your favourites away…

JAMES. Don't use that word! I *hate* that word.

Everyone I know interests me. Everyone provides different stimulation, different shades and tones to the day.

Why would I favour one human soul over another? What kind of creature would I be if I did that? The baker is my favourite when I need fresh bread. My musicians are my favourites when I want music. You're my favourite when I need advice and you screw your face up in that earnest little scowl and start…

MARGARET (*cutting him off*). They're a provocation, James! If you keep people like… Daisy close by you, they think you're taunting them.

JAMES. I am. How dare they tell me I should value their wealth, their mouldy family names, their ugly, bloody, history and fat estates over natural beauty and raw talent.

He would have been one of the greatest architects in Europe. I miss him. It really hurts. It's horrible, Margaret.

A beat.

MARGARET. If they've killed Cochrane they've come very close. They could *destroy* you!

JAMES (*indicating mirror*). Who cares, I'm too ugly to live. Look.

A beat.

MARGARET. Most of us are much uglier.

JAMES. The young aren't.

MARGARET. Well…

Time will fix that one, won't it?

JAMES. They're like the waves of the sea. A tide rising and beating on our backs.

DAISY and RAMSAY enter, each carrying something.

What do you want!?

They stop dead, look at each other, look at JAMES.

RAMSAY. Your wine?

DAISY. You wanted some white cheese.

JAMES. No, I tell you what I want, I want to be left alone.

They look at each other again and then move to exit. DAISY *exits,* RAMSAY *waits, pointedly holding the door for* MARGARET. *After a moment* JAMES *notices him.*

What do you want, Ramsay!

RAMSAY (*looking pointedly at* MARGARET). Sorry… you said you wanted to be alone.

JAMES. Piss off, you stupid little prick!

RAMSAY *exits, angry.*

Come back to Edinburgh.

A beat.

MARGARET. Will you change?

JAMES. Don't be stupid.

A beat.

MARGARET. It's all about choices, James.

JAMES (*bitter again*). Is it? Is it really? And I've had so many of those, haven't I? I don't remember choosing to marry you, Margaret, do you remember choosing to marry me? I'll just go and live in Tuscany, shall I? Make a wee pilgrimage to Rome and never come back. It's not like I'm imprisoned on the throne of Scotland or anything, is it!?

(*Points at the mirror.*) Happy birthday, darling. Now you can watch your life slipping away moment by tedious moment.

You see *this* is when I need the choir! We need beauty we can rely on! Music. Food and drink.

I asked for wine and cheese, where the fuck are my wine and cheese?

He heads for the exit, shouting.

Ramsay!

Where's my bloody choir!?

He exits.

MARGARET *uncovers the mirror and looks at herself again.*

JAMIE *enters.*

He comes to see what she's doing.

He laughs in delight. He touches his own reflection.

He pulls faces, tries to startle his reflection.

JAMIE. Is that me?

MARGARET. Yes.

JAMIE stops clowning for a moment, just studying his reflection, taking it in.

JAMIE. I look like him. My father.

MARGARET (*kisses him*). You're lucky, you're going to break hearts.

Will you see him this time? He's only gone to his rooms.

JAMIE. Did he ask to see me?

Her silence answers him. He turns away from the mirror.

MARGARET. Promise me. Say it.

JAMIE (*sulky*). He's still my father. I'll forgive him.

MARGARET. Good, now will you bring me my jewellery box?

He pulls it over. It's big.

MARGARET is considering her reflection. She is wearing a lot of lavish jewellery.

She takes off a necklace. Then she's pulling off more jewellery from her wrists, hair.

All these lovely things I had made to brighten the long winters. All the jewels.

She gives them all to him and looks at herself with nothing.

Jamie… I thought I needed jewels. I thought they were my flowers.

JAMIE. Flowers?

MARGARET. I thought I was an old barren stick of a bush and I needed flowers to soften me. That's what I always thought.

She stretches out her hand to her own reflection.

I'm soft enough. I'm young enough. I like my face.

JAMIE. I always think you're beautiful.

MARGARET. I'm not. I'm not at all, but it doesn't matter. I like my face, Jamie. I *like* her.

(*Points.*) Look, she's not frightened of anything.

JAMIE *touches her neck.*

JAMIE. You've one left.

MARGARET. Ah… this little gold cross was my first jewellery. My mother gave it to me.

She tucks it into her dress.

I'll put it next to my skin.

You know what I think, Jamie? I think who you are in just your skin is *all* you are. What you wear next to your skin should remind you of that.

He doesn't know what to say to that.

I'll put those jewels away safe. We might need them if your father decides he needs an orchestra.

MARGARET *is looking at her reflection.*

I like this woman. I don't know her but I like her.

I don't know what she's going to do.

I can't wait to find out what she's going to do. First she's going to find her darling boy Ross. Have you seen him?

JAMIE. He was hanging about in the garden.

MARGARET. Oh, go and find him, Jamie. I can't wait to see him.

JAMIE hurries off. MARGARET considers herself in the mirror a beat longer, then covers it and leaves.

The Garden, the Next Day

JAMIE *is practising his moves in the garden.* ROSS *is stalking him. After a while* JAMIE *notices.*

JAMIE. I can see you there.

> ROSS *stops trying to sneak up on him and moves closer. When he's close he launches himself at* JAMIE. *He has a knife. He tries to stab him.*

> JAMIE *fights him off easily. He pushes* ROSS *down and kicks at him.*

What are you doing!? What are you *doing*!?

Give me that!

> *He grabs the knife off* ROSS. ROSS *is hurting and very upset. Close to tears.*

ROSS. He told me to.

JAMIE. You could have killed me!

ROSS. He told me to.

JAMIE. Who told you to?

> ROSS *says nothing.*

Dad told you to kill me?

> ROSS *says nothing.*

Dad told you to stab me?

ROSS. He says stuff like that and then he says he doesn't mean it. I don't know what he means.

I told him you'd be too strong for me.

He says if I loved him I'd at least try.

A pause.

JAMIE. Well, I suppose you love him.

ROSS. It's not nice in Edinburgh. I can't ride my horse and they won't feed me till I'm nearly asleep. It's always special food, for the parties, it's too spicy for me but I'm not allowed to eat in the kitchen. Can I come home?

JAMIE. No.

ROSS. Would Mum let me come home?

JAMIE. Yes. But I won't.

ROSS. He says you'll never be King.

JAMIE. Why not?

ROSS. Because one day I'll be big enough to kill you.

A pause.

I got a dog. He's grey, he's lovely. Do you want to see?

JAMIE. No.

The Queen's Room, Stirling, Later

DAISY *is led on by* ANNABELLA *and* PHEMY. *She is scared and hostile.*

DAISY. What? What?

ANNABELLA. Queen just wants a word.

PHEMY. No harm.

MARGARET *enters. They settle themselves round her.* MARGARET *is smiling, friendly.*

MARGARET. So.

Daisy.

Is that your real name?

DAISY. Yes.

MARGARET. Do you know why I asked to talk to you?

DAISY. You can't get rid of me. You can't make me go away.

MARGARET. Why do you think I'm going to ask you to do
that?

DAISY. You can't do anything to me. I'm not going to eat your
food and I'm not going to drink your drink. You can glower
at me all you like. I'm not going anywhere.

MARGARET. You think we're going to poison you? Why
would we poison you?

DAISY *won't reply.*

Daisy, do you think you're beautiful?

DAISY. Your eyes can answer that for you, can't they?

MARGARET. I want to know what you think.

DAISY. Like the Queen of Heaven.

MARGARET. That's what you think.

DAISY. That's what they tell me. Why would they lie?

MARGARET. When did they start telling you that?

Who was the first person that told you that?

A beat, DAISY *doesn't like this.*

DAISY. My mother.

MARGARET. How old were you?

DAISY. I don't know! Small. I was always the pretty one.

MARGARET. Prettier than your sisters? Did you have sisters?

DAISY. I don't have to talk to you, you know. You can't make
me.

MARGARET. You didn't have sisters?

DAISY. None that lived. No.

MARGARET. Ah! So you were precious to your mum.

DAISY. My mother's dead these five years. What's your point?

MARGARET. You are very pretty. There's no denying it. I
wouldn't take that from you.

DAISY. Well, you couldn't, could you?

(*Looks at* ANNABELLA.) What are you looking at?

(*To* MARGARET.) Your husband loves me. That's not my fault.

MARGARET. Well, he loves a lot of people, Daisy, that's the thing. That's the problem, isn't it?

You're very like him, aren't you?

DAISY. Like who?

MARGARET. My husband.

DAISY (*suspicious*). What do you mean?

MARGARET. Well… beautiful. For want of a better way of putting it. He's quite dazzling, isn't he?

A beat.

DAISY. Well… he's the King.

MARGARET. And you love him.

A beat.

DAISY. Yes.

He's the King.

MARGARET. How old are you, Daisy?

(*As* DAISY *doesn't answer.*) Do you know how old you are?

DAISY. I'm seventeen.

MARGARET. How old are you, Phemy?

PHEMY. Fifteen, we reckon.

MARGARET. Is Phemy pretty, Daisy?

DAISY (*shrugs*). She's alright.

MARGARET. Will she be prettier when she's seventeen?

DAISY. Mebbe. If she gets some proper clothes and puts her hair about her.

MARGARET. When will she be prettiest? What's the prettiest year Phemy's ever likely to have?

DAISY. Aw God, girl like her?

(*To* PHEMY.) You're skinny and you've got that kind of soft look to you, eh? Like uncooked bannock. I reckon seventeen will be your year. See you make the most of it, eh?

MARGARET. And you, Daisy? When will your year be?

A beat. DAISY *glares at her.*

DAISY. The worms will be eating your eyes before you ever see it, old woman.

MARGARET *moves to the mirror.*

MARGARET. I want to show you something… Phemy, help me.

PHEMY *helps her shift the mirror into the centre of the room.*

This is a new mirror. It was a present from the King.

DAISY. He gives me jewels.

MARGARET. Yes, I know.

DAISY *crosses to her.* MARGARET *takes the cover from the mirror. She stands in front of it.*

See?

DAISY *looks from the reflection to* MARGARET.

DAISY (*laughs*). Well, that's what you look like, sure enough.

MARGARET. Now look…

She gently pulls DAISY *in front of the mirror.* DAISY *sees her own reflection. She goes very still, her eyes wide.*

After a moment PHEMY *and* ANNABELLA *move in behind her.* ANNABELLA *makes a startled sound.* PHEMY *gapes for a moment, then she starts to giggle.*

DAISY. Oh.

PHEMY. That's me!

MARGARET. It is.

PHEMY. I've got blue eyes!

MARGARET. Dark blue, like a summer dusk. What colour did you think they were?

PHEMY. Plain grey!

PHEMY *doubles over laughing.* ANNABELLA *is still studying her reflection.*

ANNABELLA. Oh, I'm as old as that.

MARGARET. I'm old too, look.

ANNABELLA. Oh, you're still a plump fruit, I'm the last apple in the barrel! Oh… what a wonder, what a wonder you've showed me… the girl is gone. The girl is gone for good. I'm my own mother.

She was a monster.

I can terrify you all!

ANNABELLA *is laughing too.*

DAISY *still hasn't reacted.*

MARGARET. Daisy.

DAISY (*quiet*). That's not right, that's not a proper mirror.

MARGARET. Look at Phemy in the mirror. Look at Annabella. You can see that it is.

DAISY *just stares.*

You are very pretty, Daisy.

Did you think you were more beautiful than that? As beautiful as the Queen of Heaven?

PHEMY. You nearly are, you know.

MARGARET. Do you think that woman in the mirror is as beautiful as the Queen of Heaven?

DAISY *doesn't answer.*

You are so like him.

That's what you look like, Daisy, but you're the King's favourite. What does that tell you?

DAISY. That's not my real nose.

MARGARET. Yes, it is.

Do you think maybe sixteen was your year? Do you think maybe it's gone already? But you're still leading half of Scotland round by the nose, Daisy. Think about it. You are bringing them all to their knees, with *that* face.

It's not your nose, is it? It's not your perfect mouth or your snowdrop figure. It's you. It's just you.

So you see, Daisy, there's no rush.

You can make a plan.

You don't need to grab everything you can before your skin fades because, look, it's fading already.

The King has given you jewels. I'll give you more.

You can leave here and have a life, Daisy, a whole life. You don't need to be a king's mistress. Why, you're barely pretty enough for that but you're still managing it.

What else might you manage?

You could *marry* a duke. You could go to Paris and sell Scottish wool. You can still dazzle the world when you're older than me. Why settle now?

DAISY *turns to and fro, still staring*.

Do you really love him?

DAISY. Yes.

MARGARET. Then go away. If you love him, go away.

I'll give you money now…

DAISY (*cuts her off*). I don't want your money! You can go to hell, you *witch*!

DAISY *runs off*.

ANNABELLA. It might have been better to kill her.

MARGARET. How could I have done that?

ANNABELLA. My mother would have done that. Maybe I could do that for you? It looks like I have it in me.

PHEMY *comes to look.*

PHEMY. It's your eyes. I never saw that. There's terrible things in your eyes.

ANNABELLA. I've seen terrible things. But I've done so little.

MARGARET. What are you talking about?

ANNABELLA. Two husbands put me aside and all my children flowed away from me like water to the sea and here I am back in the room I was born in.

And it all comes round again…

PHEMY. What?

ANNABELLA *exits without saying anything else.*
MARGARET *follows her.*

MARGARET. Annabella?

At the same time DAISY *is dragging bags on in the King's rooms, unpacking.*

Cover the mirror, Phemy.

She exits. PHEMY *takes off the mirror as we move into –*

The King's Room, Stirling, Later

DAISY *is sitting crying and muttering to herself. She has pulled out a beautiful dress which she has spread, inside out, on her lap. She is scrubbing at its seams with something.*

RAMSAY *enters. She startles, then glares at him for a moment. She goes back to scrubbing.*

RAMSAY. What are you doing?

DAISY. I'm poisoning her dress.

RAMSAY. Whose?

DAISY. *Hers!* He wants to leave it for the bitch. A birthday present. Congratulate the old crone on still being alive. Well, I'll fix it.

He comes to watch what she's doing. She's scrubbing harder.

RAMSAY. What are you using?

DAISY. Wormwood and copper salt.

RAMSAY. Copper salt?

DAISY. It kills rats, it should see her off.

RAMSAY. Won't she smell it?

DAISY thrusts the dress at him. He sniffs.

Hmmm, maybe not.

It won't kill her, you know.

DAISY. It kills rats.

RAMSAY. You said that.

You're an idiot.

DAISY. Away and eat yourself.

RAMSAY. Poisoned dresses are something out of children's stories.

DAISY. It kills rats.

RAMSAY. If you want to kill her, kill her! Put a knife in her.

DAISY (*still working*). I can't.

RAMSAY. Why not?

DAISY. I couldn't stab anyone.

RAMSAY. So pay someone to do it.

DAISY. They'd catch me. They'd hang me.

RAMSAY. Then learn to live with the bitch because that will
not work!

*He grabs the dress off her roughly and holds it against her
skin. She screams and struggles. He pins her for a moment
then lets her go.*

*She looks at the place he touched with the dress, hyper-
breathing in panic.*

DAISY. You've killed me!

RAMSAY. No.

DAISY. Look! Look! It's all coming up red! You've killed me!

RAMSAY. I've given you a skin rash.

DAISY. You've killed me!

RAMSAY. Then why aren't you dead!?

DAISY. I'll die. I'll die tonight!

RAMSAY. You won't. Because poisoned dresses only kill
people in children's stories. You're a child. You're an idiot.

Why does he love you!

Why!?

Pause.

DAISY. Why does he love her?

RAMSAY. That's duty. That's all that is. Duty.

DAISY. He still loves her.

RAMSAY. He hasn't slept with her in years.

DAISY. Oh, do you think? Is that what he tells you?

RAMSAY. He doesn't even *like* her.

DAISY. I don't like her.

RAMSAY. Well, you can't kill her with that.

He snatches it from her. DAISY *is examining her injured arm.*

DAISY. And I don't like you.

He thinks you're ugly now.

He only keeps you out of pity.

RAMSAY. There's no pity in him.

He keeps me because I love him. More than my life. More than anything in my life. I love him best of all. I'm the only person who does.

DAISY. I'm not going back to Edinburgh with him. I'm done with the lot of you. I'm going to Paris.

I'm going to be rich.

You can do what you like.

DAISY *exits.* RAMSAY *shakes out the dress. Looking at it.*

JAMES *enters.*

JAMES. Ramsay, can we get out of here yet? What are you doing with that?

RAMSAY. It's… I was admiring it.

JAMES. It's sweet, isn't it? It's a present for the Queen. I taught her to wear that colour, you know.

RAMSAY. Did you?

JAMES. She had no idea, it brings out the colour in her eyes. Whatever age does to her face she'll always have magnificent eyes.

She'll know that's what I mean, she usually understands.

RAMSAY. Does she?

JAMES. Well, come on! Wrap it up. And the jewels there. Take them to her women. Tell them she's to have them all on her birthday next month.

(*Moving off.*) How long does it take to saddle a fucking horse.

JAMES *exits. Carefully* RAMSAY *starts to fold the dress.*

PHEMY *comes to take it from him.* RAMSAY *exits as* PHEMY *turns into –*

The Garden, a Few Weeks Later

A sunny summer's day in the garden. ANNABELLA *seems to be looking for something on the grass.*

MARGARET *takes the dress from* PHEMY *and holds it against her, twirling as if dancing.*

MARGARET. Can you believe I ever wore this colour? God, what was I thinking?

JOHN *enters.*

John! Hullo. We heard you arrive. Where have you been?

JOHN. I was talking to Prince James.

MARGARET. Oh good, he'd had enough of us today, hadn't he, Annabella? We've had a few glasses, Lord John, and I'm afraid we're getting a bit silly.

ANNABELLA. You speak for yourself.

MARGARET (*to* JOHN). It's my birthday.

JOHN. I know.

MARGARET. Is that why you're here? What did you bring me for my birthday?

JOHN. What do you want?

MARGARET. The King left me this…

She considers it.

Do you know, Phemy? I don't think I'll ever wear that. But I doubt it'll fit anyone else. Should we cut it up for remaking?

PHEMY. Seems a shame.

MARGARET. It's the colour of another time, when my head was full of fear and jealousy and poison… Burn it.

PHEMY (*shocked*). No! You can't!

MARGARET. I can. But make sure you *never* tell the King.

She gives the dress to PHEMY.

JOHN. I know he's the man for fashion but if you want the truth I've always thought the King's taste was a bit… gaudy.

MARGARET. And you're so restrained, aren't you, Lord John?

As she exits PHEMY *sees something moving through the grass.*

PHEMY. Annabella! Annabella! There's a whole load of them scuttling off this way.

ANNABELLA. Oh, Mary Mother of God, well, don't scare them! They're running fast enough as it is.

ANNABELLA *hurries after* PHEMY.

MARGARET. We got these new birds. A birthday gift from Oslo. They're so beautiful, John! Little fat… fat… *fat* chickens with a comb that goes like this. (*Mimes a comb over one eye.*)

They wink at you! Seriously. And they can run!

One of the hens was broody and this morning… fat little chicks everywhere. They won't be ruled by their mother. What's the news from Edinburgh?

JOHN. All peaceful. For now. The King's barely left his rooms these last weeks.

One of his favourites, that Daisy girl, has left him.

MARGARET. Oh! Don't move!

She thinks she has seen a chick in the stones near him. She pounces.

Did you see it! Did you see it! It *ran.*

MARGARET *is now very close to* JOHN.

I did that. *I* did. I showed her sense and she took it as a gift. She's gone. *Gone!* See what I can do?

JOHN. Margaret, you can do more than that.

MARGARET. I think you're right.

He kisses her.

She doesn't push him away but after a moment she steps back, a little shocked, a little uncertain, watching him.

What does that mean?

JOHN. What do you think it means!?

He steps towards her. She stops him.

MARGARET. It'd be treason.

JOHN. You're joking, aren't you?

ANNABELLA *crosses upstage, looking for chicks. Her search is unconvincing, most of her attention is on* MARGARET *and* JOHN.

Do you think he would care if you took me to your bed? Do you think he would even *notice*?

MARGARET. Yes.

I think he'd notice.

ANNABELLA. Chick… chick… chick…

MARGARET *gives her a look,* ANNABELLA *exits.*

MARGARET. John… the reason I haven't taken you to my bed is that I don't want to.

JOHN. Are you sure about that?

MARGARET. Yes.

Otherwise I would have done it.

I'm sorry. I just need to be honest with you.

JOHN. Well, I'm not a child. And I'm not an idiot. And I know what's been going on here.

MARGARET. Oh, God, I feel it… I *feel* it. You've no idea. And it's… seeing how you want me?… There have been days when that was all that kept my back straight, otherwise I'd have shrivelled like a winter leaf…

But that's madness. Madness. Why would I want to be mad?

JOHN. I care for you, you stupid woman. Like he never did! You don't have to be frightened.

MARGARET. I'm not. I'm tired of being frightened. I'm tired of being mad. I'm tired of bobbing about wherever my heart hurls me and I'm choosing to never do that again.

I've looked in my own eyes now and I know who I am.

Phemy sings about love all the time.

When I tell Phemy about this she'll look at me as if I've said that I'm tearing off my face, as if I'm only going to be half-alive for the rest of my days, as if this is the saddest, stupidest thing any woman could ever do.

Phemy is fifteen years old and she thinks a new dress is life's greatest thrill.

I have three living sons. Men I made.

I have my work.

You think I'd risk that just because I'm shaking at the thought of touching you? In a few months I won't even remember what that felt like.

JOHN. You're still sleeping with him.

MARGARET. I'm sleeping alone. And I'm fine.

JOHN. I don't believe you. He has Scotland. He has you. He doesn't value either of you. He doesn't deserve either of you.

MARGARET. He's the King.

A pause. JOHN *is processing all of this, getting more and more angry.*

The hawks might get these chicks if I don't find them...

Will you help me look?

JOHN. There's plague in the south again. They've closed the gates at Berwick. Just south of the border I saw cows howling in the byre with no one to milk them and children pulling at dead arms that'll never lift them again.

God can take our lives in an hour, in a minute... and here you are, watching years pass, waiting. What are you waiting for, Margaret?

MARGARET. I'm not waiting at all.

JOHN. Nor am I.

We're gathering. In Edinburgh.

MARGARET. We?

JOHN. All the men who love Scotland.

And all the men that can be called to bear arms.

MARGARET. An army.

JOHN. I want to do this without blood, Margaret. I want you beside me.

MARGARET. Oh, I see, I see...

JOHN. What?

MARGARET. There's more than one reason to want to take a queen to bed, isn't there?

A beat.

JOHN. Yes. More than one reason. But they're all good reasons.

MARGARET. Were you planning on killing him before or after we had our night of passion? I'm glad marriage is on the table though. You'd need to marry me, wouldn't you?

JOHN. It needn't come to killing.

But you want what I want.

MARGARET. I just told you I didn't.

JOHN. And I'm telling you I don't believe you. You say you've looked in your own eyes. Well, I'm looking in them now and I know what I see.

MARGARET. You see what you want to see.

ANNABELLA *is back on*.

ANNABELLA. Are you needing us, Queen Margaret?

JOHN. Did she call you?

ANNABELLA. We've got them all. I held them all safe in my skirt, every one. Now let's go inside.

JAMIE *enters with an armed* GUARD *on either side of him*.

JAMIE. Mum? Lord John says I should go to Edinburgh and talk to the parliament. What do you think? I think he's right, it'll be my parliament one day.

MARGARET (*to* JOHN). What have you told him?

JOHN. What he says. That he should come and talk to the parliament that'll be his one day.

JAMIE. What should he have told me?

JOHN. We call a parliament...

MARGARET. Only the King can call a parliament!

JOHN (*ignoring this*). The young Prince shows them he's willing to serve the Three Estates and this country. And you are standing beside him. And so am I.

MARGARET. And the King?

JOHN. That's up to him.

MARGARET. And you said you wanted to do this without *blood*?!

ANNABELLA. Leave the children alone! Leave the children alone! Leave us alone!

She's in bits, shaking, PHEMY *comforts her.*

PHEMY. Annabella? Princess Annabella? What is it?

JAMIE. Christ, what's all the fuss! Mum? I won't go if it upsets you.

But I'm not a child. My father won't teach me to be a king. I need to learn for myself.

JOHN. Hear him? He's nearly grown.

MARGARET. Jamie, he wants to put you in your father's place.

JAMIE. That would be for parliament to decide.

MARGARET. Oh, listen to yourself, you stupid boy! You think civil war would be a great adventure, do you!?

JAMIE. I'm not a stupid boy. I'm fourteen years old. I need my own court, my own men and my own household. I'm going to Edinburgh with Lord John.

JAMIE *exits.*

MARGARET *calls after him.*

MARGARET. Jamie!

He doesn't stop.

(*To* JOHN.) You said you wanted to hold Scotland together. You said you wanted peace.

JOHN. How can we have peace without a king? Your husband is no king.

MARGARET. Give me one chance. *Please!* Let me talk to King James.

JOHN. What good will that do?

MARGARET. Let me try.

JOHN. You think you can bring him before his parliament and make him apologise to every man there? You think you can make him go down on his knees and swear he'll undo every wrong he did, give back all the land he's stolen, swear to keep all the promises he's broken… and better than that… make us believe him? You think you can do that?

MARGARET. Let me try.

A beat.

JOHN. Well… you can come and talk to him. No harm.

He exits.

ANNABELLA. Your bairn gone to be a man. You'll never win him back now.

MARGARET. I will try.

ANNABELLA. When they say they're men and pick up a sword with an edge, they're lost. They're gone. Make your heart a stone or it'll break like an egg.

MARGARET. Phemy, we're going to Edinburgh. Will you help me get ready?

PHEMY. Aye, Margaret.

MARGARET exits, PHEMY is following, she sees something on the ground.

Aw! He wasn't looking, eh?

He trod on a chick. Wee thing. He's smashed it, the brute.

The King's Room, Edinburgh Castle

MARGARET *enters. She can't speak.*

JAMES. Margaret? What's happened?

What are you doing here? What do you want?

MARGARET *drops to her knees and bows her head, stretching her arms out to him.*

MARGARET. Please.

JAMES. What are you…?

Stop it! Stop that, it's horrible. Get up.

She doesn't. He goes to her and pulls her up.

Get up!

What do you think you're doing?

MARGARET. You won't help me but you have to.

You won't want to help but you have to. You have to, James. Please.

JAMES. Are you ill?

MARGARET. It's not me. It's Jamie.

JAMES is instantly cold.

JAMES. Oh. Is it.

MARGARET. They're making him into a weapon to destroy you. But that'll destroy him, James. It will!

JAMES. What are you telling me?

MARGARET. I'm begging you. I'm begging you to save him.

JAMES. Save him? Save him from his own treason?

MARGARET. Yes!

It's not… *treason*!

He's just a boy, James! He's our boy!

JAMES. If you say so.

MARGARET. No! Not now! Not this! Not now!

He's your son.

He's our son.

JAMES. Don't ever, ever go down on the floor like that again. That was hideous. You were hideous.

MARGARET. I don't care.

JAMES. Well, I do!

A beat.

I don't even understand what you want. What do you expect me to do?

MARGARET. Call a parliament. Let them tell you what they need.

JAMES. Rule the way they like. No. No, I'm not their puppet and I'm not yours. No.

MARGARET. I'm begging...

JAMES. Stop that! I told you to stop that!

A beat. JAMES *is really upset, getting himself under control.* MARGARET *waits.*

I want you to answer something. I want you to answer honestly.

MARGARET. Alright.

JAMES. Who do you love best in the world? Who do you love above your life?

MARGARET. You know the answer to that.

My boys... But...

JAMES (*cutting her off*). Yes! Yes! Your boys! *Your boys!* Not me! Never me since...

Ever since that first mewling, bloody, slimy *thing* popped out of you it's been the same!

It's all for them, isn't it? All for *your* sons.

Show me one human being on this earth that loves me above any other human soul. Just one!

MARGARET. Oh, stop feeling sorry for yourself, you great wobbling lump of self-pity! It's pathetic.

JAMES. Oh, thank Christ. She's back. You're back. Come here.

He hugs her.

I missed you. Why don't you visit more often?

MARGARET. Because you chose to make war on your own son, James, and now it might kill you both.

A beat.

I'm thinking about my sixteenth birthday.

JAMES. Are you?

MARGARET. Tell me what you remember best about that day?

JAMES. That you finally stopped pestering me.

MARGARET. We'd been married for years. I was a woman grown. I was getting old!

JAMES. Well… what can I tell you. You always looked like you might have some growing left to do. Scrawny, stretched-out thing.

MARGARET. I thought you didn't want me to be Queen. Not really.

JAMES. I can't say I haven't regretted it at times.

MARGARET. I thought I was too ugly.

JAMES. No, you were never that.

MARGARET. I wanted to do my duty. To do everything I'd been told I had to do.

JAMES. I know you did. You made my ears bleed!

(*Imitating Danish accent.*) 'I am your wife. Take me to your bed. Let me be your wife!'

You started hitting me.

MARGARET. I did not!

JAMES. I could show you the scars.

MARGARET. And you wouldn't tell me when. You'd never tell them to prepare the bed. You waited till it was my birthday feast, you waited till they were all too drunk to notice us slipping away...

JAMES. Aye, because otherwise the filthy buggers come and *watch*!

MARGARET. You barred the door...

And you were so...

(*Getting emotional.*) You were so..

JAMES. Yes, I was fantastic. We know. Moving on.

MARGARET. No. No. You were so kind. You were so gentle.

JAMES. And fantastic...

MARGARET (*ignoring this*). And everything they'd told me, everything they'd prepared me for... I didn't even need to think about it. It wasn't duty. It wasn't duty, James. It was love.

JAMES. Of course.

Of course it was.

MARGARET. And Jamie came from that. That was the seed that made him. That's why I love him, more than my breath. Because he's yours too. He's part of you too.

A beat.

JAMES. What do you want me to do?

MARGARET. Call a parliament.

JAMES. Alright...

MARGARET. Apologise to them...

JAMES. Apologise? *Apologise!?* For what!!

MARGARET. For being a self-centred, self-pitying arse who's continuously abused his loyal, patient, long-suffering subjects!

JAMES. Well, I'm not saying *that*.

I'll think of something.

Don't look at me like that! I'll do it. You know I can do it.

MARGARET. Thank you.

She goes to kiss his hand. He pulls it back.

JAMES. Don't you fucking *dare*!

He embraces her. A hug.

JOHN *enters.*

MARGARET *breaks away from* JAMES.

MARGARET. The King is ready to summon a parliament.

JOHN. Is that right?

JAMES. Yes, yes, call them all in. They'll come galloping if they think there's a state dinner in it, won't they?

MARGARET *drops a formal curtsey.*

MARGARET. Do I have your permission to leave Your Majesty?

JAMES. Are you going to keep this up all day? Because it is seriously tedious. Yes, go on, bugger off, but don't go far. I need to talk to you later.

MARGARET *exits. She throws a triumphant look at* JOHN *as she passes.*

JOHN. She's got a bonny colour in her face. She's as beautiful as an angel by the throne of God with that light in her face, isn't she?

JAMES *says nothing, watching* JOHN, *suspicious.*

That's just the way she looks after...

He trails off, watching JAMES, *mocking.*

JAMES. After what?

JOHN. Och... not for me to say. You'd know better than me, eh? Or you would have done once.

Didny know what you had there did you?

JAMES. What I have.

JOHN. If you say so.

He holds JAMES's gaze a moment then he exits. JAMES starts to dress for parliament, at the same time –

The Great Hall / Parliament Hall, Edinburgh

PHEMY *and* ANNABELLA *are dressing* MARGARET *for parliament.* PHEMY *holds* MARGARET's *jewellery box, offering it to her. She refuses more jewellery.*

MARGARET. No. Just the necklace.

ANNABELLA. You're shaking. A queen's never frightened. You're a queen.

The procession into parliament. The Members of Parliament assemble. JOHN *takes his place before the royal thrones.*

JAMES *enters, dressed as a penitent.*

JOHN. As we are summoned by our King and by God, the Three Estates of Scotland are hereby called to service.

JAMES (*quiet, just to* MARGARET). It was Lord John's idea that I should apologise, wasn't it?

MARGARET. It's the best thing, James, you know...

JAMES (*cutting her off*). That's what I thought.

MARGARET. James...

JAMES (*indicating* JOHN). Shh! Parliament. Serious business.

JAMES. There's no agenda today, my lords. I'm just going to talk to you. I've been told, I understand, that I owe you all an apology.

There's a story that's come to my attention, a few lines, a fable, with a moral, oh, how we love a moral, don't we, boys? A lion, trapped by hunters, is freed by little mice, they nibble through his ropes and set him free.

Then he's a humbler, wiser lion, who understands at last that he really, really, *really* needs the little people...

But you know what?... I really, really don't...

He takes off his penitent clothing, revealing sparkling clothes beneath.

Behold your King.

This lion cannot be tamed and it cannot be tied down.

It's time you finally realised what should have been blindingly obvious.

This is who I am.

This is how God made me.

I was your opportunity to serve greatness and you *blew* it.

God made me a king... but I can't be the king of mice. Your tiny rodent brains couldn't even comprehend what I offered you.

I was your glitter. I was your sparkle before the dark. My lords, *this* is a tiny glimpse of what you'll be missing now. Hell mend the lot of you.

JAMES *dips* RAMSAY *and pulls him into a prolonged and passionate kiss.*

Good luck finding someone else to govern Scotland the way you want.

Whatever you do now... I'm finished with you.

JAMES *exits with* RAMSAY. *There is instant uproar. Utter fury.*

In the middle of this, JOHN *walks forward with* JAMIE *and stands ready to speak.*

As soon as MARGARET *sees this, she strides forward and pulls the staff out of his hands.*

She bangs it on the floor, deliberate, determined blows. She keeps going till she has silence again.

MARGARET. No, no, that's enough. We'll have no more of this.

Men of Scotland? Lords of Scotland? Rulers of Scotland? God help us all. I'll send a message to the nations of the world, shall I? I'll them if they want to invade all they have to do is put on fancy dress and show their arses. You'll all just run around shrieking like a bunch of geese, won't you?

Be quiet! Now! Be quiet and listen to me!

(*To* JAMIE.) Jamie, sit down, will you, I'm talking.

(*As he hesitates.*) Jamie!

He sits down.

Well, if you've all finished having hysterics can someone remind me what you're supposed to be doing here? What was it again? Oh yes, ruling Scotland. In fact I think we just heard your *King* giving you specific instructions to get on and do that job any way you liked. So this is your plan, is it? To stand here howling obscenities? Is anyone going to attempt any parliamentary business or will we have another shouting session? It's time to do the job you came for, gentlemen.

JOHN. And how do you think we can do that!? The King is head of his parliament. He's left us! We have no king!

MARGARET. You have a Queen!

I have the King's trust. I can take the King's place!

LORD. Aye, pillage some more of our gold, you'd like that, wouldn't you?

MARGARET. Like it? Like it? Have you blown your nose and lost your brain? Who would want the job of ruling Scotland? I'm Danish, you ignorant, abusive lump of manure! I come from a rational nation with reasonable people.

You know the problem with you lot? You've got fuck-all except attitude. You scream and shout about how you want things done and how things ought to be done and when the chance comes look at you! What are you frightened of? Making things worse? According to you things couldn't get worse for Scotland!

You wear me out, do you know that? You drive me mad.

Would one of you please explain to me why it is I still love you so much? Would someone please tell me why a rational woman, born in a reasonable country, would rather live here and be your Queen than exist in quiet, happy, peace anywhere else on earth?

I am the Queen of Scots. And no, I don't always like that. But I do love it. Always.

I was twelve years old when I came here. I didn't understand a word anyone said to me. I was frightened, I was lonely, I had no friends on this side of the North Sea. But you talked slowly till I understood. You showed me that the more frightened you are the better the joke you can tell about it, you taught me you can find friends anywhere you share food and drink if you just wait and see how to join in the conversation. By the time I was thirteen this was my home.

You let me be.

You let me grow.

You taught who I am.

I am the Queen of Scots.

Shall I show you how well I learned that lesson? This is yours.

MARGARET *takes her box of jewels and spills them all over the floor.*

I am your Queen and these are yours.

The comfort of community is warmer and softer than cold gold could ever be. I'm sorry that it's taken me nearly fifteen years to understand that, to understand how to be your Queen. I'm sorry I never told you any of this. I should have known that the only way to let you understand how much I care, was to tell you exactly what I think of you.

I've seen the worst of you, and you're murderous, miserable, men. You've seen the worst of me, I've been a proud, overdressed, self-centred woman. But the best in you pulls me above that, and the best in you, with my help, can sustain this parliament and this nation.

I give you my jewels. I give you my self. I give you all I know. I wasn't even born here but I'm offering Scotland my life. I'm your Queen, I'm still here look at me.

Am I not the Queen of Scots?

A few calls of assent.

Will you help me unite this country in peace?

The assent grows.

Will you help me make Scotland's law? Will you let me do all I can in her name?

Gentlemen, will you help me rule?

There are a chorus of 'Ayes' around the room.

Then tomorrow we can begin. Together you and I will govern Scotland!

There's a cheer and general applause. JOHN *moves to* MARGARET.

Are you going to oppose me?

JOHN. No.

You were magnificent.

MARGARET. Thank you. I've never been so scared in my life.

The Queen's Room and King's Room

ANNABELLA *and* PHEMY *are in the Queen's room,*
ANNABELLA *has a drink.*

JAMES *is in the King's room, looking over the plans for his*
cathedral.

Years have passed, ANNABELLA *is watching as* MARGARET
conducts the business of the Three Estates, but this is a memory.

ANNABELLA. That was a good day. A good, good day. Why
can't it stop there?

You held them back for a few years, Margaret. You bought
us a few years' peace. You barred the door against war with
your own arm. Here's to you.

She raises her glass.

MARGARET *and parliament disappear.*

RAMSAY *enters* JAMES*'s room.* JAMES *is reading a letter*
he's written.

RAMSAY. Your Majesty… We're in danger.

JAMES. Yes probably. (*The letter.*) I'm petitioning Rome to
have her made a saint. She probably wouldn't want to be a
saint. I couldn't think what else to do. I couldn't think how
to give her anything else, now.

RAMSAY. James, Your Majesty, are you listening to me?

JAMES. She'd no business dying so quickly. She was strong.
She was healthy… she… We could have had one more
conversation. Just that at least. Who can I talk to now?

RAMSAY. James… I'll always be here for you. My whole life…

JAMES. You don't even understand my jokes! You just laugh!

PHEMY. What's going to happen? What's going to happen now?

ANNABELLA. Nothing you or I can help, Phemy. Nothing we
can stop. We're two wee souls and the world is rolling over us.

ANNABELLA *shakes her head. She turns away.* PHEMY
follows.

RAMSAY. You have to get ready to defend yourself, Your Majesty. Please. They're going to bring war on you!

JAMES. Are they? How staggeringly unimaginative of them.

RAMSAY. The traitors are coming for you now. They're gathering round your son. We have to go now, Your Majesty. Please.

JAMES. Yes, yes, alright.

They're moving down.

I won't run though. I won't. What's the point of that?

RAMSAY. There's no time to run. They're on us. Their army is moving against us.

JAMES. Seriously?

RAMSAY. They're here! They're here now!

JAMES. All of them?

RAMSAY. Every enemy you have!

JAMES. That… must be quite an army.

RAMSAY. We're outnumbered. They've cut off our escape.

JAMES. Then it's today, isn't it? This is the time. No choice then, is there? There never was.

JAMES and RAMSAY exit or move to the battlefield.

The army is gathering, or better, if possible, the parliament is transforming into an army. JAMES and RAMSAY are on one side, a massed force, with JAMIE and JOHN at the back at the other side.

JAMES is standing looking over at the opposing army. It's a bright, sunny day.

RAMSAY stands behind him.

RAMSAY is terrified, trying to hold it in.

The sound of a huge army. Rhythmic shouting. Drums. Swords beaten on shields.

(*Wonder.*) Listen to them. It's like a wave, ready to break.

RAMSAY. Oh, sweet Jesus. I won't leave you, I'm with you, I'll stay with you, James.

JAMES kisses RAMSAY.

JAMES. Run. Run, Ramsay. Live. Here they come!

RAMSAY exits. JAMES puts down his sword and waits.

JAMIE. Are you ready? Ready for my command. Charge!!

The army breaks over him and he goes down.

Then JAMIE is standing over his father's dead body.

The scene transforms into –

The Queen's Room, Stirling, Coronation Day

JAMIE is looking at himself in the true mirror.

Then he is facing the ghost of his mother, MARGARET.

JAMIE. We needed you.

I can't feel you when I pray.

I can't see you. The mirror shows what's really there. You're not there.

I can't feel you! Where are you? Where are you?! *Mum…!*

Slowly MARGARET moves away. JAMIE breaks down.

I'm sorry. I'm sorry. I couldn't forgive him. I killed him. I'm sorry.

MARGARET has gone.

JAMIE starts to tear off his clothes.

He picks up a spiked chain from the floor and starts to wind it round his body.

ANNABELLA enters.

ANNABELLA. What's that?

JAMIE. What you wear next to your skin tells you what you are.

I'm a son who killed his father.

ANNABELLA. So is that what you're wearing for your coronation?

JAMIE. Yes.

ANNABELLA *considers him for a moment.*

ANNABELLA. What about a shirt over it maybe?

She gets it. He lets her put it over his head.

Arms up… that's the boy…

And something to keep you a bit warmer maybe?

She puts more clothes on him, coaxing him like a child.

And it is your coronation, maybe we should dress you up a wee bit, eh? You're Scotland today after all… maybe some gold? What do you say?

She gets a box.

There's only you and me who loved them enough to remember what they were, Jamie. If we don't carry that out into the world, where will it go?

(*Taking a ring out, admiring it.*) Ah, this was my father's ring. Your great-grandfather. He would have loved you. He was a poet.

Well, everyone knows that. You like the poetry, eh, Jamie?

She puts it on his finger.

Now… this was your great-grandmother's. Queen Joan. She was like your mother. Came hundreds of miles to be here and never left. Part of you now. Dark and light together.

She puts another jewel on him.

And you love the hunt and the football, that's my brother, your grandfather. We'll give you his chain here. And this was your grandmother's, oh, lovely Mary, a wee bit of France we'll pin on you.

Does so.

You never heard a laugh like hers! She loved to laugh.
You've got her smile I think.

You know what your mother gave you. We'll give you a wee
minding of her though, eh?

She puts one of MARGARET*'s jewels on him.*

And now you can wear your father's crown. Now you're
Scotland.

JAMIE. I promised her I wouldn't make war on him. I promised
her I'd forgive him.

ANNABELLA. I know. But you didn't.

And now you have to go out there and show them their King.

That's what she'd want you to do now, to be King of Scots.

Don't worry about what kind of king you're going to be.
Scotland herself doesn't know what kind of nation she is half
the time but I've learned that there's no sense being
frightened of what you don't know. Time to walk out in the
world again and find out.

As he hesitates.

Don't be scared, Jamie. It's not all on you. King or not, all
you can do is what one wee soul can do. Just be one man and
do your best. Scotland will do what Scotland does.

Love that. Trust that. Trust that and remember who you are.

JAMES. Yes.

ANNABELLA. On you go then, son. On you go. You can do it.

*The Three Estates fill up again. They start to stamp, a
thunderous noise that grows and grows as* JAMIE *walks out
into the floor of the parliament.*

One last deafening stamp.

Silence.

He looks at them, they look at him. Fade lights.

End.

NATIONAL THEATRE OF SCOTLAND

Artistic Director and Chief Executive: Laurie Sansom
Chair: Seona Reid DBE

The National Theatre of Scotland has earned a significant national and international reputation for its daring and originality. Being a theatre without walls and building-free, it presents a wide variety of work that ranges from large-scale productions to projects tailored to the smallest performing spaces. In addition to conventional theatres, the Company has performed in airports, schools, tower blocks, community halls, ferries and forests.

The Company has toured extensively across Scotland, the rest of the UK and worldwide. Notable productions include *Black Watch* by Gregory Burke which won four Laurence Olivier Awards amongst a multitude of awards, a radical reimagining of *Macbeth* starring Alan Cumming, presented in Glasgow and at the Lincoln Center Festival and subsequently, Broadway, New York, and *Our Ladies of Perpetual Succour*, adapted by Lee Hall from Alan Warner's novel, *The Sopranos*.

The National Theatre of Scotland creates much of its work in partnership with theatre-makers, companies, venues and participants across the globe. From extraordinary projects with schools and communities, to the ground-breaking online *5 Minute Theatre* to immersive pieces such as David Greig's *The Strange Undoing of Prudencia Hart*, the National Theatre of Scotland's aspiration is to tell the stories that need to be told and to take work to wherever audiences are to be found.

w: **nationaltheatrescotland.com**
t: 0141 221 0970

The National Theatre of Scotland is core funded by the Scottish Government. The National Theatre of Scotland, a company limited by guarantee and registered in Scotland (SC234270), is a registered Scottish charity (SC033377).

The Scottish Government
Riaghaltas na h-Alba

**EDINBURGH
INTERNATIONAL
FESTIVAL**

Every August, the giants of the arts gather in the stunning city of Edinburgh for the International Festival. For three exhilarating weeks the city becomes an international cultural epicentre with the finest creators and performers from the worlds of classical music, theatre, opera and dance offering intense, personal and exciting experiences to those who come from Scotland, the UK and overseas.

As a vibrant, innovative organisation, involved in commissioning and producing new work from the very best artists working internationally, while also nurturing grassroots arts engagement on its doorstep, the Festival contributes to many aspects of life, be it culture, economy, education and society, and enhances the lives of people not just in Edinburgh and Scotland, but around the world.

The 2016 Edinburgh International Festival runs from 5–29 August.
Find out more at **eif.co.uk**

The Edinburgh International Festival is supported by The City of Edinburgh Council and Creative Scotland.

Scottish Charity No: SC004694

National Theatre
of Great Britain

Director of the National Theatre: Rufus Norris
Executive Director: Lisa Burger

Founded in 1963, and established on London's South Bank in 1976, the National Theatre is dedicated to making the very best theatre and sharing it with as many people as possible. We stage up to thirty productions at our South Bank home each year, ranging from reimagined classics – such as Greek tragedy and Shakespeare – to modern masterpieces and new work by contemporary writers and theatre-makers. The work we make strives to be as open, as diverse, as collaborative and as national as possible.

We want to inspire artists and audiences to think in new ways, to constantly reimagine the act of making theatre. Much of that new work is researched and developed at the NT Studio: we are committed to nurturing innovative work from new writers, directors, creative artists and performers.

The National's work is also seen on tour throughout the UK and internationally, and in collaborations and co-productions with regional theatres. Popular shows (such as *War Horse* and *The Curious Incident of the Dog in the Night-Time*) transfer to the West End and occasionally to Broadway; and, through the National Theatre Live programme, we broadcast live performances to 1,500 cinemas in forty countries around the world.

Our extensive Learning programme offers talks, events and workshops for people of all ages in the new Clore Learning Centre, and reaches nationwide through programmes such as Connections, our annual festival of new plays for schools and youth theatres. National Theatre: On Demand In Schools has made three acclaimed, curriculum-linked productions free to stream on demand in every secondary school in the country. Online, you'll find a rich variety of innovative digital content on every aspect of theatre.

The National Theatre and Headlong Theatre production of Duncan Macmillan's *People, Places and Things* is at Wyndham's Theatre in the West End from March 2016.

Box Office and information: +44 (0)20 7452 3000
National Theatre, South Bank, London SE1 9PX
nationaltheatre.org.uk
Registered Charity No: 224223

Production Team (2016 production)

Producer	Margaret-Anne O'Donnell
Production Manager	Chris Hay
Company Manager	Mandy Whittaker
Stage Manager	Cynthia DuBerry
Deputy Stage Manager	Emma Skaer
Assistant Stage Manager	Jo Phipps
Assistant Stage Manager	Ali Biggs
Production Electrician	Paul Claydon
Lighting Programmer	Liam Jones
Lighting Supervisor and Re-lights	Marec Joyce
Lighting Technician	Jon Meggat
Lighting Technician	Abbi Fearnley
Production Sound Engineer	Andrew Kirkby
Production Sound Technician	Fergus Lockie
Sound No1	Karen Szameit
Sound No2	Amy Spencer
Costume and Wardrobe Supervisor	Louise Robertson
Wardrobe Technician	Nicky McKean
Wigs and Make-Up Technician	Michelle Lyons
Wigs Technician	Kirstin McCubbin
Wardrobe Supervisor (pre-tour)	Stephanie Thorburn
Production Carpenter	Jes Baines
Production Carpenter	Mike Hall
Stage Supervisor	David Mason-Hill
Stage Technician	Iain Ramponi
Assistant Production Manager (pre-tour)	Chris Holmes
Touring Communications Manager	Sarah Wilson

Original casting (2014 production) by Charlotte Bevan and Laura Donnelly

Hammered dulcimer made and supplied by Tim Manning
Border pipes made and supplied by Hamish Moore
Set built and painted by Set-up (Scenery) Ltd

www.nickhernbooks.co.uk

 facebook.com/nickhernbooks

 twitter.com/nickhernbooks